Date Due

DEC 2 1 1993			

BRO DART   CAT. NO. 23 233   PRINTED IN U.S.A.

Theory of
Energy Transfers
and Conversions

Theory of Energy Transfers and Conversions

Federico Grabiel

Space Systems Division
Hughes Aircraft Company, Culver City
and
Loyola University, Los Angeles

John Wiley & Sons, Inc.   New York   London   Sydney

Library of Congress Catalog Card Number: 67-23440
Printed in the United States of America

Dedicated to
My Parents

Preface

This book presents the main body of my investigations concerning the laws of energy transfers and conversions. A linear theory of energy transfers and conversions is developed that encompasses the second and third laws of classical thermodynamics and their consequences as particular cases. The theory associates with every intensive parameter a quantity that is extensive and additive and is a function of state. This quantity is here called the coparameter or associated extensive parameter. The coparameter of the temperature is the entropy function. For a given system, a coparameter change can be expressed in terms of the change in another coparameter, using the relation between their respective intensive parameters as expressed in the equation of state.

Chapters 3 to 18 present results that, as far as I am aware, are essentially new and unpublished. Appendix A contains, with slight modification and some additions, material already published in reference [2]; it has been included here to make readily accessible concepts and theorems that are used frequently throughout the work. Appendix B presents background material that is applied at various places in the book; Appendices C and D contain, within the framework of the theory presented and as applications of it, results that are well known. The appendices have been written in more leisurely fashion than the chapters wherein the theory is presented, and they are intended to aid the less experienced readers.

In Chapters 12, 15, and 17, conditions for equilibrium are given in very general form, and some of those theorems are then applied in Appendix D.

Chapter 18 presents results, believed to be new, relating to the behavior of systems far from equilibrium—systems receding from equilibrium, as well as systems moving towards equilibrium. The fundamental laws regulating systems at negative temperatures are particular cases of some of the results derived in Chapter 18.

Constant confrontation, in the book, of the predictions of the theory with data from observation and experimentation has not been deemed necessary in view of the fact that the results of the theory contain those of classical thermodynamics and others that are well known and readily accessible. When concrete illustrations of the theoretical results have been given, they have generally been chosen from phenomena other than heat.

The book has not been written as a textbook in the usual American style, and thus it includes fewer examples than is customary, and no problems or exercises. However, with additional material, examples, and problems, it has been used in the form of notes as a textbook for courses at both Loyola University of Los Angeles and Mount St. Mary's College.

That the material has been accessible to undergraduates is shown by the fact that theorem 11-2 is a joint contribution of five students: Robert Herbelin, William Jerkovsky, Thomas Gurski, Richard Fortner, and Sharon Lisle (now Mrs. Robert V. Writer). A partial formulation and proof of theorem 12-6 originated with the first four of these students. These contributions were not made in response to assignments given by the professor; they resulted from inquiries originated by the students themselves. In my opinion their value is enhanced by the fact that the students were thinking critically and creatively, not in a relatively virgin field, but in an area well studied by several generations of scientists, since the theory in which the students were working is essentially an extension of classical thermodynamics. Such inquiries originated by students are worth more than many problems assigned by a teacher and formulated in the textbook. Furthermore, the discovery and *thorough* formulation and examination of a few questions, in depth and from various angles, is more fruitful to the student than the *hasty* solution of a multitude of problems and exercises.

The presentation of the theory follows the rigorous form of well-distinguished definitions, assumptions, theorems, and interpolated discussions and motivations. Such precision in theoretical formulation and development is of definite aid for tracing back to their sources the discrepancies that may be detected between the results of the theory and the particular aspect of nature that the theory is expected to represent; corrections of errors and intelligent modification of hypotheses are then markedly facilitated.

Utility is not the sole criterion for employing the rigorous manner of presentation that has been chosen—the human mind delights in clearness of ideas, and precision of distinctions is indispensable for the attainment of depth of analysis and beauty of synthesis.

I desire to express my gratitude to Sister Cecilia Louise Moore, C.S.J., head of the department of physical sciences at Mount St. Mary's College, Los Angeles, where this theory was presented, for the first time, to a very competent group of students. Hughes Aircraft Company, Culver City plant, donated the typing and reproduction services, even though the theory presented in this book has no relation to my responsibilities in the company. To the management of that corporation, which continually demonstrates respect for individual persons as well as awareness of social responsibility, I also wish to acknowledge publicly my appreciation. The actual typing of most of the manuscript was the responsibility of Mrs. Patricia Umphres, who accomplished this task in a professionally superior manner. Mrs. Ann Davidson donated her time to type Chapter 18 and the many dozens of corrections and additions to the manuscript. I want to express my appreciation to Ruth Flohn for the care with which she edited my manuscript. I also want to thank Frank and Virginia Mullin, Susan Mary Raycraft, and Sharon Roome, for their assistance in typing the manuscript and proofreading the galleys. Finally, I express my deepest gratitude to Dr. Solomon J. Klapman, Senior Scientist in the Space Systems Division of Hughes Aircraft Company, who read and discussed with me the entire manuscript, offering criticisms and suggestions that substantially improved the book.

Los Angeles, Calif.   FEDERICO GRABIEL
March 1967

Contents

Theory of
Energy Transfers
and Conversions

1

Introduction

This monograph is the result of an inquiry and a dissatisfaction:

The inquiry: Reading the literature on thermodynamics, one constantly comes upon the phrases "energy conversion" and "energy transfer," but the derivation of the thermodynamic relations seems to be carried out for only one or the other of them (although usually later applied to all kinds of phenomena). The author found himself always asking these questions: Is this relation, as derived, valid for only one or for all kinds of energy transfers? Is it valid for energy conversions and, if so, for some or for all kinds of energy conversions?

The dissatisfaction: A most important theorem of thermodynamics states that the quantity entropy is a function of state, and the predominant demonstration of this theorem proceeds as follows: (a) it is shown that the change in entropy is independent of the path when the transformation between states consists of only isothermal and adiabatic segments and the system remains *sufficiently close* (!) to equilibrium during the transformation; (b) it is then demonstrated that an arbitrary path between states can be approximated to within any degree of accuracy by a path composed exclusively of isothermal and adiabatic segments; (c) the independence of the entropy change from this last type of path is then extended to the arbitrary path to which it is an (as good as desired) approximation. That entropy is a function of state follows then as a corollary.

Step (c) in the procedure is based upon the (usually implicit) assumption that the limit of a process of approximation possesses the same properties as the approximating elements. This is not universally true, however, and in every instance it is necessary to demonstrate that the property of interest, possessed by the approximating elements, is *conserved under passage to the limit.*

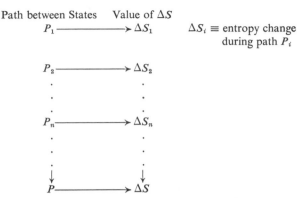

Figure 1-1   Diagram illustrating the commutativity discussed in the text.

As an extremely simple illustration we may consider the set of functions $\{x^s, s > 0\}$. Every element of this set is endowed with the following property: continuity over the *closed* interval $[0, 1]$. But this property is *not* possessed by the function $f(x) = \lim_{s \to \infty} x^s$, *or* by the function $g(x) = \lim_{s \to 0} x^s$.

What is involved in the assumed conservation of the property (that entropy is a function of state) under passage to the limit is the *continuity* of the property with respect to the parameter used to characterize the passage to the limit, or in other words, the *commutativity of the functional correspondence with the passage to the limit* (see Figure 1-1).

If by f we symbolize the functional correspondence $f : P_i \to \Delta S_i$ for any i [that is, $\Delta S_i = f(P_i)$ for all i], then the assumption implicit in step (c) above is but an expression of the following commutativity:

$$\lim_{i \to \infty} [f(P_i)] = f\left(\lim_{i \to \infty} P_i\right) = f(P).$$

In fact, with reference to Figure 1-1,

Step (a) asserts that $\Delta S_i = f(P_i)$ is a constant quantity independent of i, under the stated conditions,

Step (b) asserts that P can be expressed as $P = \lim_{i \to \infty} P_i$, and

Step (c) then affirms that $\Delta S = f(P)$ has the same value as every ΔS_i. In other words,

$$\Delta S = f\left(\lim_{i \to \infty} P_i\right)$$

$$\Big\| \text{ assumed equality}$$

$$\lim_{\to \infty} \Delta S_i = \lim_{i \to \infty} f(P_i) = \text{constant value}.$$

That such a commutativity requires demonstration in every case of interest is evident, since it does not hold universally for every functional correspondence and every passage to limit.

Some authors avoid the indicated weakness by postulating the existence of the entropy function and the thesis of the theorem. While unobjectionable from the standpoint of the theory of formal systems, this procedure is open to the criticism that scientific theory is more than a formal system, one of the differences being that its postulates have close interconnections with knowledge obtained experimentally. That the conclusions deduced from the postulates must have some kind of correspondence with experiential results is obligatory. A desirable characteristic, although not indispensable, is that the postulates be closely related to those experiences that *give birth to the scientific theory*, and that they be expressed in terms which are as close as possible to those which are primitive in the theory. Although a set of postulates that are far removed from the experiential foundations of the science may be *formally* aesthetic, it can hardly be said to be *scientifically* elegant (i.e., in the context of the experimental science). Moreover, such an approach is rarely suitable pedagogically.

The method of C. Caratheodory [12]*, while very elegant from the mathematical point of view, is open to the objections listed in the preceding paragraph and has also the disadvantage of requiring a mathematical apparatus that may be more than what is strictly necessary. A theory of physics should aim at using instruments (especially mathematics) that are as simple as possible and sufficient to reach the objectives.†

In this context we would like to quote the words of Maurice A. Biot, which we fully endorse: "It should be borne in mind that Applied Mathematics is an art as much as it is a science. In physical theory it is of paramount importance to acquire an intimate grasp of the reality behind the mathematical symbols. The formalism alone or even numerical solutions do not by themselves bring to light the significant qualitative features which lead to deeper insight and constitute an essential part of any truly comprehensive theoretical treatment. The commonly accepted notion

---

* Numbers in square brackets refer to the references listed at the end of the book.

† The theory presented in this book uses a small amount of elementary set theory, a subject that until recently had found no application in the physical sciences. This elementary set theory, however, is used here *only* to attain a more adequate and precise *mathematical formulation* (or *representation*) of the physical facts underlying the theory (i.e., experiments performed with apparatus of finite dimensions, etc.), and indeed the reader, if he so chooses, may follow the whole development by substituting in his mind points for sets. In Caratheodory's presentation, however, the theory of Pfaffian forms— or an equivalent mathematical theory—is indispensable for the *development* of the physical theory from its postulates.

that all problems are solved once exact equations have been established which can be fed into automatic computers is a fundamental fallacy. The criterion of adequacy of a physical theory is not necessarily based on pure logical structure and generality. The theory must be associated with other advantages of a conceptual and pragmatic nature. This obviously involves a judgment of values which lies beyond the scope of mathematical principles." [7], pp. X–XI.

In this book a *unified linear* theory of energy transfers and conversions is developed, the unification resulting from a formulation that includes transfers as particular cases of conversions. The theorems are deduced from a general abstract formulation of the conversion process and its associated problem, so that their theses have unlimited applicability *within the domain of the processes satisfying the linear conditions* found in the postulates of the theory.

The most important result establishes that, associated with every intensive parameter, there is a quantity that is extensive, additive, and a function of the state of the system; it is here called the associated extensive parameter, and more commonly, the *coparameter*. When the intensive parameter is temperature, the coparameter is the entropy function. If the system undergoes a process in which there is work of expansion or contraction under the influence of the intensive parameter pressure, the reversible part of the coparameter change is the change in volume of the system.

Any coparameter change can be expressed in terms of the change in another coparameter, given that we know the equation of state relating the intensive parameters, and the relation holding between their associated energy transfers. Thus, for example, knowing the equation of state connecting the pressure P with the temperature T in a system, and the relation between ΔQ and ΔW, it is possible to establish the relation between ΔS (change in T-coparameter) and the equivalent change in the P-coparameter. This justifies the use that is made of entropy change calculations for processes in which no ΔQ is involved, as well as the method commonly employed, consisting in the determination of the ΔS for an alternative process taking place between the same terminal states and involving ΔQ-transfer.

The work is presented using the most elementary concepts of set functions, these being summarized in Chapter 2. To make the presentation self-contained, a few basic definitions are included at the beginning of Chapter 3; these are given in more detailed form in reference [2] of the list at the end of the book.

2

Mathematical Preliminaries

In the presentation of a theory, the following aspects may be distinguished:

1. The physical theory itself.
   (a) The primitive concepts of the theory.
   (b) The postulates of the theory.
   (c) The physical content of the theory.
2. The mathematical presentation of the theory.
   (a) The mathematical instruments selected for the mathematical representation of the physical systems and relations to which the theory is to apply.
   (b) The mathematical theories and algorithms used for the development of the theory from its postulates.

As far as aspect 2(b) is concerned, our work will not require any mathematical apparatus beyond the differential and integral calculus.

For 2(a) we have selected to mathematically represent physical systems by sets of points in space, *a geometrical point of the set corresponding to one and only one material "point" of the system.*

Nota Bene. It is *not necessary*, for the presentation of our theory, to make the above choice; the whole theory may be developed by representing "large" systems by sets of points and "small" systems (like the bulb of a thermometer, or an electron) by mathematical points—and until now this is what has been most commonly done in physical theories. The reader, if he chooses, may consider as a mathematical point what we throughout our study denote as a δ_p-cell, δ_p-set, or simply δ-cell. Also, the material in this chapter, up to but excluding definition 2-2, has for its only purpose the mathematical specification of those systems to which the theory is to be applied; in consequence it can be disregarded by a reader who will be satisfied by considering that the theory to be developed is designed to apply to the physical systems studied in classical physics and physical chemistry, plus perhaps a few other (molecular and atomic) systems.

Only the following concepts and operations of elementary set theory will be needed. Consider two sets of points, S_1 and S_2; then

α   The set-theoretic union $S_1 \cup S_2$ is the set consisting of all the points belonging to S_1 or to S_2 (or to both).

β   The cartesian product $S_1 \times S_2$ is the set of all ordered couples (s_1, s_2), where $s_1 \in S_1$ and $s_2 \in S_2$.

A topological space is a set (containing all other sets that are to be of possible interest) in which one can identify the *neighborhoods* of each of its points. These neighborhoods then permit us to work with the concept of *continuity* in the space. For a precise definition of this material the reader may consult [1] or similar presentations of the fundamentals of topology. A space in which there exists a distance function, for example, is a topological space, since the distance function (also called metric function) can be used to characterize neighborhoods. In most situations the spaces used in classical physics and quantum mechanics are metric spaces.

Two subspaces, or sets, of a topological space T are *homotopic* if and only if *one of them can be transformed into the other by a continuous deformation.* This formulation provides for a sufficiently clear intuitive idea of homotopic sets. For a more precise formulation, let $I \equiv \{t \mid t \text{ real number}, 0 \leq t \leq 1\}$; then

Definition 2-1.   Let X be a topological space, and S and S' be subspaces of a topological space Y. Subspaces S and S' are *homotopic* if and only if there exists a continuous mapping f from the cartesian product $X \times I$ to Y such that $f(x, 0) \in S$ and $f(x, 1) \in S'$.

The mapping f of definition 2-1 is called a *homotopic mapping.* Figure 2-1 illustrates the definition.

Naturally, in a homotopic mapping each point of S traverses a continuous path that may be represented as a continuous function of the parameter time.

We shall consider that each physical system to which our theory is to apply admits a mathematical representation of one of the following three types:

1. A homotopic image of a sphere.
2. A homotopic image of a torus.
3. A set-theoretic union of finite numbers of sets of types 1 and/or 2.

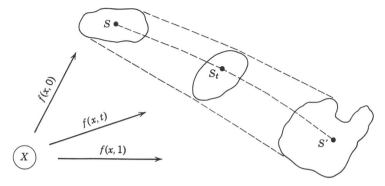

Figure 2-1 Subspaces S, S_t, and S' are homotopic.

Examples of (1) may be a star, an amoeba, a cloud; of (2) the rings of Saturn, a doughnut, the body of a mammal, the inner tube of an automobile tire; of (3) the block of an automobile engine, a pair of scissors.

Definition 2-2. A *numerical set function* is a single-valued correspondence having for domain the class of admissible sets of the space, and for range the field of real or complex numbers.
   A single-valued function will also be called a *univalent* function.

Only real-valued set functions will be of interest in this investigation. *Example* of a set function: the weight of an object.

Definition 2-3. A set function is *additive* iff $F(S_1 \cup S_2) = F(S_1) + F(S_2)$, where S_1 and S_2 are arbitrary disjoint sets.

Representing by $\omega(S)$ the three-dimensional *measure* or volume of set S, we may state

Definition 2-4. The set function $F(S)$ is *point-continuous* iff $\lim_{\omega(S) \to 0} F(S) = 0$ for every S.

Definition 2-5. A set function $F(S)$ is *continuous* at S_{t_0} iff $\lim_{t \to t_0} F(S_t) = F(S_{t_0})$, S_{t_0} being a homotopic image of S_t.

Lemma 2-1. $F(S)$ is continuous at $S_{t'}$, iff for any $\epsilon > 0$ there always exists a $\delta > 0$ such that $|t - t'| < \delta$ implies $|F(S_t) - F(S_{t'})| < \epsilon$, where S_t and $S_{t'}$, are homotopic images.

The proof of lemma 2-1 is analogous to the proof of the corresponding theorem for real functions of a real variable.

Lemma 2-2. If F is an additive set function, then $\dot{F} = (d/dt)F$ is likewise an additive set function.

PROOF.   That $\dot{F}$ is a set function is immediate from the definition of set function. The additivity follows from the linearity property of the derivation operator:

$$\dot{F}(S_1 \cup S_2) = \frac{d}{dt}[F(S_1) + F(S_2)] = \dot{F}(S_1) + \dot{F}(S_2).$$

3

The Fundamental Theorems
on Functions of State

A transfer or interchange can exist only between two things or parts of the universe; likewise, two things or parts of the universe are required for any interaction. For the quantitative study of transfers it is then indispensable that the two things or sections of the universe participating in the transfer be clearly identified. The following concepts, notations, and theorems will be used continually throughout the theory.

Convention. The whole universe will be divided into two parts, called, respectively, *system*, and *surroundings, environment*, or *exterior*. They will generally be symbolized by the letters $\mathcal{S}$ (system) and $\mathcal{E}$ (environment).

The subdivision can be characterized in two ways: (1) by defining $\mathcal{S}$; (2) by defining the *boundary* $\mathcal{B}$ between $\mathcal{S}$ and $\mathcal{E}$. System and boundary may be defined by space specifications, matter specifications, or a mixed (space and matter) specification.

As an illustration of the use of a mixed specification of a system, we may consider the system identified in the following manner: $\mathcal{S}$ consists of the condensed water in the atmosphere of the earth, or $\mathcal{S}$ consists of the fluid matter in a (given) human body.

Definition 3-1. The *state* of a system at a certain instant is determined by the *set of its properties* at that particular instant.

Definition 3-2. A *process* or *transformation* is determined by associating a state of $\mathcal{S}$ with each instant t of time within an interval $t_0 \leq t \leq t_1$.

Definition 3-3. The number of properties that is necessary and sufficient to characterize the state of $\mathcal{S}$ is the *number of degrees of freedom* of $\mathcal{S}$.

Definition 3-3 implies that the values of all the properties of S may be known (by calculation) once the values of the *characterizing* properties are known, and there are as many of these as the system has degrees of freedom. Any such set of properties is called a *complete* set of *generalized co-ordinates*, or of *characterizing parameters*, of S. It follows that a process is determined by specifying, as functions of time, the values of a complete set of generalized parameters of S.

Nota Bene. Process has been defined in terms of state of S, and state of S in terms of the set of properties of the system. Now, no property can be measured at an instant; what is measured is some kind of mean value during a certain time interval (no matter how small). Therefore, "state of S at instant t" is a very specific idealization, unless it so happens that S is, during the whole measuring process, in a state of perfect quietude. The consequences of this idealization extend themselves to the definition of process. Also, the number of degrees of freedom of S is determined, not only by the system and the process being studied, but also by the *degree of refinement of the study*. The nature of the process strongly influences the degree of refinement needed in the study.

Lemma 3-1. Suppose that $\{X_1, X_2, \ldots, X_n\}$ is a complete set of characterizing parameters for a process $\mathfrak{F}$ undergone by S. Then $\{X_1, X_2, \ldots, X_{n-1}, Y\}$ is also a complete set of characterizing parameters for $\{S, \mathfrak{F}\}$ iff Y is a strictly monotonic function of X_n.

PROOF. The sufficiency is immediate. For the necessity observe that, if the function $Y = Y(X_n)$ is not strictly monotonic over the interval of concern, there will be at least one value Y' that will be in correspondence with at least two values X_n', X_n'' (refer to Figure 3-1). But, because X_n is an element of the set $\{X_1, \ldots, X_{n-1}, X_n\}$ of characterizing parameters, X_n' and X_n'' are in correspondence with two different states A' and A'' of S; therefore Y' will be in correspondence with at least two different states of S and hence cannot be one of the characterizing parameters of $\{S, \mathfrak{F}\}$.

The initial and final states of a process (associated respectively with the instants t_0 and t_1) are called the *terminal* states of the transformation.

Definition 3-4. Two system transformations or processes are *coterminal* iff their initial states are identical and their final states are identical. A *cyclic* process is one in which the terminal states are identical.

Definition 3-5. An *equivalence relation* $\simeq$ defined over a set S of elements is a binary relation (over S) having the following three properties:
    (a) Reflexivity: if $s_1 \in S$, then $s_1 \simeq s_1$.
    (b) Symmetry: if $s_1 \in S$ and $s_2 \in S$, then $s_1 \simeq s_2$ implies $s_2 \simeq s_1$.

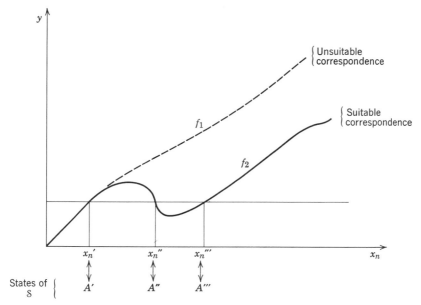

Figure 3-1 f_1 is a strictly monotonic function of X_n; f_2 is not strictly monotonic.

(c) Transitivity: if s_1, s_2 and s_3 are elements of S, then $s_1 \simeq s_2$ and $s_2 \simeq s_3$ imply $s_1 \simeq s_3$.

It is easy to prove that an equivalence relation defined over S yields an *exhaustive* subdivision of S into *disjoint* subsets (see, for example, [10], pp. 11–21, or [11], pp. 4–7). These subsets are called *equivalence classes* because any two elements of the same equivalence class are equivalent to each other (from the standpoint of the binary relation $\simeq$), and no two elements of S, belonging to different equivalence classes, are equivalent to each other. It is this characteristic of decomposing a set exhaustively into disjoint equivalence classes that makes the concept of an equivalence relation such a useful instrument in mathematics and in the other sciences. It is used primarily for purposes of classification and definition, and secondarily in demonstrations.

Lemma 3-2.   Coterminality of processes is an equivalence relation.

Temporarily denote by C the set of all equivalence classes of coterminal processes, any one such equivalence class being represented by $c \in C$, then

Definition 3-6a.   A correspondence associating to each $c \in C$ a single real number is a *function independent of the path*.

Definition 3-6b.   A *function of couples of states* is a univalent function having for domain the set of all couples of states and for range a subset of the real numbers.

It is easily demonstrated that there exists a one-to-one correspondence between the set of functions independent of the path and the set of functions of couples of states.

Definition 3-7.   A univalent function defined upon the states of S (i.e., having for domain the abstract space of all states of S) is called a *function of state*.

The following theorems are of immediate demonstration:

Theorem 3-1.   Let f be a function of state over a domain $\mathfrak{D}$ of states of a system, and let a and b represent arbitrary elements of $\mathfrak{D}$. Then the function $\Delta f = f_b - f_a$ is independent of the path between states a and b.

Theorem 3-2.   To every function independent of the path corresponds a function of state defined to within an arbitrary constant.

PROOF.   See theorem A-4 (Appendix A) and its demonstration.

We shall prescind from adding the constant to our symbolism (i.e., we shall assign the value zero to the arbitrary constant); and, if we use Δf to represent the function independent of the path, f will stand for the corresponding function of state.

Theorem 3-3.   The sum of two functions independent of the path is also a function independent of the path.

Theorem 3-4.   If $f = \beta g$, where g is a function of state and β a fixed number, f is also a function of state.

Theorem 3-5.   If the relation $\Delta f = \beta \, \Delta g$ is valid, Δg being a function of couples of states and β a fixed number, Δf is also a function of couples of states.

Theorem 3-6.   If a conservation relation of the form $\Delta f = \Delta g + \Delta h$ exists, and f and g (f and h) are functions of state, h (g) must also be a function of state.

Theorem 3-7.   If a conservation relation of the form $\Delta f = \Delta g + \Delta h$ exists, and (1) f is a function of state, and (2) Δg (Δh) is not independent of the path, Δh (Δg) cannot be independent of the path.

Theorem 3-8 (Basic State Function Theorem).   If a conservative relation of the form $\Delta f = \sum_{i=1}^{n} \beta_i \, \Delta f_i$ exists, β_i representing a pure number for every i, a necessary condition for f to be a function of state is that *either* (1) f_i is a function of state for every value of i, or (2) there are at least *two* values of i for which Δf_i is not independent of the path.

PROOF. Suppose first that for some value of i, say $i = n$, f_i is not known to be a function of state, while f_i is a function of state for $i \neq n$. Then $\Delta f = (\sum_{i=1}^{n-1} \Delta f_i) + \Delta f_n$, and the term in parentheses is independent of the path by theorem 3-3. Denote the parenthetical term by Δg. Then $\Delta f = \Delta g + \Delta f_n$, where Δf and Δg are independent of the path. By theorem 3-6, then, Δf_n must also be independent of the path.

On the other hand, if Δf_n is known to be dependent on the path, then, by theorem 3-7, $\Delta g = \sum_{i-1}^{n-1} \Delta f_i$ must also be dependent on the path. But this implies that for at least one value of i among $i = 1, \ldots, n - 1$ the function Δf_i must be dependent on the path, for otherwise Δg would be independent of the path by theorem 3-3.

Definition 3-8. Two given quantities u and v will be said to be *interconvertible* iff there exists a number k such that $u = kv$. Quantities that are not interconvertible will be called *mutually irreducible* or *independent*.

Definition 3-9. Two functions x and y of physical or physicochemical transformations will be said to be *interchangeable* iff, for arbitrary coterminal transformations a and b, the relation $kx_a + y_a = kx_b + y_b$ holds, k being a suitable constant.

In other words, two functions of transformations or processes are interchangeable if and only if their linear combination is a function independent of the transformation (i.e., independent of the path).

Suppose that a given quantity x is decomposable into the sum of two or more other quantities called terms or components of the decomposition: $x = \sum_{i=1}^n x_i$. Each term x_i in turn may be written as the product of a unit of measure e_i and a magnitude $|x_i|$. Hence, we may write $x = \sum_{i=1}^n |x_i| e_i$, and to say that the quantities x_i are mutually irreducible is equivalent to saying that the units of measure e_i are mutually irreducible or independent, since the quantities $|x_i|$ are pure (dimensionless) numbers. Then we have

Theorem 3-9. If a quantity is decomposable into mutually irreducible components, that decomposition is necessarily unique.

PROOF. It suffices to establish the demonstration for the case of two components; the extension to any finite number is immediate.

To prove the necessity, deny the conclusion by temporarily assuming that the decomposition is not unique. We may therefore write

$$x = \sum_{i=1}^{2} |x_i|\, e_i = \sum_{i=1}^{2} |x_i'|\, e_i, \tag{3-1}$$

and in consequence

$$(|x_1| - |x_1'|)e_1 + (|x_2| - |x_2'|)e_2 = 0$$

The non-uniqueness of the decomposition would imply that at least one of the coefficients, say $(|x_1| - |x_1'|)$, is different from zero; we may in consequence divide by it and obtain

$$e_1 = \frac{-(|x_2| - |x_2'|)}{(|x_1| - |x_1'|)}\, e_2,$$

which is of the form $e_1 = ke_2$, indicating that $\{e_1, e_2\}$ are interconvertible, and thus contradicting the hypothesis of the theorem. Therefore of necessity $|x_i| = |x_i'|$, $i = 1.2$, and the decomposition is unique.

Theorem 3-10. Suppose that f is a state function, and Δg and Δh are functions dependent on the path. Then the relation $\Delta f = \Delta g + \Delta h$ demands interconvertibility of the measure units $\{e_g, e_h\}$ and interchangeability of the magnitudes $\{|\Delta g|, |\Delta h|\}$.

PROOF.   Because f is a function of state, Δf is independent of the path; and, selecting any two arbitrary paths (labeled as primed and unprimed), we must have

$$\Delta f = |\Delta g|\, e_g + |\Delta h|\, e_h = |\Delta g'|\, e_g + |\Delta h'|\, e_h = \Delta f'.$$

Because Δg and Δh are dependent on the path, however, in general $|\Delta g| \neq |\Delta g'|$ and $|\Delta h| \neq |\Delta h'|$, and the decomposition of Δf is not unique. By theorem 3-9 it then follows that the measure units are interconvertible: there exists a k such that $e_g = ke_h$. Substituting this in the expression corresponding to (3-1) of theorem 3-9, it follows that $k\,|\Delta g| + |\Delta h| = k\,|\Delta g'| + |\Delta h'|$. The magnitudes $|\Delta g|$ and $|\Delta h|$ are therefore interchangeable.

It is evident that we may also say that the quantities $|\Delta g|\, e_g$ and $|\Delta h|\, e_h$ are interchangeable. In fact, it suffices to put $x_a = |\Delta g|\, e_g$, $x_b = |\Delta g'|\, e_g$, $y_a = |\Delta h|\, e_h$, and $y_b = |\Delta h'|\, e_h$, with $k = 1$ in definition 3-9.

Appendix A

The First Law of Energy Transfers and Conversions

This appendix essentially reproduces, with a few modifications and extended additions, the material of reference [2]. In it use will be made of the definitions and notations introduced in the first part of Chapter 3 of the text. The results of this appendix are applied in various places throughout the main body of the book and in the other appendices.

The first statements about nature, in the form of "conservation principles," may be attributed to the earliest Greek philosopher-scientists, insofar as historical records show. For the history of the inductive principle that today is called the law of conservation of energy, the reader may consult references [22], [23], and [24].

Besides definitions 3-1, 3-2, 3-4, 3-6a, and 3-6b, as well as lemma 2-2, the following notions are used in the formulation and study of the first law of energy transfers and conversions (which, from now on, will be abbreviated as F.L.).

Mass (or *matter*) *transfer*. This concept will be borrowed from general physics; it is thus undefined in our theory.

Definition A-1. The state of S will be said to be modified by *heat transfer* when the change (in state) is effected by one of the two following experimentally defined methods: (a) heat conduction, (b) heat radiation.

Our presentation therefore is borrowing from experimental general physics the definitions of three kinds of phenomena: mass transfer, heat conduction, and heat radiation. For these, the reader may consult, for example, [44], pp. 675–682, [45], [46], [47], [48].

Definition A-2. The state of a system will be said to have been modified by *heat convection* when a mass transfer has been effected in which the temperature of the mass transferred differs from the temperature of the system receiving or delivering it.*

Definition A-3. *Work transfer* will be said to have occurred when the state of a system has been changed by any other method exclusive of heat transfer and heat convection. Evidently, mass transfer without heat convection is here being considered a form of work transfer.

Based upon numerous observations and experimental results, the following generalization could be made about the middle of the nineteenth century.

First Law. If a system has had heat transfer and/or heat convection with its surroundings, while undergoing a cyclic process, then work transfer must have also occurred during the transformation, and in the direction opposite to that of the heat-transfer and/or heat-convection.

Observe that this formulation of the F.L. rests exclusively upon the ideas of heat transfer, heat convection, state of the system, and cyclic process—all of which can be related in a direct manner to experimental observations. Let us now analyze the formulation.

Theorem A-1. The F.L., as just formulated, follows as a consequence of the definitions given for cyclic process and work transfer.

PROOF. If S has received, let us say, heat transfer, as a consequence its properties (at least one of them) have changed. But if the final state of S is identical with the initial state (cyclic process), the changed properties of S must have returned to their original values. This return, however, must be due to some phenomena other than heat transfer (or heat convection). Therefore work transfer must have occurred in the direction opposite to that of the heat transfer.

Notice that heat convection could not be responsible for the return of a system to its original (initial) state if the system was displaced from this initial state by heat transfer, for the mass of the system would be changed and S would not have undergone a cyclic process.

Theorem A-1 can be immediately extended to the case in which there are several separate heat transfers during the cyclic process. It is also easily extended to the situation in which heat convection (which is a combination of heat transfer and work transfer) enters into the process.

---

* For a definition of temperature, the reader may consult a general physics textbook or reference [38].

Theorem A-2. The F.L. implies that, in an arbitrary conversion, the work transferred (symbol: ΔW) stands in a fixed ratio to the heat transferred (symbol: ΔQ). Furthermore, the magnitude of this ratio depends only on the units employed to measure the work and the heat transferred.

PROOF. Only the first assertion of the conclusions will be demonstrated, the second assertion following in an obvious way.

The hypothesis H of the theorem is of the nature of an implication, which may be written as follows:

$$H: \begin{cases} H_{11}\text{—}\Delta Q > 0, \\ H_{12}\text{—cyclic process,} \\ H_{13}\text{—}\Delta W < 0. \end{cases}$$

The conclusion demands that $|\Delta Q|/|\Delta W| = k$, independent of path (process) between terminal states.

The proof will proceed by contradiction. Assume that

$$S_1 \xrightarrow{a} S_2: \quad \frac{|\Delta W_a|}{|\Delta Q_a|} = k, \qquad \text{in process } a \text{ for going from state } S_1 \text{ to state } S_2;$$

$$S_1 \xrightarrow{b} S_2: \quad \frac{|\Delta W_b|}{|\Delta Q_b|} = l \qquad \text{in process } b \text{ for going from state } S_1 \text{ to state } S_2;$$

with $k \neq l$. Now choose a and b such that $|\Delta W_a| = |\Delta W_b|$, and form the cycle $S_1 \xrightarrow{a} S_2 \xrightarrow{-b} S_1$. While traversing this cycle the system has undergone the heat transfer

$$|\Delta Q_a| - |\Delta Q_b| = \frac{|\Delta W_a|}{k} - \frac{|\Delta W_b|}{l} = \frac{(l-k)|\Delta W_a|}{kl}.$$

If, say, $l > k$, then $|\Delta Q_a| - |\Delta Q_b| > 0$, and the denial of the conclusion of the theorem has led us to the set of relations $\begin{cases} Q > 0, \\ \text{cyclic process,} \\ W = 0. \end{cases}$

This set of relations contradicts the implication in the hypothesis of the theorem, and therefore it also contradicts the F.L.

If the same units of measure are used for ΔW and ΔQ (by including the constant factor of proportionality k in the appropriate way in the measure units of ΔW or of ΔQ), then $|\Delta W|/|\Delta Q| = 1$, and the F.L., in consequence of this and of theorem A-2, may be formulated in the following way.

First Law. In cyclic processes $\Delta W + \Delta Q = 0$.

Convention. From now on both ΔQ and ΔW will be expressed in the same units of measure. A positive sign will be associated with work or heat transferred from $\mathcal{E}$ to $\mathcal{S}$. A negative sign will mean that the transfer is from $\mathcal{S}$ to $\mathcal{E}$.

A process or transformation is characterized by two sets of data:

(a) A couple of states of $\mathcal{S}$, between which the process occurs; the terminal states of the process.

(b) The path (sequence of subprocesses) that $\mathcal{S}$ follows between the two terminal states. This path is equivalent to giving the set of all intermediary states of $\mathcal{S}$ (i.e., the set of states of $\mathcal{S}$ associated with the instants in the open interval of time $t_0 < t < t_1$).

The F.L., as stated, affirms a property for a *particular* case of (a) above (that in which the terminal states of the process are identical), the property asserted further being independent of (b). The property is as follows: the algebraic quantity $(\Delta W + \Delta Q)$ is zero for a particular class of terminal states, which is defined by the property that any transformation of the class has coincident terminal states.

Is it possible, from the F.L., to deduce a property that holds for a wider class of terminal states but still remains independent of (b)? Can, perhaps, this wider class be unrestricted? Figure A-1 illustrates schematically the problem that has been posed.

If the problem admits of an affirmative solution, then a quantity (the quantity indicated above; label it ΔE) will have been found that is a numerical invariant under transformations between any two fixed states of the system. That is, we will have at hand a *uniform* (or univalent) function that has for range the real numbers, that has for domain the set defined by (a) above (the set of all couples of states of $\mathcal{S}$), and that is independent of (b) above.

In the investigation of the query that is of concern use will be made of the following

Lemma A-1. For a uniform function, the property of being zero over any cycle of its domain is a necessary and sufficient condition for the property of additivity with respect to path.

PROOF. Notice that additivity with respect to path is but a particular case of the additivity of a set function (see definition 2-3, or reference [4]). If $F(X, Y)$ stands for the value of the function associated with the path from point X to point Y, additivity with respect to path means that $F(A, B) + F(B, C) = F(A, C)$ when the paths $\{A, B\}$ and $\{B, C\}$ are disjoint (refer to Figure A-2).

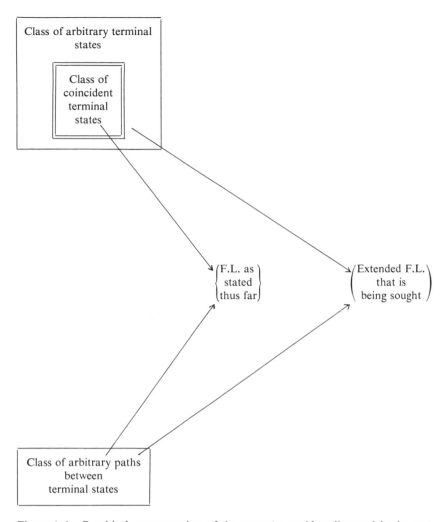

Figure A-1 Graphical representation of the *extension problem* discussed in the text.

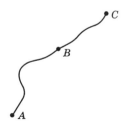

Figure A-2 Path from state *A* to state *C*, passing through state *B*.

Notation.   A path will be denoted by $\{X, Y\}$ where X and Y are the terminal points (states) of the path; a number associated with $\{X, Y\}$ will be denoted by (X, Y).

Demonstration of Necessity.   Subdivide the cycle $\{A, A\}$ into any finite number of disjoint parts, say $\{A, A\} = \{A, B, C, D, A\}$. By the additivity property, the right side of that equality of paths leads to the numerical equation $(A, B) + (B, C) + (C, D) + (D, A) = (A, A)$. But (A, A) is precisely the value associated with the path $\{A, A\}$ on the left side of the equality of paths. Hence both sides of the equality of paths are associated with the same value (A, A). The question now is: what is this value (A, A)? Consider path equality $\{A, B\} = \{A, A, B\}$. To this corresponds the numerical equality $(A, B) = (A, A) + (A, B)$. Because the function is uniform, from properties of the real number system it follows that $(A, A) = 0$. Now consider a different (arbitrary) path decomposition, $\{A, B\} = \{A, B, C, D, A, B\}$. By the additivity property this equality of paths leads to the following numerical equalities: $(A, B) = (A, B) + (B, C) + (C, D) + (D, A) + (A, B) = (A, A) + (A, B)$. Therefore $(A, A) = 0$ is independent of the decomposition of $\{A, A\}$ into parts.

Demonstration of Sufficiency.   Given that $\{C, C\}$ implies $(C, C) = 0$, we are to show that $\{A, B, C\} = \{A, B\} + \{B, C\} = \{A, C\}$ implies $(A, B) + (B, C) = (A, C)$. Because the hypothesis provides information only about cycles, we shall incorporate each of the above three terms as one of the terms associated with a cycle, and then apply the hypothesis to each of those cycles. Thus:

$$(A, B) + \cdots + (B, A) + \cdots = \quad \cdots \quad = 0$$

$$(B, C) + \cdots + (C, B) = \quad \cdots \quad = 0$$

$$(A, C) + (C, A) = 0$$

$$\overline{(A, B) + (B, C) + (B, A) + (C, B) = (A, C) + (C, A)}$$

| desired
terms | undesired
terms | desired
term | undesired
term |

To get rid of the undesired terms, form a cycle with them and apply the hypothesis; thus, from the equality above:

$$(A, B) + (B, C) = (A, C) + (C, A) - (B, A) - (C, B)$$
$$= (A, C) + (C, A) + (A, B) + (B, C)$$
$$= (A, C) + (C, C)$$
$$= (A, C) \text{ since } (C, C) = 0 \text{ by hypothesis.}$$

Notice that in the algebraic manipulations immediately above use was made of the relation $(A, B) = -(B, A)$. This follows from the hypothesis, for the correspondences $\{A, B\} \leftrightarrow (A, B)$, $\{B, A\} \leftrightarrow (B, A)$, and $\{A, A\} \leftrightarrow (A, A)$ and the equality $(A, A) = 0$ imply

$$\underbrace{(A, B) + (B, A)} \longleftarrow \qquad \longrightarrow \{A, B\} + \{B, A\} = \{A, A\}$$

$$0 = (A, A)$$

Observe that the relation $(A, B) = -(B, A)$ is truly a special case of additivity: additivity over a cycle. The sufficiency part of the lemma in essence asserts that this particular additivity implies the general additivity (over an arbitrary path).

Now we are in a position to demonstrate

Theorem A-3. The function $(\Delta Q + \Delta W) = \Delta E$ is a function independent of the path.

PROOF. The F.L. asserts that the function ΔE vanishes over any cycle. Hence, an assertion about cycles is to be used to obtain another assertion concerning coterminal processes which are not cycles. There is a *general* method applicable to this kind of problem when the function in question is additive. In fact, with the following

Notational Agreement. Denote transformations (processes) by Roman numerals, and states of S by Latin numerals; $I(\Delta X)_1^2$ will mean the value ΔX associated with process I from state 1 to state 2. Then

Given: A function F (of cycle) having the same value for all cycles with the same point of departure. Thus, $F(I) = F(II)$ and, because the function is additive with respect to path (lemma A-1), also

$$F(\text{I direct}) + F(\text{I inverse}) = F(\text{II direct}) + F(\text{II inverse}).$$

Method: Make $\{\text{II inverse}\}$ identical to $\{\text{I inverse}\}$. Then $F(\text{I inverse}) = F(\text{II inverse})$ and substitution in the above equality yields $F(\text{I direct}) = F(\text{II direct})$ for arbitrary $\{\text{I direct}\}$ and $\{\text{II direct}\}$ (refer to Figure A-3).

Applying the method to our particular case, we shall study the two cycles

$$(1) = \text{II}(2) \longleftarrow (2) = \text{I}(1);$$
$$(1) = \text{II}(2) \longleftarrow (2) = \text{II}(1)$$

from the standpoint of the function $\Delta E = \Delta Q + \Delta W$. [Notice that, in the symbolism used immediately above to specify the cycles, Roman numerals (processes) operate upon Latin numerals (states of S) to yield other Latin numerals].

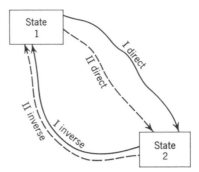

Figure A-3   II inverse is taken identical to I inverse.

By applying the F.L., the following relations are obtained:

$$I(\Delta W)_1{}^2 + I(\Delta Q)_1{}^2 + II(\Delta W)_2{}^1 + II(\Delta Q)_2{}^1 = 0$$

$$II(\Delta W)_1{}^2 + II(\Delta Q)_1{}^2 + II(\Delta W)_2{}^1 + II(\Delta Q)_2{}^1 = 0$$

which immediately lead to the equality $I(\Delta W)_1{}^2 + I(\Delta Q)_1{}^2 = II(\Delta W)_1{}^2 + II(\Delta Q)_1{}^2$, or $I(\Delta E)_1{}^2 = II(\Delta E)_1{}^2$, thus demonstrating the thesis of the theorem.

Observe that ΔQ and ΔW are each a function of three variables: initial state, final state, and process (path). On the other hand, ΔE is a function of only two variables: initial state and final state, and is *invariant under path changes*.

Theorem A-4.   Associated with the function ΔE independent of the path, another function E may be constructed that is a uniform function having for domain the abstract space of all states of the system, and for range a subset $[O, M]$ of the real numbers. The function of state so constructed is unique to within a constant.

PROOF.   Again a general method is applicable for the construction of a function of state (also called a *potential function*) out of a function independent of the path.

Method of Construction: Choose a *base state* S_0 and define E as being E_0 at S_0. Then define E at any *arbitrary* state S_a by the function $E_a = E_0 + (\Delta E)_0{}^a$.

That the function constructed by this method satisfies the requirements imposed by the theorem is quite evident. Notice that, to every function ΔE independent of the path, an infinity of functions of states E may be associated, any two of which differ by a constant. In other words, a function independent of the path defines a function of states to within a constant. This lack of uniqueness in the function E is not a consequence of the method of constructing the function, but is inherent in the nature (as given by the definition) of the function independent of the path. The function E that has been defined (starting with the functions ΔQ and ΔW) is called the *energy function*.

Notice that the statement (not uncommonly found as an expression of the F.L.) "in a cyclic process there is no loss of energy" is redundant, for the definition of cyclic process includes global (with respect to the whole cycle, not necessarily over any one portion of it) unchangeability of the characterizing parameters (of state), and $\Delta E = \Delta Q + \Delta W$ is defined in terms of the changes in these parameters.

The F.L. as extended adds or *makes explicit* new knowledge because it relates the energy E, which has global invariance for all cyclic processes, to two concepts, ΔQ and ΔW, having the following characteristics:

1. They are predicated on *exchanges* between S and $\mathcal{E}$ and are not predicable on S itself;

2. They do *not* possess *global invariance* under global transformations (i.e., they are not independent of the path).

The new function, energy, on the contrary:

1. Is predicated on the *system* itself; it is a function of the states of the system;

2. *Possesses* global invariance under cyclic processes.

The F.L. then states two equivalent relations connecting those entirely dissimilar concepts and their measuring quantities:

(a) In a cyclic process $\Delta E = \Delta Q + \Delta W = 0$.

(b) In an arbitrary, general transformation from state 0 to state a:

$$.E_a = E_0 + \sum (\Delta W + \Delta Q),$$

or, equivalently,

$$(\Delta E)_0{}^a = (\Delta W)_0{}^a + (\Delta Q)_0{}^a.$$

It has been established that a function that is zero over any cycle has the following two properties: (1) it is additive; (2) it is independent of that path. In fact:

Theorem A-5. A function is independent of the path iff it is additive and uniform.

PROOF. That independence of the path implies uniformity follows by the general method used for constructing E out of ΔE (see proof of theorem A-4). The implication of additivity is then a consequence of lemma A-1. In fact, a function independent of the path must assume the value zero over any cycle, for otherwise, by going over the same cycle a different number of times, we would obtain a multiple-valued function. The function being uniform and zero over any cycle, its property of additivity is asserted by lemma A-1.

To prove the converse consider any two arbitrary paths B_i and F_i, $i = 1, \ldots, n$. Then

$$(A, B_1) + (B_1, B_2) + (B_2, B_3) + \cdots + (B_n, C) = (A, C)_B$$

by additivity, and

$$(A, F_1) + (F_1, F_2) + (F_2, F_3) + \cdots + (F_n, C) = (A, C)_F$$

by additivity. But by uniformity $(A, C)_B = (A, C)_F$. Hence (A, C) is independent of the chain of intermediate steps and is a function exclusively of the initial and the final states: it is a function independent of the path.

Observe that the additivity holds over the path, while the uniformity exists over couples of states.

Notice also that in proving additivity we have used the fact (see proof of lemma A-1) that independence of the path provides an *equivalence relation* for paths—and an *invariant*—and thus enables us to make an exhaustive classification into disjoint classes. Each equivalence class then *characterizes* an entity: the number (A, C), this number being an invariant under changes of path.

The F.L. has been extended from cyclic processes to general transformations in two ways: by means of functions independent of the path, and by means of the properties of additivity and uniformity. It has further been shown that the two methods of extension are transformable one into the other. Figure A-4 illustrates the procedure that has been followed in this study.

Some treatments of the F.L. start by postulating that the sum $(\Delta Q + \Delta W)$ is independent of the path. In addition to greater theoretical value, the weaker postulate adopted here also possesses the following advantage: the experimental verification of this postulate ($\Delta Q + \Delta W$ independent of the cycle) requires the experimental characterization and identification of only one state, whereas the experimental verification of the postulate "$\Delta Q + \Delta W$ independent of path" demands the experimental characterization and identification of two states. The difference becomes doubly significant because of the fact that the experimental verification must be realized over a statistical sample.

Observe finally that it has been implicitly shown that functions such as Q and W cannot exist, for ΔQ and ΔW are not independent of the path. Nevertheless, ΔQ and ΔW are *additive*—but they are *not uniform*. Notice also that, by reason of dimensional balance, the relation $\Delta E = \Delta Q + \Delta W$ could not be written were it not that the measuring units of ΔQ and ΔW are interconvertible (definitions 3-8 and 3-9 and theorems 3-9 and 3-10).

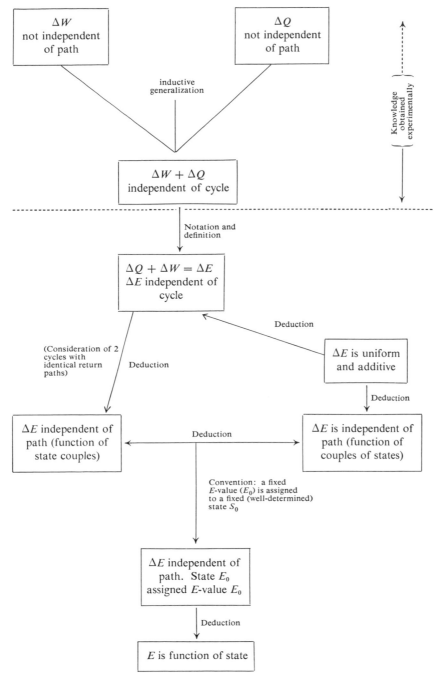

Figure A-4 Methods used for extending the first law from cyclic processes to general processes.

If in applications of the F.L. it is understood that the increment in every term extends from the same initial state (for all terms) to the same final state (for all terms), the indices denoting the states may be omitted and the F.L. written as $\Delta E = \Delta W + \Delta Q$. For purposes of calculation each of the terms may be subdivided as seems most convenient. The term ΔW is usually decomposed into subterms according to the different types of forces associated with the various kinds of work transfers that may be significant in each particular case.

A frequently useful decomposition of the forces associated with some of the various kinds of work transfer is:

External forces acting on S
$\begin{cases} \text{1—forces acting on the boundary } \mathcal{B}. \\ \quad \text{Examples: pressures, surface tensions,} \\ \quad \text{frictions on the boundary.} \\ \text{2—forces acting over the volume of } S. \\ \quad \text{Examples: gravity, magnetic forces.} \end{cases}$

Another very useful decomposition rests upon the concept of conservative force.

Definition A-4.   A force is *conservative over a region R* iff the work that is performed between any two arbitrarily fixed points of R is independent of the path.

Thus, with each conservative force field (i.e., a conservative force defined over a region R) there is associated a function—the work function—that is independent of the path. From the preceding development of our theory we know that with every function independent of the path it is possible to associate a function of state, defined to within a constant. This function of state cannot be the conservative force field, because this field is a vector field and with every point of R it associates a *triplet* of numbers (the three space components of the force at that point of space). A function of state, on the contrary, is a scalar (single number) point function in the abstract space of all the states of S (each "point" of this abstract space representing a state of S). Figure A-5 illustrates the situation.

The fact that a triplet of numbers is more awkward to handle in calculations than a single number leads to the formulation of the following problem: is it possible to construct a scalar point function that, associated with the conservative work function, is *equivalent* (in its mathematical consequences) to the conservative force field that originally produced the conservative work function? The answer to this query has been found to be in the affirmative, and the point function so constructed is called the potential function.

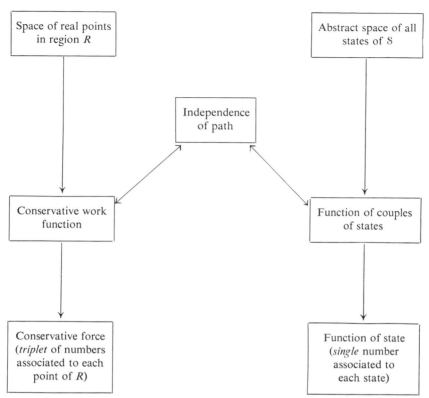

Figure A-5 Summary of preceding analysis, leading to the formulation of the concept of a potential associated to a conservative force field.

Definition A-5. A force **F**, function of position, is said to be derived from a *potential* ϕ iff it is expressible as the *gradient* of a scalar point function ϕ; that is, iff the following relations are satisfied:

$$F_x = \frac{\partial \phi}{\partial x}, \quad F_y = \frac{\partial \phi}{\partial y}, \quad F_z = \frac{\partial \phi}{\partial z}; \quad \text{i.e., } \mathbf{F} = \text{grad } \phi.$$

The gradient expresses the equality of the three components of the vector point function **F** to the three directional derivatives of the scalar point function ϕ along the decomposition axes.*

Definition A-6. A three-dimensional set will be said to have a *tear* or *hole* if it is possible to find a closed curve interior to the set and such that it cannot be shrunk to a geometrical point without leaving the set. The

---

* There is no universal agreement on the sign of the relation between **F** and ϕ. Some authors define $\mathbf{F} = -\text{grad } \phi$.

three dimensional set will be said to have *n tears or holes* if it is possible to find *n* closed curves interior to the set and such that each of them cannot be shrunk to a geometrical point without leaving the set, the *n* curves remaining at all times disjoint (throughout the whole shrinking process).

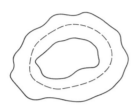

Figure A-6 Example of a doubly connected region (a homotopic image of a torus).

Nomenclature. A set having no tear or hole is said to be *simply connected.* Otherwise the set is called *multiply connected.*

It is easy to see that the sphere or any homotopic image of the sphere is simply connected. On the other hand, the torus or any homotopic image of the torus is doubly connected (in Figure A-6 the dotted curve is interior to the torus and cannot be shrunk to a point without leaving the torus). A pair of scissors and any of its homotopic images are triply connected.

Theorem A-6. In a simply connected region, the necessary and sufficient condition for a force to be conservative is that it be derived from a potential.

PROOF. See, for example, [26], pp. 70–82.

The theorem can be extended to multiply connected regions by transforming them into simply connected regions by means of "cuts." See, for example, [27], pp. 191–199.

From the definitions it follows that potential energy difference has a sign opposite to that of potential difference, the physical reason for the oppositeness being shown in Figure A-7. The formulation in the figure is with reference to a conservative force *internal* to the system, and to work transfers between S and Ɛ. The diagram could equally well have been filled with a formulation in terms of a conservative force *external* to the system, but *always* with reference to work transfers between S and Ɛ (not internal work transfers). In the second type of formulation, when the work is done *by* a conservative force which is external, S has received work transfer; hence there has been energy in-transfer into S, and the system is now in a state of greater potential energy, but of lesser potential. The reverse occurs when the work is done *against* the external conservative force.

In both formulations, however, the work transfer referred to must take place between S and Ɛ, and must not be of the nature of an internal work transfer—for in this case there is no energy transfer into or out of

(Conservative force internal to system)

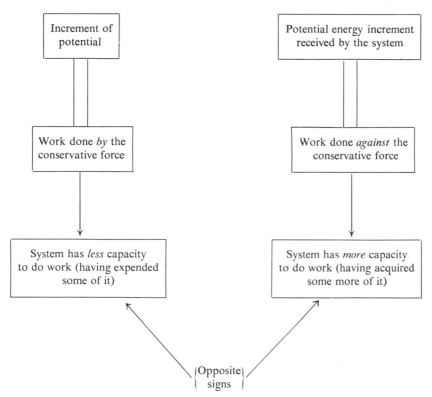

Figure A-7 The potential energy difference has a sign opposite to that of the potential difference.

the system, and thus no increment or decrement of potential energy or of potential. Internal work transfer takes place in an energy conversion, not in energy transfers between $\mathcal{S}$ and $\mathcal{E}$. That is what happens, for example, in the system composed of earth and sun, in which there are alternate energy conversions between the potential and the kinetic forms of energy: $\Delta E = \Delta E^{g} + \Delta E^{v}$.

Consider, on the other hand, the system composed of two magnets, and let them be disposed as shown Figure A-8. Then bring an external

Figure A-8 A *single* system composed of two magnets.

agency (from $\mathcal{E}$—for example, muscular exertion by the experimenter) to bear an external force upon $\mathcal{S}$ and separate the two magnets by a certain distance.

The external force has acted *against the internal conservative magneto-static force of the system*, and the system has received energy in-transfer ΔE^p; as a consequence, in its new state $\mathcal{S}$ has more capacity to do work than it had in its original state.* If, on the contrary, the initial state of $\mathcal{S}$ is one in which the two magnets are held apart by an external agency, and then they are allowed to come together, the *internal* conservative magneto-static force of $\mathcal{S}$ has performed work (overcoming the external agency); there has been an energy out-transfer from $\mathcal{S}$ to $\mathcal{E}$, and $\mathcal{S}$ has in its final state less capacity to do work than it had in its initial state, but it now is in a state of greater potential.

The concept of conservative force field has been defined in terms of a global property (invariance with respect to path transformations). Its existence has then been characterized in terms of a scalar field (the potential) over the region. The existence of a conservative force field may also be characterized in terms of local properties: the vanishing of the curl (or rotor) vector field at every point of the region. See, for example, [28], pp. 60–78, 83–87.

Now that the concept of conservative force is at hand, and a necessary and sufficient condition for its existence is available, the decomposition suggested for the work transfer term may be indicated:

External forces acting on $\mathcal{S}$
$$\begin{cases} 1\text{—forces that are conservative.} \\ \quad \text{Examples: gravitational, electrostatic,} \\ \quad \text{magnetostatic forces.} \\ \\ 2\text{—forces that are not conservative.} \\ \quad \text{Examples: frictional forces, electro-} \\ \quad \text{magnetic forces, etc.} \end{cases}$$

In some kinds of situations it becomes necessary to focus attention upon the kinetic energy of the whole system or of some of its internal parts. This is especially important in open systems, where transport of matter occurs side by side with other kinds of energy transfers; such is the case, for example, in biological systems, meteorology, astrophysics, and continuous industrial processes.

Let L and K symbolize potential and kinetic energies, respectively, as defined in mechanics.

Theorem A-7. L and K are functions of state.

---

* Within the conceptual structure to be introduced in Chapter 5, this added capacity to do work would be measured by $\Delta E_c{}^p$.

Definition A-7. The *internal energy* U of S is defined by the relation $U \equiv E - K$; the *total energy* E_T of S is defined by $E_T \equiv U + L + K$.

Theorem A-8. The internal energy and the total energy are functions of state.

If ϕ stands for the potential function, then $\Delta_1{}^2 W_c = \phi_1 - \phi_2$ is the work transfer into the system against the internal conservative force or forces. The $(\phi_1 - \phi_2)$ is energy gained if $\phi_1 > \phi_2$, for then the potential energy of S is greater in state 2 than in state 1—the system has acquired capacity to do work; it has acquired energy. It is easy to see that $\Delta_1{}^2 W_c = \phi_1 - \phi_2 = L_2 - L_1 = \Delta_1{}^2 L$.

From the definitions of conservative force and of potential it follows that $\Delta_1{}^2 W_c$ is independent of the path and ϕ is a function of state; from what has been explained concerning the relation between potential and potential energy, $L = -\phi$. By theorem 3-4, then, L is a function of state. That K is a state function is an immediate consequence of its definition in mechanics. Finally, that U and E_T are functions of state is a consequence of their definitions and of theorems 3-4 and 3-3. Theorems A-7 and A-8 have thus been demonstrated.

For the correct application of the F.L. it is indispensable to include as terms in the "energy balance" (the F.L.) all types of mass and energy transfers that could possibly be significant (i.e., non-negligible) in the phenomenon being studied. To illustrate this assertion, if the system is subjected to (among other things) a variable field of force, the existence of which is unknown to us, the application of the principle of conservation of energy (the F.L.) would lead to erroneous results. In fact, ignorant of that variable field of force, we would use an insufficient number of parameters to characterize the states of S; that is, unknowingly we would be using an *incomplete* set of generalized parameters, thus not achieving a true characterization. As a consequence, states that in reality are different could be identified in the study. Also, work transfers due to the ignored field of force would be neglected. Naturally, the two kinds of errors just specified are not independent; each is a consequence of the other.

A general methodological principle of scientific investigation is the following: whenever the application of the F.L. to a phenomenon causes some difficulties (i.e., the energy-transfers do not balance), an attempt is made to postulate some new form of energy transfer (associated with the phenomenon) that will restore the conservation of energy property.

It has already been explained in this appendix that the F.L. is more than the definition of a quantity: it implies the existence of a quantity having a very particular *invariant* property. This law demands that the sum of *all* the energy transfers between *any* two specified states be independent of the path; if it were possible to find just one single process between a pair of states that did not satisfy this condition, the phrase "principle of conservation of energy" could not properly be employed, but the concept of energy transfer would still be usable.

It is evident that, in the application of the F.L. to any particular system and phenomenon, the decomposition of the terms of the F.L. equation will be used that suits best the specific case being studied. Because every term of the equation has the physicochemical interpretation of an "energy term or component" (especially if the interconvertibility of mass and energy according to the equation $E_m = mc^2$ is included), the F.L. is often written in the forms

$$\sum_{i=1}^{n} \Delta E_i = 0 \quad \text{and} \quad \Delta E_n = -\sum_{i=1}^{n-1} \Delta E_i,$$

with one or the other being used according to convenience.

4

The Second Law of Energy Transfers and the General Gradient Law

It is observed in scientific studies that some quantities characterizing properties of systems are functions of the amount of volume occupied by the system. Examples are mass (for a given mass density) and charge (for a given charge density). Other quantities expressing values of properties of systems, on the other hand, are independent of the amount of volume of the whole system. Examples of these are temperature and pressure. The first type of quantity is usually called *extensive*; the second type, *intensive*.

Because extensive quantities associate a number with a system, and a physical system is represented geometrically by a set of points in space, it is evident that extensive quantities may be adequately represented by set functions.

Intensive quantities, being independent of the space occupied by the system, are ordinarily predicated on mathematical points of space and mathematically represented by point functions. This, of course, implies a specific idealization, for the concept and definition of any property of a physical system has for its immediate or remote point of departure necessarily a physical experiment and measurement, and no physical measurement can be performed at a mathematical point (which has zero one-dimensional measure). Any physical measurement must be taken over a necessarily finite volume of space, and associates with that finite volume of space a real number; a physical measurement should thus be represented mathematically by a system function or set function. The difference between the *mathematical representations* of intensive and extensive properties is thus to be found in the properties of the set functions that are used for one or the other of the representations.

Note. The reason why point functions have been used almost exclusively for the mathematical representation of intensive properties is that the mathematical analysis of point functions has been incomparably more developed than the analysis of set functions. We may as well, however, use set functions in our study until the point is reached at which the mathematics of set functions may be inadequate, passing then to representation in terms of point functions, and using the appropriate integrations and transformation theorems. The reader may consult on this matter [3], [4], [5], [6], and [49].

Let S represent both the system of interest and the set of points that represents it mathematically; the starting point of our investigation is the following concept:

Definition 4-1.   A δ_p-*set* (or δ_p-*cell*) is the smallest subsystem (or subset) of S at which property p is measurable.

It follows from definition 4-1 that a δ_p-cell must have:

1. Three-dimensional measure δ.
2. The proper shape for the measurement of physical property p.

Two advertences are in order:

(a) δ_p-cells are associated with both intensive and extensive parameters because they are associated with any measurement.

(b) The δ_p-cell is a *function of the instrument* being used to measure property p. In the notation "δ_p-cell," therefore, the symbol p stands for three variables: a property of the δ_p-cell (and therefore of S), the quantity used to measure that property, and the instrument employed to measure it. For example, the property may be temperature, the quantity used to measure it may be brightness (or length of a column of mercury), and the instrument employed may be a thermometer.

The above will lead to no confusion in what follows, however, and in general the letter p will represent an intensive property or parameter. When the discussion centers around only one such parameter, the index p may be dropped without danger of ambiguity, and a δ_p-cell will simply be called a δ-cell.

Definition 4-2.   *Extensive properties* of systems are those that can be adequately represented mathematically only by univalent set functions that are additive and point-continuous.

It is the additivity property that expresses (mathematically) the fact that an extensive property depends for its value on the amount of volume of the system. The property of being point-continuous is the mathematical representation of the physical assumption that the value of the quantity varies continuously with the volume. In other words, definition 4-2 *expresses mathematically* the following *hypotheses* concerning *physical qualities* of those properties that are called extensive: (1) they vary in value with the volume; (2) that variation is continuous.

Definition 4-3. *Intensive properties* of systems are those having the following three characteristics:

(a) They are representable mathematically by univalent set functions.

(b) The set functions representing intensive properties are not additive.

(c) If $p(S)$ represents the value of intensive property p at S, and S_1, S_2 are δ-sets, then *either* $p(S_1 \cup S_2) = p(S_1) = p(S_2)$ *or* $p(S_1 \cup S_2)$ is not physically defined.

Evidently, characteristic (b) expresses mathematically the fact that properties that are called intensive do not depend for their values on the total volume of the system. Characteristic (c) expresses the fact that, if an intensive property is predicated of a system larger than a δ-cell (and such a system is, for example, $S_1 \cup S_2$), it must have a constant value throughout that system. If an intensive property is not constant throughout a system S larger than a δ-cell, that intensive property cannot be predicated of the whole system S but only of the δ-cells contained in it.

Extensive and intensive properties of systems will be measured by extensive and intensive *parameters*, respectively. Observe that these two types of properties are real in the sense that actual measurements directly (without mathematical operation other than establishing a correspondence) yield the numerical values of these parameters. "Mean values" do not fall under either of the above two categories, and they are not the values yielded directly by physical measurements. Likewise, specific values are neither extensive nor intensive properties [they are not additive nor do they satisfy condition (c) of definition 4-3] but they are not real, since they express the ratio (a mathematical operation!) of the measurements of two distinct extensive properties.

From the definition of the δ_p-set of a parameter p it follows that the δ_p-set can suffer only translations and rotations. In fact, because a δ_p-cell cannot change its measure δ, any deformation other than a rotation or translation would force a change of shape; but the original δ_p-cell was the *smallest* set with the proper shape for the measurement of p—hence the instrument for the p-measurement would not fit into the distorted image of the δ-cell. Thus:

Theorem 4-1. A δ-cell can suffer no deformation other than translations and rotations while remaining a δ-cell (for the same parameter).

In what follows, unless specifically stated otherwise, rotations of δ-sets will be neglected. This will imply no loss of generality, as the reader can easily see.

The first law (see [2])* states a conservation principle obeyed by energy transfers and conversions. It enunciates a necessary condition that is to be observed *globally* by the process (i.e., without reference to the *local* conditions in the system or the surroundings—in other words, without reference to the properties of δ-sets of S or of $\mathcal{E}$). It states nothing concerning two very important questions:

(a) The *compatibility* of energy transfers and conversions with the conditions that may hold in local areas (or δ-sets) of the system.

(b) The *direction* of the energy transfers with relation to the local conditions within S or between S and $\mathcal{E}$.

Two generalizations from experience, the second law of energy transfers and the general gradient law, provide answers to these questions. To express them adequately we need the following

Nomenclature. By ΔE^p we shall understand an energy transfer "associated with" an intensive parameter p.

For example, if p is temperature ($p = T$), then ΔE^p is that form of energy transfer associated with T and called heat transfer (of which we admit two types: refer to definition A-1 in Appendix A). If p is pressure, ΔE^p is compressibility work transfer (of which there can be more than one type also). If p is fluid density, then ΔE^p is fluid mass transfer.

Usually we shall have to deal simultaneously with more than one parameter p; these parameters will be distinguished by an index attached to p-thus p_1, p_2, etc.

By a *gradient* of the intensive parameter p we shall understand a difference in value of p at two different δ-sets within S, or at two δ-sets lying on opposite sides of a boundary.

For any property p_i, the value of parameter p_i at δ_p-cell S_δ will be symbolized by $p_i(S_\delta)$. The ΔE^{p_i}-transfer between cells $S_{\delta 1}$ and $S_{\delta 2}$ will be designated by $\Delta E_{12}{}^{p_i}$. The gradient existing (it could naturally be zero) between $S_{\delta 1}$ and $S_{\delta 2}$ will be symbolized by $\Delta p_i(\delta 1, \delta 2)$.

Second Law of Energy Transfers. If there exists only one kind of energy transfer within S or between S and $\mathcal{E}$, or if two or more energy transfers occur simultaneously but independently of each other (i.e., uncoupled), then

    1. A *necessary* condition for ΔE^p-transfer to take place between δ_p-cells $S_{\delta 1}$ and $S_{\delta 2}$ is that $p(S_{\delta 1}) \neq p(S_{\delta 2})$.

---

* See also Appendix A.

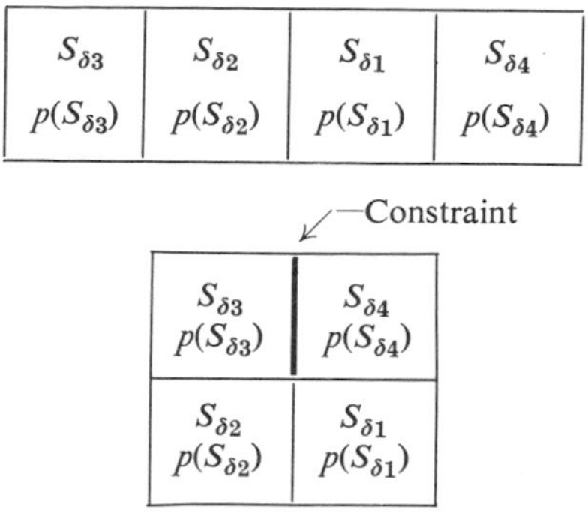

$S_{\delta 3}$	$S_{\delta 2}$	$S_{\delta 1}$	$S_{\delta 4}$
$p(S_{\delta 3})$	$p(S_{\delta 2})$	$p(S_{\delta 1})$	$p(S_{\delta 4})$

↙—Constraint

$S_{\delta 3}$	$S_{\delta 4}$
$p(S_{\delta 3})$	$p(S_{\delta 4})$
$S_{\delta 2}$	$S_{\delta 1}$
$p(S_{\delta 2})$	$p(S_{\delta 1})$

Figure 4-1 Two possible schematic arrangements of the four δ_p-cells referred to in definitions 4-4a and 4-4b.

2. If $p(S_{\delta 2}) > p(S_{\delta 1})$, then the *direction* of ΔE^p-transfer is from $S_{\delta 2}$ toward $S_{\delta 1}$.

Now suppose that $p(S_{\delta 2}) > p(S_{\delta 1})$ (see Figure 4-1).

Definition 4-4a. $(S_{\delta 1} \cup S_{\delta 2})$ is a *quasi-isolated subsystem* of S iff *any one* of the three following conditions holds:

α There exists no ΔE^p-transfer into $S_{\delta 2}$—from a third $S_{\delta 3}$ with $p(S_{\delta 3}) > p(S_{\delta 2})$—and no transfer out of $S_{\delta 1}$—into a fourth $S_{\delta 4}$ with $p(S_{\delta 4}) < p(S_{\delta 1})$.

β $\Delta E_{14}^p = 0$ and $\dot{E}_{21}^p > \dot{E}_{32}^p$ during the time interval of concern.

γ $\Delta E_{32}^p = 0$ and $\dot{E}_{21}^p > \dot{E}_{14}^p$ during the time interval of concern.

Naturally, when conditions α holds, $(S_{\delta 1} \cup S_{\delta 2})$ is an isolated subsystem of S as far as the property characterized by p is concerned.

Definition 4-4b. $(S_{\delta 1} \cup S_{\delta 2})$ is a *quasi-static subsystem* of S iff *either* of the two following conditions holds:

α $\Delta E_{14}^p = 0$, $\dot{E}_{12}^p = 0$, and $\dot{E}_{32}^p > 0$,

β $\Delta E_{32}^p = 0$, $\dot{E}_{21}^p = 0$, and $\dot{E}_{14}^p > 0$,

where, as before $p(S_{\delta 3}) > p(S_{\delta 2})$ and $p(S_{\delta 4}) < p(S_{\delta 1})$.

The intuitive content of definitions 4-4a and 4-4b is immediate.

General Gradient Law

I. The existence of $\Delta p(\delta 1, \delta 2) > 0$ is a sufficient condition, in the absence of constraints, for $\Delta E_{12}^p > 0$.

II. If $(S_{\delta 1} \cup S_{\delta 2})$ forms a quasi-isolated subsystem of S, then $\Delta E_{12}^p > 0$ implies $(d/dt) \Delta p(\delta 1, \delta 2) < 0$.

III. If $(S_{\delta 1} \cup S_{\delta 2})$ forms a quasi-static subsystem of S, then either $\dot{p}(S_{\delta 2}) > 0$ (if condition α of definition 4-4b holds) or $\dot{p}(S_{\delta 1}) < 0$ (if condition β holds).

The intuitive significance of the general gradient law is also sufficiently immediate as to require no elaboration.

Observe that, while there is a conservation law imposing a condition upon the ΔE^p-transfer (the first law; see [2] or Appendix A), there is no equivalent law of conservation for the "transfer of p" indicated in the general gradient law.

From now on we shall use the following abbreviations:

> S.L. for second law of energy transfers,
> G.G.L. for general gradient law,
> E^p-transfer for ΔE^p-transfer.

Above, and in what follows, the phrase "in the absence of constraints" should be understood in the sense "in the absence of sufficiently strong constraints."

The S.L. and the G.G.L. are, naturally, intimately related to the second law of thermodynamics, of which they are, in a sense, extensions and generalizations.

5

The Convertibility Equation. The Increment of the Associated Extensive Parameter, Its First Two Properties: Additivity and Extensiveness

Consider a system S that either is available or its construction is under consideration. The following problem may be presented for study: if an energy transfer ΔE^p is introduced from environment $\mathcal{E}$ into the system, what proportion of that ΔE^p may be returnable from S to $\mathcal{E}$? (See Figure 5.1.)

The part of ΔE^p that is returned to $\mathcal{E}$ from S may be returned in the form of E^p-transfer itself or as another energy transfer to which the ΔE^p received by S has been converted within the system. The latter situation is more common, for most often an energy transfer is introduced into a system in order to obtain from that system energy in another—and, for the moment, more useful—form.

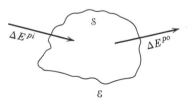

Notations and Nomenclature.

$\Delta E^{pi} \equiv$ input energy transfer or *in-transfer*.

$\Delta E^{po} \equiv$ output energy transfer or *out-transfer*.

Figure 5-1 System S receiving from environment $\mathcal{E}$ the input ΔE^{pi} and returning to it the output ΔE^{po}.

Retransfer phenomenon: $po = pi$

Conversion (or conversion-transfer) phenomenon: $po \neq pi$. The conversion phenomenon will also be called *energy conversion*.

The out-transfer may consist of more than one kind of energy transfer; thus, $\Delta E^{p_k o}$ will stand for system output p_k.

The energy converter (symbol: $\mathcal{C}$) may be considered as that part of $\mathcal{S}$ for which $pi \neq p_k o$ for at least some one k. $\mathcal{C}$ may, on occasion, be the whole of $\mathcal{S}$.

The conversion process may also have more than one *conversion product*; the symbol $\Delta E^{p_i c}$ will stand for conversion product p_i. Those conversion products that leave $\mathcal{C}$ will be called *conversion outputs* and denoted by ΔE^{pco}. Every converter output is a conversion product, but not vice versa; a conversion product that is not a converter output will be called a *retained conversion product* and symbolized by ΔE^{pcr}—such a product stays within $\mathcal{C}$ and accumulates there. A ΔE^{pco} that is retained in $\mathcal{S}$ will be denoted by ΔE^{pcor}. Finally, that part of ΔE^{pi} that does not enter $\mathcal{C}$ but is retained within $\mathcal{S}$ will be denoted by ΔE^{pir}.

That the problem formulated at the beginning of this chapter is not meaningless or trivial follows from the fact that the retransfer (like any transfer) is subject to the S.L., while the conversion must obey the first law [2]. In fact, the first law imposes the condition

$$\Delta E^{pci} = \sum_j \Delta E^{p_j c} = \sum_k \Delta E^{p_k cr} + \sum_l \Delta E^{p_l co},$$

where ΔE^{pci} represents the input to $\mathcal{C}$, as well as the condition

$$\Delta E^{pi} = \Delta E^{pci} + \Delta' E^{pi} = \sum_k \Delta E^{p_k cr} + \sum_m \Delta E^{p_m ir} + \sum_j \Delta E^{p_j cor} + \sum_l \Delta E^{p_l o}.$$

Figure 5-2 represents the analysis as carried out thus far.

As an illustrative example of system and converter, we may take the human body as the system and its digestive tract as the converter. In the eating of a dish of food the system will receive as many inputs as organic chemicals are contained in the intaken food. The converter outputs, however, will consist of as many chemicals as the digestive process manufactures out of the food received, as well as heat transfer from the combustion of some of the chemicals. The products of body elimination are clearly system outputs, but system output is also the energy that leaves the body in the form of heat transfer. The chemicals that are stored in the body are retained conversion outputs.

If the converter is muscular tissue, the inputs to $\mathcal{C}$ consist of the blood supply to the muscle and of the output from the nerves to the muscle; the converter output is mechanical motion, which is the same as the system output.

The preceding is a very simplified treatment of the processes of nutrition and muscular action, but it suffices to show how our analysis of transfer and conversion processes is applicable to familiar real processes.

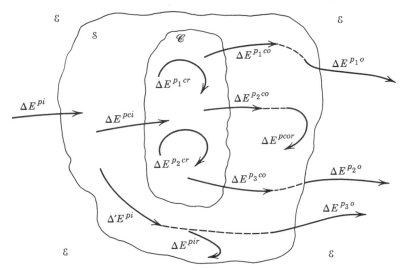

Figure 5-2 Schematic of a system having energy transfers with its environment, showing in-transfer, out-transfers, retransfer, conversion products, conversion outputs, and retained conversion products.

Our inquiry necessitates a consideration of the types and origins of conversion, treated *only* from the standpoint that is of significance for our study.

Definition 5-1. A conversion is *ideal* iff it has only one conversion product. A process is a *complete conversion* iff the input to $\mathcal{S}$ is not found (in kind) in the set of outputs of $\mathcal{S}$. An *identity* conversion is that process in which converter input and conversion product are identical in kind.

An ideal conversion is characterized by $\Delta E^{pci} = \Delta E^{pc}$ with $pci \neq pc$. In an identity conversion $\Delta E^{pci} = \Delta E^{pc}$ and $pci = pc$. A complete conversion is characterized by the relations

$$\{\Delta E^{pi} = \sum \Delta E^{p_k o}, \qquad p_k o \neq pi \quad \text{for every } k\}.$$

In an identity conversion necessarily $pi = pci = pc = pco$ if all the corresponding quantities are non-null. Obviously, the identity conversion may be considered as a degenerate case of a conversion phenomenon.

A conversion can in general have two sources:

A. The structure and nature of the matter of the converter itself. This may be manifested by (1) the structural constitution of the chemicals in the converter (e.g., explosive chemicals), or (2) the mathematical relation holding between the characterizing parameters of the converter (the equation of state).

Thus, if the converter is composed of an ideal gas, with $pci = T$ and $pco = P$, there is a definite functional relation between pco and pci: $pco = (nR/V)\,pci$. If the converter is a real gas, with the same parameters for pci and pco, the functional relation is still of direct proportionality, but with a different coefficient and perhaps a different exponent (non-linear).

On the other hand, if the converter is a chemical explosive, it is the physicochemical structure of the compound, rather than its physical equation of state, that is of interest for the conversion.

B. The kinematic or dynamic relations of different parts of the converter with respect to each other. Thus, if the converter consists of the couple {earth, body} with $pci = h$ (altitude over sea level) and $p_1 co =$ velocity potential, then, if the distance between the centers of mass of the two parts of the converter is diminishing, we have $\Delta E^{pci} =$ potential energy of gravitation; $\Delta E^{p_1 co} =$ kinetic energy; $\Delta E^{p_2 co} =$ frictional energy loss. There is a *double conversion* in this example, for $\Delta E^{p_2 co}$ becomes the $\Delta E^{p_2 ci}$ of a second conversion (with a different converter!) with $\Delta E^{p_{21} co} =$ heat transfer, and $\Delta E^{p_{22} co} =$ energy of deformation (of atmospheric air during motion, and of body and solid earth upon impact). Both conversions occur simultaneously.

Notice that the existence of a ΔE^{pci} and a converter does not suffice to produce an energy conversion; needed also is the absense of constraints to the conversion, just as the G.G.L. specifies that the existence of a p-gradient is sufficient for an E^p-transfer *if* there are no constraints to the ΔE^p-flow.

Observe also that, if the first law is to be obeyed by the process, it is necessary that ΔE^{pi} or ΔE^{pci} include all the in-transfers to $\mathcal{S}$ or to $\mathcal{C}$ that eventually take part in the process (independently of whether or not those in-transfers occur simultaneously or millions of years apart). Thus, if the converter is a chemical explosive, ΔE^{pci} includes not only the energy transferred from detonator to converter (which transfer may be of a photochemical, mechanical, etc., nature) but also the energy transfer that, perhaps long before, was introduced into the converter in chemical form.

It is seen that conversions of type B, because they essentially depend upon kinematic and dynamic relations between parts of the converter, of necessity depend upon a gradient—the word gradient being used here, not in the sense of a gradient of a potential, but with the same meaning that it has in the G.G.L. and the S.L. More precisely:

Definition 5-2. A system $\mathcal{S}$ is said to possess a *gradient of a quantity q with respect to the parameter s*, over the interval $[s_i, s_f]$, iff q, a quantity associated with $\mathcal{S}$, is a strictly monotonic function of s over $[s_i, s_f]$.

The parameter s will usually be designated as the *parameter of the gradient.*

Observe that this definition of gradient subsumes the one given in the discussion of the S.L. and the G.G.L.

In the absence of constraints, the existence of such a gradient is also sufficient for the realization of type B conversions.

A seeming exception to the above is the extremely idealized situation that would fall under Newton's first law of motion, but such cases enter into the conceptual scheme just introduced by placing q = distance (from some reference point) and s = time.

Definition 5-2 makes the existence of a gradient a necessary and sufficient condition for the existence of any motion or process. Thus, by way of illustration, the existence of a gradient may be shown to be a necessary and sufficient condition for real mechanical motion of a body—and in two ways:

1. The effective force, in any direction, upon any body is the difference between the forces acting, along the same direction, on opposite sides of the body, for otherwise the necessary and sufficient conditions for equilibrium $\left(\sum_i \mathbf{F}_i = 0, \sum_i \mathbf{M}_i = 0 \right)$ would be fulfilled. Here q is force and s is position. In Figure 5-3, $F(s_2) > F(s_1)$.

2. The acting force is the derivative of the momentum, and the necessary and sufficient condition for real motion of an unconstrained body is that $F_a = (d/dt)(mv) \neq 0$. But this means the existence of a gradient of $q = mv$ with respect to the parameter time.

The existence of a gradient is also necessary and sufficient for a conversion of the first class of type A, the one typified by the chemical explosive as converter. In fact, it will later be shown that there exist quantities which are functions of state and such that, in the absence of constraints, their diminution as a function of time is a necessary and sufficient condition for the evolution of any chemical process, indeed, for the evolution of any physicochemical process.

Based upon the preceding considerations and subject to further examination in terms of its consequences, it suffices to postulate a

Conversion Hypothesis.   An energy conversion in a system S has as a necessary condition the existence of a gradient of some quantity q

Figure 5-3   Body will move iff there exists a gradient $F(s_2) - F(s_1) \neq 0$.

associated with S. In the absence of constraints, the condition is also sufficient.

Observe that the constraint need not be of the nature of a "wall"; it may, for example, be a force. Thus, in meteorology, the gradient of atmospheric density (q) with respect to the parameter distance from the surface of the earth (s) is, for values of s below a certain one, constrained from operating by the gravitational force.

The parameter of the gradient may vary from case to case, and some conversions may also have associated with them more than one gradient. The parameter of the gradient will be symbolized by s, and this parameter is to be distinguished from the quantity, q or p, on which the gradient is predicated; the letter q represents the *parameter of the conversion*, and the letter p the intensive *parameter of the transfer*.

Now, for an in-transfer ΔE^{pi} there must be a *pi*-gradient from ε to S by the S.L. There will be a lowest or minimum available *pi*-value in S; denote it by $p_0 i$.

Analogously, the S.L. demands that, for an out-transfer ΔE^{po}, there be a *po*-gradient from S to ε. Denote by $p_0 o$ the lowest or minimum *po*-value available in ε.

Finally, the conversion hypothesis demands that, for an energy conversion ΔE_c^q, there be a q-gradient within C. Denote by q_0 the lowest or minimal available q-value in C.

Nota Bene. The q-parameter of the conversion need not be identical with the *pci* of ΔE^{pci} or with the $p_k co$ of $\Delta E^{p_k co}$ for any k.

Because all three phenomena listed above are subject to the same conditions, it is expedient to unify the symbolism. We proceed as follows.

Formulation of the Problem

1. Given an in-transfer to C, what part of it may be converted?

2. Given a product of C, what part of it may be out-transferred?

3. In the case of no conversion, given an in-transfer into S, what part of it may be retransferred?

In every case we have an input (from S to C, from C to S, or from ε to S) and an output (from C to S or to ε, or from S to ε), and in every case also a parameter of the gradient is associated with the process.

Unified Notation.

Conversion or transfer parameter: p

$$\text{Input:} \quad \Delta E^p \qquad \text{Output:} \ \Delta E_c^p$$

$$\text{Gradient parameter:} \ s \text{ or } t$$

The symbol $\Delta E_c{}^p$ has been chosen for the output because a *retransfer is a particular case of a conversion phenomenon*, since *it is a type of identity conversion* (definition 5-1)—a type characterized by the fact that $pi = pci = pc = pco = po$ and $\Delta E^{pi} = \Delta E^{po}$. This is reflected in the fact that *the S.L. and the G.G.L. are particularizations of the conversion hypothesis*, which is an extension of the other two.

In our unified treatment of all three processes, $\Delta E_c{}^p$ will be called the *convertible* part of ΔE^p; it is that part of ΔE^p that is convertible (or transferable) by virtue of the existence of a p-gradient. $\Delta E_{ic}{}^p$ will represent the remaining part of ΔE^p: the part that will not be converted or transferred by virtue of a p-gradient; it will be called the *inconvertible* part of ΔE^p.

For the present we shall study uncoupled energy transfers and conversions, that is, energy transfers and conversions that do not influence one another even if they occur simultaneously. In consequence we may study each transfer or conversion as if it occurred in isolation from all other transfers and conversions. On another occasion we shall study coupled transfers and conversions.

Nomenclature. With respect to a possible E^p-transfer from S to $\mathcal{E}$, the *minimum p-value in $\mathcal{E}$ that is available* for E^p-transfer (by means of a p-gradient from S to $\mathcal{E}$) will be denoted by p_0. Generally p_0 will be the p-value in that part of $\mathcal{E}$ (the part that may be called the "outer system") that is to receive the out-transfer from S. In case of a conversion, p_0 (or q_0) is the minimal value of p (or of q) that $\mathcal{C}$ may use to effect the conversion (following the conversion hypothesis).

The symbol $A_o{}^p$, called the *absolute zero value of the parameter p*, represents the lowest p-value that can be *conceptually predicated* of the whole universe $U = S \cup \mathcal{E}$.

From the definition it follows that p_0 is a *local* property of $\mathcal{E}$—a property in that part of $\mathcal{E}$ that is adjacent to S. On the contrary, $A_0{}^p$ is a *global* property of U; in the whole universe no p-value lower than $A_0{}^p$ can be found. Also observe that p_0 is defined as a *real* property, actually existing at some locality of $\mathcal{E}$. The absolute zero value $A_0{}^p$, on the other hand, is *defined* as an *ideal* property of U; nothing has been said thus far regarding the possibility of its actual (real) existence in some locality or p-cell of U (in Chapter 16 some investigations related to this problem will be carried out).

Finally, observe that, concerning *one and the same* intensive parameter p, with different phenomena depending on that parameter there may be associated different lowest available p-values; thus, for example, if S is a bathysphere several thousand feet below the surface of the ocean, and S_2

is an open-hearth furnace in a steel plant, and the phenomenon of interest in both cases is heat transfer, the lowest available temperature for heat transfer in the first instance will be quite different from that in the second.

Suppose now that there exists a system S which has received a ΔE^p in-transfer. Then the following *logical decomposition* of ΔE^p becomes non-trivial:

$$\Delta E^p = \Delta E_c^{\ p} + \Delta E_{ic}^{\ p} \tag{5-1}$$

Observe that the fact that $\Delta E_{ic}^{\ p}$ will not be converted or transferred by virtue of the existence of a p-gradient (prescinding from constraints) is ultimately dependent on the existence of the minimal available value $p_0 > A_0^{\ p}$ in the receiving system (for an in-transfer, the receiving system is S; for an out-transfer, it is $\mathcal{E}$; in a conversion, both the supplying and the receiving system are the same: $\mathcal{C}$). This is so because it is the existence of p_0 that ultimately accounts for the depletion of the p-gradient that produces $\Delta E_c^{\ p}$.

Definition 5-3. A process is said to be *free of parasitic conversions* iff either the conversion is ideal (definition 5-1) or the process is a retransfer.

Any internal E^p-transfer in S (one that is neither an in-transfer nor an out-transfer) is thus considered to be parasitic.

The following theorem holds:

Theorem 5-1. In a process free of parasitic conversions, the equality $p_0 = A_0^{\ p}$ necessarily implies $\Delta E_c^{\ p} = \Delta E^p$ in the absence of constraints, and the inequality $p_0 > A_0^{\ p}$ implies $\Delta E_{ic}^{\ p} > 0$.

PROOF.   Immediate.

As examples we may consider

$p = $ temperature T,
ΔE^T-transfer $=$ heat transfer,
$A_0^{\ T} = $ absolute zero temperature,

$p = $ pressure P
$\Delta E^P = $ pneumatic energy transfer,
$A_0^{\ P} = $ perfect vacuum,

$p = $ altitude h
$\Delta E^h = $ gravitational energy conversion,
$A_0^{\ h} = $ point of maximal gravitational potential.

Table 5-1 also presents illustrations of processes and quantities that are particular cases of a unified theory of energy transfers and conversions.

Table 5-1

The second row shows energy transfers and conversions associated with different kinds of intensive parameters (top row). The third and fourth rows show processes that are particular cases of these energy transfers and conversions, and the bottom row contains quantitative relations associated with these processes

	Distance from attracting body, h	Pressure, P	Density, δ	Distance from attracting body, s
Temperature, T				
Heat transfer ΔQ	Gravity potential-energy conversion, $\Delta\Omega_g$	Compressibility (PV) work transfer, ΔW_{pv}	Fluid mass transfer, ΔM	Electrical potential-energy conversion, $\Delta\Omega_e$
Isothermal process	Weight transfer along equipotential	Constant P process (e.g., heat transfer with volume transfer)	Constant δ process (e.g., volume transfer with mass transfer)	Charge transfer along equipotential
Adiabatic process	Weight transfer with gravity-gradient (distance) transfer	Zero volume transfer (e.g., changing P with heat transfer or with mass transfer)	Zero fluid transfer (e.g., changing δ with volume transfer)	Charge transfer with electrical-gradient (distance) transfer
$\Delta Q = T\,\Delta S$ $= S\,\Delta T$	$\Delta\Omega_g = \dfrac{W}{g}\cdot\Delta h$ $= \dfrac{\Delta W}{g}\cdot h$	$\Delta W_{pv} = \cdot P\,\Delta V$ $= V\cdot\Delta P$	$\Delta M = \delta\cdot\Delta V$ $= V\cdot\Delta\delta$	$\Delta\Omega_e = Eq\,\Delta s$ $= E\cdot\Delta q\cdot s$

In Appendix A of Chapter 3 the existence of a new function of the state of S is demonstrated on the basis of the first law; this function is called energy. Nothing in what has been said thus far implies that, if S has $A_0{}^p$ for p-value (for any one parameter p or for all of them), it necessarily has zero energy.

From an analysis of the factors and conditions entering into any conversion or retransfer it is seen that the inconvertible term $\Delta E_{ic}{}^p$ in (5-1) can have two sources:

1. The *actual existence* of a transfer or a conversion subject to the two stipulated conditions. That is, the fact that there has been a process fulfilling the following two conditions:

   (a) The process requires a p-gradient;
   (b) There exists a p-lowest bound p_0 in the receiving system, such that $p_0 > A_0{}^p$;

suffices to account for a certain measure of inconvertibility in the process, *independently* of the *manner or mode* in which the process is carried out. The *mere fact that there has been an input* by means of which ΔE^p has been added to the energy content of S implies (under the two conditions above) that a part—denote it by $\Delta E_t{}^p$—of ΔE^p will be "inconvertible" (in the case of a retransfer this means that the $\Delta E_t{}^p$-portion of ΔE^p will not leave as an out-transfer; in a conversion it means that the $\Delta E_t{}^p$-portion will not be converted).

2. The *particular manner* in which the conversion or transfer has been carried out. This portion of $\Delta E_{ic}{}^p$ will be denoted by $\Delta E_l{}^p$; it follows from the existence of "losses" internal to the transfer or conversion (like those caused by internal unconstrained p-gradients) or "losses" associated with the transfer across the boundary (like, for example, friction on the boundary).

The last term in (5-1) can thus be further decomposed as follows:

$$\Delta E_{ic}{}^p = \Delta E_t{}^p + \Delta E_l{}^p. \tag{5-2}$$

$\Delta E_t{}^p$ is inconvertibility *intrinsic to the existence of a transfer or conversion subject to conditions* (a) and (b); it must in consequence be directly proportional to the total amount of input ΔE^p.

$\Delta E_l{}^p$ is inconvertibility *intrinsic to the particular process or method* by which the conversion or transfer takes place. The subscript l stands for "loss" because $\Delta E_l{}^p$ is very often the result of a *parasitic conversion* accompanying the desired (intended) conversion. Otherwise, it is the result of *parasitic internal p-gradients* (and their associated parasitic internal transfers) accompanying the intended transfer. Frictional losses exemplify a parasitic energy conversion; turbulence, and heat transfer internal to the system, exemplify parasitic internal p-gradients and transfers.

Nota Bene.   Ultimately, conditions (a) and (b) are responsible for both ΔE_t^p and ΔE_l^p, because those two conditions regulate all convertibility and all transfer in the theory (by the S. L. and the conversion hypothesis), but in ΔE_t^p they work *upon the input*, while in ΔE_l^p they work *upon the disturbances* (parasitic conversions and internal gradients) present in the actual process.

As an example, internal (to S) multidirectional p-gradients will, depending on the constraints, be cancelled either partially or entirely. In thus bringing the whole system (or parts of it) to a lower p-value, this cancellation of internal p-gradients also effects a loss of convertibility or transferability because the *tendency* for energy conversion (or transfer) is proportional to the gradient (see below). Turbulence is one such case in which loss of convertibility is brought about by the existence of multidirectional internal gradients. On the other hand, frictional loss is a parasitic energy conversion followed by a heat transfer obeying conditions (a) and (b); if it were not for these conditions, the output of the frictional conversion would be available for useful further conversion instead of becoming a partial or total loss (on occasions, frictional dissipation will bring about more than one measurable kind of parasitic conversion: mechanical deformation, etc.).

Figure 5-4 illustrates the application of expressions (5-1) and (5-2) to the

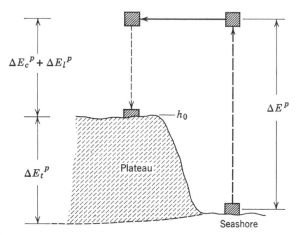

Figure 5-4   Process illustrating the physical significance (for this particular case) of the quantities entering into relations (5-1) and (5-2).

case in which a weight is raised to a higher (and perhaps laterally displaced) position and then dropped. The quantities indicated are *proportional* to the distances shown in the sketch. Were the atmosphere above the plateau of very thick density (like molasses), the term ΔE_i^p would be very large because of the high frictional conversion (which in this case, as usual, is a *parasitic* conversion), and the term ΔE_c^p (measuring the conversion to energy of motion) would then be correspondingly small.

As long as no further conditions are imposed on the terms of the decomposition

$$\Delta E^p = \Delta E_c^p + \Delta E_{ic}^p = \Delta E_c^p + (\Delta E_t^p + \Delta E_l^p),$$

this equality represents a *logical decomposition of* ΔE^p. The next task is to determine a mathematical, calculable expression for ΔE_{ic}^p in terms of characterizing parameters of the system and the process—such quantitative expression, of course, yielding conclusions that agree sufficiently well with results of experiments.

Now, ΔE_{ic}^p has been made to depend on the existence of a p-gradient and a p-lowest bound $p_0 > A_0^p$ in the receiving system. As a consequence, ΔE_{ic}^p must be a function of the value p_0, and furthermore the relation ought to be one of direct proportionality: because a p-gradient $(p - p_0)$ is necessary for convertibility, to higher p_0 there correspond a smaller p-gradient available for energy conversion (or transfer), and hence also a larger ΔE_{ic}^p.

Assumption. ΔE_{ic}^p is a *linear* function of p_0. Thus

$$\Delta E_{ic}^p = \beta p_0 = \Delta E_t^p + \Delta E_l^p = \beta_t p_0 + \beta_l p_0.$$

Remains to consider the coefficients of the linear function.

Because ΔE_t^p is *independent* of the losses producing ΔE_l^p, the most appropriate way to study ΔE_t^p is by analyzing its functional structure in cases where ΔE_l^p is negligible with reference to the measuring instruments available. Hence, temporarily assume $\Delta E_l^p = 0$; this will in no way affect the generality of the functional structure that is to be obtained for ΔE_t^p.

Assumption.   The coefficient β_t is a *linear* function of ΔE^p.

Hence $\beta_t = \alpha_t \Delta E^p$, and we may write $\Delta E^p \overset{no}{\underset{l}{=}} \Delta E_c^p + \alpha_t \Delta E^p \, p_0$, where the symbol $\overset{no}{\underset{l}{=}}$ signifies that the equality holds under the condition $\Delta E_l^p = 0$.

To investigate the structure of α_t, observe that, if ΔE^p is received at $p = p_0$, there is no possibility of having a p-gradient available for out-transfer or for conversion, and thus $\Delta E_c^p = 0$ and $\Delta E_t^p = \Delta E^p$. Therefore $p = p_0$ implies $\alpha_t = 1/p_0 = 1/p$.

On the other hand, if ΔE^p is received at a p-value that may be considered infinite for all practical purposes, it follows that, no matter what portion of that ΔE^p has been converted, there will still remain p-gradient (for an infinite gradient is never exhausted), and $\Delta E_t{}^p = 0$. Hence, in this case

$$\lim_{p \to \infty} \Delta E^p = \Delta E_c{}^p, \quad \text{and} \quad \lim_{p \to \infty} \alpha_t = 0 = \lim_{p \to \infty} \frac{1}{p}.$$

The expression $\alpha_t = 1/p$ has been deduced from the consideration of the two extreme cases. For intermediate values of p, to a larger p-value corresponds a larger available p-gradient $(p - p_0)$, and hence more ΔE^p is available for conversion before depletion of the p-gradient (this depletion following from the G.G.L.); therefore, the smaller in consequence will $\Delta E_t{}^p$ be. Thus, α_t should be inversely proportional to p, the value of ΔE^p reception.

That the function p^{-1} satisfies the lower bound case $p = p_0$ is but a consequence of the first assumption stated above, which adopted the first positive power for p_0.

In the foregoing derivation it has been implicitly assumed that the finite quantity ΔE^p is received at the fixed value p of the intensive parameter. When the in-transfer is received at varying p, we obtain (remembering that $\Delta E_t{}^p$ is independent of the losses producing $\Delta E_l{}^p$):

$$\Delta E^p = \Delta E_c{}^p + \Delta E_{ic}{}^p = \Delta E_c{}^p + \Delta E_t{}^p + \Delta E_l{}^p$$

$$= \int_{t_1}^{t_2} \dot{E}_c{}^p \, dt + \left[\int_{t_1}^{t_2} \frac{\dot{E}^p}{p} \, dt + \beta_l \right] p_0, \tag{5-3}$$

where $E = dE/dt$, $t = $ time, and $C = $ integration path for process being considered.

Theorem 5-2. The quantity

$$\left[\int_{t_1}^{t_2} \frac{\dot{E}^p}{p} \, dt + \beta_l \right] = \Delta P^{ap}$$

is additive and extensive.

PROOF. Let us start with considerations extrinsic to the expression for ΔP^{ap}. In (5-3) the left side, ΔE^p, may be of the nature of a heat transfer, a mass transfer, a convective transfer, or a work transfer (see Appendix A), and in any case it is univalent, additive, and point-continuous; therefore, ΔE^p is an additive and extensive quantity. As a consequence, both $\Delta E_c{}^p$ and $\Delta E_{ic}{}^p$ must also be additive and extensive. But $\Delta E_{ic}{}^p = \Delta P^{ap} p_0$, and p_0 is a constant; hence ΔP^{ap} must satisfy the condition of being an extensive quantity.

An intrinsic examination of the expression for ΔP^{ap} likewise shows that the first term

$$\Delta P_t^{ap} = \int_{t_1}^{t_2} \frac{\dot{E}^p}{p} \, dt$$
$$\scriptstyle C$$

is an additive and extensive quantity. In fact, if p is constant throughout the whole boundary $\mathcal{B}$ where the E^p-transfer takes place, it is evident that the integrand $\dot{E}^p/p$ is both univalent and additive, for E^p possesses those two properties and p is a constant. If p is not constant throughout $\mathcal{B}$, then

$$\dot{P}_t^{ap} = \lim_{\Delta b \to \delta_p} \sum_{\Delta b \in \mathcal{B}} \left(\frac{\dot{E}^p}{p}\right)_{b'} = \sum_{\delta_p \in \mathcal{B}} \left(\frac{\dot{E}^p}{p}\right)_{b'}$$

where Δb is a part of the boundary $\mathcal{B}, \delta_p(\mathcal{B})$ is a δ_p-cell of $\mathcal{B}$, and b' denotes a point interior to Δb or interior to $\delta_p \subset \Delta b$. (Instead of considering δ_p-cells of $\mathcal{B}$, the boundary may be idealized to be two dimensional, and the δ_p-cells taken interior to S but tangential to $\mathcal{B}$.) Because $(\dot{E}^p/p)_{b'}$ is univalent and additive for each b', the above finite sum for $\dot{P}_t^{ap}$ will also be univalent and additive, and these properties will be conserved by the integral

$$\Delta P_t^{ap} = \int_{t_1}^{t_2} \dot{P}_t^{ap} \, dt$$
$$\scriptstyle C$$

by virtue of the linearity and continuity properties of the definite integral, and the additivity property of the definite integral with respect to domains of integration. The subscript t in the integrand of the last expression is not the variable time with respect to which the integration is carried out. (Observe that the additivity that has been established is additivity with respect to subsets of S, not additivity with respect to subsets of the process path C—the latter follows immediately from the integral expression for ΔP_t^{ap}.) Furthermore, because $\lim_{\omega(S) \to 0} \dot{E}^p = 0$, while $p > 0$, it follows that $\lim_{\omega(S) \to 0} \Delta P^{ap} = 0$. Therefore ΔP_t^{ap} is an extensive quantity.

For dimensional reasons the second term $\beta_l = \Delta P_l^{ap}$, which is as yet undetermined in its analytical structure, will have to satisfy in that structure the condition of being an extensive quantity as an externally imposed necessity.

Nomenclature.   The quantity

$$\Delta P^{ap} = \Delta P_t^{ap} + \Delta P_l^{ap}$$

$$= \int_{t_1}^{t_2} \frac{\dot{E}^p}{p} \, dt + \beta_l$$
$$\scriptstyle C$$

will be called the increment of the *extensive parameter associated to p* and, more briefly, the change in the *p-coparameter* (*p* being the parameter). When there is no possibility of confusion, the letter *p* may be dropped.

When the *p*-value of energy transfer is a function of the position of the δ_p-set on the boundary, expression (5-3) assumes the form

$$\Delta \dot{E}^p = \int_{t_1}^{t_2} \left[\int_{\mathcal{B}} \dot{E}_c^p \, db \right] dt + p_0 \left\{ \int_{t_1}^{t_2} \left[\int_{\mathcal{B}} \frac{\dot{E}^p}{p} \, db \right] dt \right\} + \beta_l p_0, \quad (5\text{-}3')$$

where *db* denotes the integrating element of boundary area. Seldom is the variation of *p*-value with boundary position sufficient to warrant the iterated integrations of (5-3'). Ordinarily the boundary can be decomposed into a finite number of pieces, in each of which the *p*-value can be considered effectively constant, and one of the integrations in (5-3') is then transformed into a sum.

Equalities (5-3) and (5-3') will be called the *convertibility equation*; form (5-3) will in general be sufficient for our discussions.

It is evident that the specific nature of each *p*-coparameter change will depend on the specific nature of the parameter *p* with which it is associated. Thus, if $p = $ temperature T, then $\Delta E^T = \Delta Q$, and

$$\Delta P^{aT} = \Delta S = \int_{t_1}^{t_2} \frac{\dot{Q}}{T} \, dt + \beta_l;$$

if a transformation is chosen for which it may be assumed that $\beta_l = \Delta S_{\mathrm{irr}} = 0$, and T is maintained sufficiently constant, then $\Delta S = \Delta Q / T$ is the T-coparameter, or *entropy*, change during $\Delta t = t_2 - t_1$.

As another illustration, if $p = P$, if $\Delta E^p = \Delta W$ is the work of compression or expansion, and if furthermore $\mathcal{T}$ is at constant P and such that $\dot{\beta}_l = \Delta P_l{}^{aP}$ is small enough to be neglected, then

$$\Delta P_t{}^{aP} = \frac{\Delta W}{P} = \Delta V.$$

The convertibility equation makes no assumption regarding the original source of ΔE^p; it offers a decomposition of ΔE^p from the standpoint of its potentiality for convertibility (and for retransfer, as a special case), giving a partial characterization of the terms of the decomposition. It is a kind of "conservation of energy relation", but of an entirely different nature from the first law. The latter stipulates that $\Delta E = \sum_p \Delta E^p$; the convertibility equation then decomposes *each* term on the right side of this equality from the standpoint of its potentiality for convertibility (into *another* ΔE^p) or for retransfer.

Among all the conceivable processes, a special class, because of its simplicity, has been very thoroughly studied in the past.

Definition 5-4.   A process will be called *reversible* iff $\dot{\beta}_l = \dot{P}_l{}^{ap} = 0$ at every instant of the process.

Because of this definition the dissipation coefficient $\dot{P}_l{}^{ap}$ will also be called the *coefficient of irreversibility* and symbolized by $\dot{P}_{irr}^{ap} = \dot{\beta}_{irr}$. Then

$$\dot{E}_l{}^p = \int_{\substack{t_1 \\ C}}^{t_2} \dot{\beta}_l p_0 \, dt = \int_{\substack{t_1 \\ C}}^{t_2} \dot{P}_{irr}^{ap} p_0 \, dt \equiv \dot{E}_{irr}^p.$$

Processes that are not reversible will be called *irreversible*. A reversible conversion must be an ideal conversion, for otherwise there would be a parasitic conversion in the process and $\Delta E_l{}^p \neq 0$.

6

Interpretation of the Coparameter Increment

In terms of the metalanguage of the science, the following interpretation may be attributed to the coparameter increment.

If $\mathcal{S}$ receives an energy transfer ΔE^p by means of a certain process $\mathfrak{F}$, the coparameter increment ΔP^{ap} is a measure of the *potentiality for inconvertibility* associated with the phenomenon $\{\mathcal{S}, \mathfrak{F}, \Delta E^p\}$. The *actual* inconvertibility associated with the ΔE^p-transfer is measured by $(\Delta P^{ap} p_0)$, which is a quantity associated with the phenomenon $\{\mathcal{S}, \mathcal{E}, \mathfrak{F}, \Delta E^p\}$.

Nota Bene. The quantity $\dot{P}^{ap}$ has the same dimensions as the quantity $\dot{E}^p/p$, but this does not mean that $\dot{P}^{ap}$ is physically the same as $\dot{E}^p/p$, any more than in mechanics the force of friction is to be physically identified with an elastic force imparting acceleration to a body, even though both forces have the same dimensions. This remark applies in particular to the irreversible term of the coparameter increment (or rate).

7

Evaluation of the Irreversible Production of the Coparameter: Parasitic Conversions. Frictional Dissipation

The second inconvertible term, $\Delta E_i^p = \Delta E_{irr}^p$, may have two primordial sources: (1) parasitic conversions; (2) parasitic transfers. Parasitic conversions take place when the conversion is not ideal. Parasitic transfers occur when there are internal energy transfers (i.e., transfers within, or internal to, $\mathcal{S}$—not just transfers from $\mathcal{E}$ to $\mathcal{S}$ or vice versa). The parasitic conversion that is most difficult to handle is frictional loss or dissipation. The parasitic transfer of most awkward behavior is that due to multidirectional p-gradients (those giving rise to multidirectional transfers); turbulent flow is the typical example of multidirectional transfer.

FRICTIONAL LOSS

From the standpoint of our study, frictional dissipation is but an energy-conversion process in which an input different from heat transfer has as conversion products (generally parasitic) heat transfer and mechanical deformation (see Figure 7-1). Generally, frictional dissipation is a parasitic conversion, but in exceptional cases (for example, when the system of interest consists of the sole of a shoe) frictional conversion may be the intended product of the converter as designed.

In most frictional conversions the heat-transfer product of the conversion by far surpasses the mechanical deformation product, to the extent that the latter is then neglected; nevertheless, the mechanical-deformation product of the frictional conversion is not always negligible (as in the

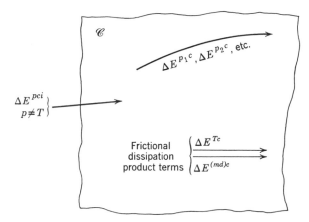

Figure 7-1 Frictional dissipation considered as an energy-conversion process.

illustration of the preceding paragraph), and in some cases it may be a very large part of the whole frictional conversion-energy product.

The frictional loss-energy product ΔE_f may be evaluated by using the first law:

$$\Delta E_f = \Delta E^{pci} - \sum_k \Delta E^{p_k c}.$$

A particular expression that covers a very large number of cases is:

$$\Delta E_f = P^e \, \Delta V - P^i \, \Delta V - \Delta E_k - \Delta E_l - \Delta Q, \qquad (7\text{-}1)$$

where P^e = exterior pressure, P^i = interior pressure, ΔE_k = kinetic energy output, ΔE_l = potential energy output, and ΔQ = heat-transfer output.

The ΔQ term in (7-1) is to be distinguished from the heat transfer of the frictional conversion output in that the first one is intended whereas the second is generally parasitic. This double source of heat transfer occurs frequently in situations in which the system performs functions of automatic control. For example, the human body is a system that, among other functions, automatically regulates its internal temperature. Now, the flow of blood within the circulatory subsystem of the body is a mass transfer (and therefore an energy transfer) and has a variety of outputs, one of them being frictional conversion (in this case the primary converter is the boundary between the blood and the vessel walls). This frictional conversion, however, does not produce sufficient heat transfer to maintain the interior of the system at the required temperature. The system must in consequence possess another source (biochemical) of heat transfer— that is, heat transfer must become an intended conversion product, over and above the parasitic heat transfer resulting from the frictional conversion produced by the blood flow (the purpose of this flow is not, essentially, heat transfer, which is but a parasitic conversion product of the blood flow).

If the mechanical deformation term of ΔE_f is negligible, $\Delta E_f = \Delta S_f \, T_0$, where ΔS_f represents the entropy increment due to the frictional conversion.

If, furthermore, the frictional conversion has no concomitant losses (i.e., no *secondary* parasitic conversions and transfers that are not negligible), $(\Delta E_f)_l = 0$ and

$$\Delta E_f = (\Delta E_f)_c + (\Delta E_f)_{ic} = (\Delta E_f)_c + (\Delta E_f)_t$$

$$= (\Delta E_f)_c + \Delta S_f \, T_0 = (\Delta E_f)_c + \frac{\Delta E_f}{T} T_0. \qquad (7\text{-}2)$$

Theorem 7-1. $\Delta S_f \nless 0$. More generally, $\dot{P}^{af} \nless 0$.

PROOF. From equation (7-2) the thesis follows immediately, under the conditions imposed upon the derivation of (7-2): negligible mechanical deformation term of ΔE_f, and absence of secondary (to the frictional conversion) parasitic coversions and transfers. It is easily seen, moreover, that the removal of those two conditions will not change the affirmed inequality. Thus, for example, if there is a mechanical-deformation term besides the heat transfer term, $\Delta E_f = \Delta E^{Tc} + \Delta E^{(md)c}$, and the sum of the two coparameters associated with the frictional conversion will have for rate of change:

$$\dot{P}^{af} = \dot{S}_f + \dot{P}^{a(md)} = \frac{\dot{E}^{Tc}}{T} + \frac{\dot{E}^{(md)c}}{p_{md}}.$$

Both terms on the right will be non-negative, since the four quantities in them are non-negative.

In the last equation the rates of change, rather than finite increments, have been used because the parameters T and p_{md} almost always obtain variable values during the conversion.

8

Evaluation of the Irreversible Production of the Coparameter: Internal Gradients

The second primordial source of the term $\Delta E_l{}^p = \Delta E_{irr}^p$ is parasitic transfers. A parasitic transfer is by its nature an undesired one. Because the objective of an in-transfer (out-transfer) is to place an energy transfer from $\mathcal{E}$ into $\mathcal{S}$ (from $\mathcal{S}$ out to $\mathcal{E}$), any other energy transfer associated with the in- (or out-)transfer, but distinct from it, is a parasitic phenomenon that we could well do without. Therefore, internal energy transfers in general, and multidirectional internal transfers in particular, are parasitic energy transfers.

In the first situation to be considered there exists a single internal unidirectional gradient. This applies with a sufficient degree of approximation, for example, to the heat conduction within a bar or to the heat radiation from star to planet.

The building block for the entire study is obtained by considering the case (Figure 8-1) in which the whole internal transfer is localized; there exists a p-gradient between two subsystems of $\mathcal{S}$, each of the subsystems

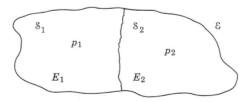

Figure 8-1 System $\mathcal{S}$ composed of two subsystems (subsystems $\mathcal{S}_1$ and $\mathcal{S}_2$ may be considered as δ-cells).

(S_1 and S_2) possessing throughout a constant value of the intensive parameter, and S being isolated from $\mathcal{E}$ with regard to E^p-transfers.

Subdivide S into subsystems S_1 and S_2, with intensive parameter values p_1 and p_2, and energy values E_1 and E_2, respectively. Because S is isolated from $\mathcal{E}$, $E = E_1 + E_2$, E being the energy of S.

Suppose that $p_2 > p_1$; then there will be a p-gradient and an E^p-transfer within S (in the absence of constraints), and $\dot{E}_1{}^p = -\dot{E}_2{}^p$. Also,

$$\dot{P}_1{}^{ap} = \frac{\dot{E}_1{}^p}{p_1} + \dot{P}_{1\,\mathrm{irr}}^{ap};$$

$$\dot{P}_2{}^{ap} = \frac{\dot{E}_2{}^p}{p_2} + \dot{P}_{2\,\mathrm{irr}}^{ap};$$

and, because of the additivity property of the coparameter,

$$\dot{P}^{ap} = \frac{\dot{E}_2{}^p}{p_2} + \frac{\dot{E}_1{}^p}{p_1} + (\dot{P}_{1\,\mathrm{irr}}^{ap} + \dot{P}_{2\,\mathrm{irr}}^{ap})$$

$$= \dot{E}_1{}^p\left(\frac{1}{p_1} - \frac{1}{p_2}\right) + (\dot{P}_{1\,\mathrm{irr}}^{ap} + \dot{P}_{2\,\mathrm{irr}}^{ap})$$

$$= \dot{E}_2{}^p\left(\frac{1}{p_2} - \frac{1}{p_1}\right) + (\dot{P}_{1\,\mathrm{irr}}^{ap} + \dot{P}_{2\,\mathrm{irr}}^{ap}). \qquad (8\text{-}1)$$

If the process has no other cause of irreversibility but the internal p-gradient in question, then

$$\dot{P}^{ap} = \dot{E}_1{}^p\left(\frac{1}{p_1} - \frac{1}{p_2}\right) = \dot{E}_2{}^p\left(\frac{1}{p_2} - \frac{1}{p_1}\right).$$

Theorem 8-1. $\dot{P}^{ap} > 0$ for the process described immediately above.

PROOF. From the preceding equations, observing that $(1/p_1 - 1/p_2) > 0$ is accompanied by $\dot{E}_1{}^p > 0$, while $(1/p_2 - 1/p_1) < 0$ is accompanied by $\dot{E}_2{}^p < 0$.

The $\dot{P}^{ap}$ increment in S has resulted from a process that is purely internal to S, although the energy that was transferred during this internal process was present in the system as a consequence of a *previous* intransfer from $\mathcal{E}$ to S (which may have occurred shortly before the internal transfer being studied, or millennia before). Because the coparameter increment (with positive sign) asserted in theorem 8-1 is not accompanied by any concomitant coparameter decrement elsewhere (in $\mathcal{E}$), it will be said to be a *coparameter production*.

Furthermore, this coparameter production is due to limitations or imperfections ("losses") that accompany the *original E^p-transfer into* S.

Thus, if any E^p-transfer into S were to take place *instantaneously* and *independently* of the *structure and materials within* S—in other words, if the process of in-transfer *had no time or space limitations*—there would be no internal p-gradient, and no internal E^p-transfer. The coparameter production results, not from the mere existence of an in-transfer and the amount of it (from this follows $\dot{P}^{ap}_{\text{rev}} = \dot{P}_t{}^{ap} = \dot{E}^p/p$) but from the peculiar time and space limitations of the process in S; given an amount ΔE^p of in-transfer to S, it is these limitations that will determine the directions and magnitudes of the internal p-gradients as functions of time.

Observe that to a $\dot{P}^{ap}_{\text{rev}} > 0$ in S corresponds a $\dot{P}^{ap}_{\text{rev}} < 0$, of equal magnitude, in $\mathcal{E}$. Hence $\dot{P}^{ap}_{\text{rev}}$ in reality represents a *coparameter flow* (from $\mathcal{E}$ to S for an in-transfer and from S to $\mathcal{E}$ for an out-transfer).

In summary, the calculated—in (8-1)—coparameter production *in* S is associated with an E^p-transfer *into* S, the energy in-transfer that produced the internal p-gradient. That in-transfer into S had associated with it a coparameter flow from $\mathcal{E}$ to S by virtue of the actual realization and quantity of the in-transfer; this coparameter *flow* has magnitude

$$\Delta P^{ap}_{\text{rev}} = \int_{t_1}^{t_2} \frac{\dot{E}^p}{p}\, dt.$$

To this coparameter flow is now added the coparameter *production* in S, given by

$$\Delta P^{ap}_{\text{irr}} = \int_{t_1}^{t_2} \dot{E}_1{}^p \left(\frac{1}{p_1} - \frac{1}{p_2} \right) dt.$$

Figure 8-2 illustrates in schematic form the quantities being considered.

Nota Bene. What is $\dot{P}^{ap}_{\text{irr}}$ associated with the *in-transfer* from $\mathcal{E}$ to S is also, in the case of *internal* transfer, $\dot{P}^{ap}_{\text{rev}}$ associated with an $E_1{}^p$-transfer internal to S. Naturally, $\Delta E_1{}^p \leq \Delta E^p$. In the case of friction, the $\dot{P}_f{}^{ap} = \dot{P}^{ap}_{\text{irr}} = \dot{P}^{af}$ is associated with an energy conversion either internal or in the boundary of the system. It is evident that frictional losses can also accompany the internal transfer; blood flow presents an illustration of this. Therefore

$$\dot{P}^{ap}_{\text{irr}} = \dot{E}_1{}^p \left(\frac{1}{p_1} - \frac{1}{p_2} \right) + \dot{P}^{af}. \tag{8-2}$$

Finally observe that, while $\dot{P}^{ap}_{\text{irr}}$ as calculated from (8-2) is irreversible coparameter production associated with the in-transfer $\dot{E}^p$ into S, the

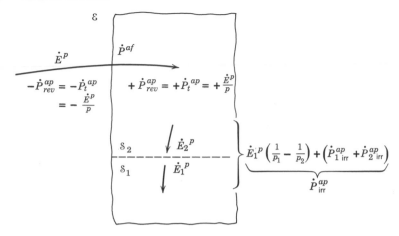

$-\dot{P}^{ap}_{rev}$ = rate of coparameter outflow from $\mathcal{E}$;
$+\dot{P}^{ap}_{rev}$ = rate of coparameter inflow into $\mathcal{S}$;
$\dot{P}^{ap}_{irr}$ = rate of coparameter production in $\mathcal{S}$.

Figure 8-2 Schematization of the coparameter flows (inflow and outflow) and of coparameter production. $\mathcal{S} = \mathcal{S}_2 \cup \mathcal{S}_1$.

term $(\dot{P}^{ap}_{1\,irr} + \dot{P}^{ap}_{2\,irr})$ in (8-1) is irreversible coparameter production associated with the internal (to $\mathcal{S}$) transfer $E_1{}^p$. Ultimately, therefore, $(\dot{P}^{ap}_{1\,irr} + \dot{P}^{ap}_{2\,irr})$ is *also* a consequence of the in-transfer $\dot{E}^p$ that is the remote cause of the internal $\dot{E}_1{}^p$. The form of the expression for the calculation of $(\dot{P}^{ap}_{1\,irr} + \dot{P}^{ap}_{2\,irr})$ is exactly analogous to (8-2), the two expressions differing only in the numerical values to be substituted.   Because each transfer produces its own parasitic transfers and friction, the complete expression for the $\dot{P}^{ap}_{irr}$ resulting from the original in-transfer to S takes the form

$$\dot{P}^{ap}_{irr} = \sum_{k=0}^{\infty} \dot{E}_k{}^p \left(\frac{1}{p_{k1}} - \frac{1}{p_{k2}} \right) + \dot{P}_k{}^{af}, \tag{8-3}$$

In (8-3), $\dot{E}_0{}^p$ stands for the original in-transfer (rate). It is to be expected that in many, if not most, cases only the first two or three terms of (8-3) will be significant.

The incremental expression corresponding to (8-2) and (8-3) would not be valid, for it would associate a *finite* $\Delta E_1{}^p$ with *fixed* values of p_1 and p_2. But at the very instant when $\Delta E_1{}^p > 0$ the quantity $(1/p_1 - 1/p_2)$ has a non-zero decrement, in virtue of the last assertion of the G.G.L. Hence the incremental expression becomes valid only in the limit $\Delta E_1{}^p \rightarrow 0$, and that limit corresponds to $\lim \Delta t \rightarrow 0$, where t is the time. The finite value ΔP^{ap}_{irr} must then be obtained by integration.

From theorems 7-1 and 8-1 there follows

Corollary 8-1.   For energy transfers which are accompanied by internal energy transfers or frictional losses or both, $\dot{P}^{ap}_{irr} > 0$.

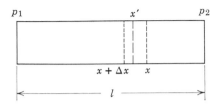

p_1 x' p_2

$x + \Delta x$ x

l

Figure 8-3   Schematic of a bar with end points at different *p*-values.

It has not been demonstrated that $\dot{P}^{ap}_{irr} > 0$ for *every* process, but only for those that are accompanied by internal transfers or by friction.

As an illustration of the preceding, consider the case (Figure 8-3) of a rectangular homogeneous bar of length *l*, one end of which is maintained at *p*-value p_2. What will be the rate of coparameter production at steady state?

Taking the section of bar from x to $x + \Delta x$ as our system for the moment, and an interior boundary x'—interior to the system $\{x, x + \Delta x\}$— we apply expression (8-2) [or the first term of (8-3)], neglecting friction:

$$\dot{P}^{ap}_{irr\ x'} = \dot{E}^{p}_{x'}\frac{P_{x+\Delta x} - P_x}{P_{x+\Delta x}P_x}, \quad x < x' < x + \Delta x.$$

Taking now this $\{x, x + \Delta x\}$ system as a subsystem of the whole bar, adding all the subsystems, and passing to the limit;

$$\dot{P}^{ap}_{irr} = \int_{p_1}^{p_2}\frac{\dot{E}^{p}_x}{P_x^2}\,dp = \int_{0}^{l}\frac{\dot{E}^{p}_x}{P_x^2}\frac{dp}{dx}\,dx.$$

In this expression x is a point interior to dp (and to dx).

Corollary 8-2.   If the solar system is considered as an isolated system as far as heat transfer goes, the entropy of the solar system is always increasing.

9

The Finite Propagation Hypothesis and the Law of Degradation

In the preceding chapter it was shown, based on the G.G.L. and the second part of the S.L., that $p_2 - p_1 > 0$ implies $\dot{E}_1{}^p > 0$, and as a consequence there follows the thesis of theorem 8-1, asserting $\dot{P}_{irr}^{ap} > 0$. The same thesis has been seen to follow likewise if $p_2 - p_1 < 0$. Vice versa, by theorem 7-1, $\Delta P^{af} \nless 0$, and then from equation (8-2) it follows that the condition $\dot{P}_{irr}^{ap} > 0$ necessitates that both $\dot{E}_1{}^p$ and $(p_2 - p_1)$ have the same sign. Therefore we have established

Theorem 9-1. For energy transfers which are accompanied by internal energy transfers, by frictional losses, or by both, the S.L. of energy transfers and the inequality $\dot{P}_{irr}^{ap} > 0$ are equivalent.

From theorem 9-1 it follows that a reversible process would require, as a necessary condition, the complete absence of internal energy transfers occasioned by a boundary energy transfer, and also the complete absence of frictional losses in all energy transfers. The internal energy transfers in turn have as a necessary condition (by the S.L.) and as a sufficient condition (by the G.G.L., part I) the existence of an internal p-gradient.

Under the conditions of parts II and III of the G.G.L., the velocity of propagation of any energy-transfer in the interior of S is not zero. With the help of the

Finite Propagation Hypothesis. Any transfer effect (flow, motion, etc.) is propagated in nature with finite velocity.

the following theorem may now be demonstrated:

Theorem 9-2. There do not exist reversible energy transfers in nature.

PROOF.   The initiation of an energy in-transfer through the boundary converts S into a quasi-static system (the cells $S_{\delta 3}$ and $S_{\delta 4}$ belonging now to $\mathcal{E}$) under condition α of definition 4-4b; then, by part III of the G.G.L., there will be an increase in the p-value at the boundary cell $S_{\delta 2}$. According to the finite propagation hypothesis, such a p-value increment will need a finite time to reach the more interior cells of S. Therefore, a p-gradient will have been temporarily introduced within S. By part I of the G.G.L. there will then be an internal energy transfer in the system, and theorem 8-1 (and theorem 9-1 as well) preclude the possibility of the process being reversible (according to definition 5-4).

The preceding demonstration applies equally well to the reverse process (transfer from S to $\mathcal{E}$) by designating as system what formerly was called environment, and vice versa. Otherwise direct use may be made of condition β of definition 4-4b (applying to an out-transfer S to $\mathcal{E}$) and part III of the G.G.L.

Corollary 9-1. The degree of approximation to reversibility in an energy transfer is directly proportional to the smallness of the p-gradient at the boundary.

PROOF.   Direct consequence of (8-2) and theorem 9-2.

Naturally, as (8-2) indicates, the magnitude of the p-gradient is not the only thing that influences the degree of approximation to reversibility of the E^p-transfer.

The inequality $\Delta P_{\text{irr}}^{ap} > 0$ for transfers and friction will now be universalized in the following assumption:

Law of Degradation. $\dot{P}_{\text{irr}}^{ap} > 0$ in every process in nature.

The generalization consists in extending to conversions *other than* frictional dissipation what theorems 7-1 and 8-1 (and 9-1) assert for frictional dissipation and for transfers. Some authors term the second law of thermodynamics what has here been called the law of degradation, when this law of degradation is applied to the case $p = T$.

Theorem 9-3.   In every process in nature $\dot{E}_l{}^p > 0$.

PROOF.   From the relation $\dot{E}_l{}^p = \dot{P}_{\text{irr}}^{ap} p_0$ and the fact that $\dot{P}_{\text{irr}}^{ap} > 0$ and $p_0 > 0$.

Nota Bene.   Referring to definition 5-2 and the conversion hypothesis, observe that, if the parameter s of the gradient were always of the nature of a distance, the finite propagation hypothesis would apply to all conversions, and the law of degradation would follow from it rather than be a generalization of the theses of theorems 7-1 and 8-1. But we are in no position to assert that every conversion parameter p or q has for gradient parameter s a quantity of the nature of a distance, and in consequence theorem 9-2 can be stated only for energy transfers, and not for all conversions as well. It is clear, however, that *the assertion of theorem 9-2 could include also all conversion processes for which the parameter s of the gradient is of the nature of a distance, as well as all processes involving conversion processes of the nature of frictional dissipation (by theorem 7-1).*

Now that the relation $\dot{P}_{\text{irr}}^{ap} > 0$ has been extended by the law of degradation to apply to all processes, irrespective of the nature of the gradient parameter s, there follows as an immediate consequence

Corollary 9-2.   There do not exist reversible processes in nature.

Now, on many occasions an energy-conversion process is employed in order to transform an available source of energy into another form in which the energy will be more readily or easily usable for the final objective desired. In view of the interpretation attributed in Chapter 6 to the coparameter increment it seems natural to formulate, as a quantitative estimate of the goodness of such a process, the following

Definition 9-1.   The efficiency (Eff) of a process is defined as

$$\text{Eff} \equiv \frac{\Delta E_c^{\,p}}{\Delta E^p},$$

where ΔE^p is the input to S in the process. If the input is $\Delta E = \sum_i \Delta E^{p_i}$, then

$$\text{Eff} \equiv \frac{\sum_i \Delta E_c^{\,p_i}}{\Delta E}.$$

Evidently $0 \leq \text{Eff} \leq 1$ from the definition, but from theorem 9-3 it follows that $0 \leq \text{Eff} < 1$.

The maximal efficiency that may be expected under certain given conditions may be easily determined with the aid of

Theorem 9-4.   The maximal (theoretical) efficiency corresponds to a reversible process.

PROOF.   From definition 9-1 we have

$$\text{Eff} = \frac{\Delta E_c^{\,p}}{\Delta E^p} = \frac{\Delta E^p - \Delta E_{ic}^{\,p}}{\Delta E^p} = \frac{\int \dot{E}^p \, dt - p_0 \int \frac{\dot{E}^p}{p} \, dt}{\int \dot{E}^p \, dt} - \frac{\int \dot{E}_i^{\,p} \, dt}{\int \dot{E}^p \, dt}$$

From theorem 9-3 and definition 5-4 it then follows that maximal (theoretical, in view of corollary 9-2) efficiency would be given by a reversible process between the given terminal states.

Corollary 9-3. If within an interval of time the function $\dot{E}^p$ does not change sign, the maximal (theoretical) efficiency is measured by $\text{Eff}_{max} = 1 - (p_0/\bar{p})$, where $\bar{p}$ is a number lying between the maximal and the minimal values of p in the process under consideration.

PROOF. From theorem 9-4 we have that

$$\text{Eff}_{max} = \frac{\int \dot{E}^p \, dt - p_0 \int \frac{\dot{E}^p}{p} \, dt}{\int \dot{E}^p \, dt}.$$

Now, the functions $1/p$ and $\dot{E}^p$ are both bounded in the interval of integration under consideration, the product $\dot{E}^p/p$ is integrable within the same interval, and furthermore the function $\dot{E}^p$ does not change sign within the interval; therefore by a mean-value theorem of the integral calculus (see, for example; [8], p. 366, or for a more extensive treatment [9], pp. 361–365) we have that there exists a value $\bar{p}$, lying between the maximal and minimal values of the parameter p in the interval, such that $\int (\dot{E}^p/p) \, dt = (1/\bar{p}) \int \dot{E}^p \, dt$. Substituting, we find that $\text{Eff}_{max} = 1 - (p_0/\bar{p})$. If p is constant throughout the process, $\text{Eff}_{max} = 1 - (p_0/p)$.

From the above it is seen that the efficiency (as defined) of a process is diminished by the quantity $\int \dot{E}_i^p \, dt$ for the process, as well as by the quantity p_0/p.

Thus, if $p = $ pressure (P) and P_0 is perfect vacuum, $\text{Eff} = 1$ for a reversible pneumatic process. On the other hand, if $P = P_0$, $\text{Eff} = 0$.

10

Third Fundamental Property
of the Coparameter:
Function of State

One of the most important theorems in physical science asserts that the entropy of a system is a function of state. A more general result is presented by

Theorem 10-1. The coparameter is a function of state.

PROOF. Consider a couple of states of S. An infinity of paths may be possible between those two states, and they are obtained by using different kinds of energy transfers, ΔE^{p_i}, in various proportions and combinations. Some of these may be in-transfers (into S or into C); others may be out-transfers (from S) or conversion products (of the nature of either a converter output or a retained conversion product). In the sequel we shall denote as energy-transfers the inputs and outputs of *both* S and C, thus simplifying the terminology and shortening the expressions without any sacrifice in precision. It suffices to prove the theorem for two arbitrary types of energy transfers, the extension to any finite number of kinds being straightforward.

Suppose that the two (arbitrarily selected) kinds of energy transfers are associated with the intensive parameters p_1 and p_2 (for example, p_1 could be temperature and p_2 pressure; then $\Delta E^{p_1} = \Delta Q$ and $\Delta E^{p_2} = \Delta W_P$). By conjoining the conservation of energy equation (F.L.) with the convertibility equation, the energy increment between the two specified states may be algebraically expressed as:

$$\Delta E = \Delta E^{p_1} + \Delta E^{p_2} = \Delta E_c^{p_1} + \Delta E_c^{p_2} + \Delta E_{ic}^{p_1} + \Delta E_{ic}^{p_2}.$$

This will be called the basic transfer, or conversion, equation.

The left side of this equation is a function of couples of states ([2] or Appendix A); therefore the right side of the equation must represent a function independent of the path. By the basic state function theorem (3-8) it follows that, either each of the four terms on the right must be independent of the path, or at least two terms on that side must not be functions of couples of states.

If all four terms were functions independent of the path, then from theorem 3-3 would follow that ΔE^{p_1} and ΔE^{p_2} would each also be independent of the path. But that these last two quantities are not independent of the path follows from corollary 9-1, and is also known from experimentation (consider, for example, the well-known case in which $p_1 = T$ and $p_2 = P$). Therefore, at least two of the four terms on the right of the basic conversion equation must not be independent of the path.

The immediate problem at hand in the demonstration of the theorem is to ascertain which, of the four terms on the right side of the basic conversion equation, are not functions of couples of states. Lemma 10-1 will be the main tool in the investigation.

Lemma 10-1. Two E^p-transfers that are not functions of couples of states must be interchangeable (definition 3-9) if their addition is to give rise to a function of couples of states.

PROOF. Corollary of theorem 3-10.

Lemma 10-2. $\Delta E_c{}^{p_1}$ and $\Delta E_{ic}{}^{p_2}$ for arbitrary p_1 and p_2 are not interchangeable.

PROOF. The interchangeability of arbitrary $\Delta E_c{}^{p_1}$ and $\Delta E_{ic}{}^{p_2}$ would imply the interchangeability of $\Delta E_c{}^{p}$ and $\Delta E_{ic}{}^{p}$, corresponding to the case $p_1 = p_2$ in which the path between states consists of a single energy transfer. But if $\Delta E_c{}^{p}$ and $\Delta E_{ic}{}^{p}$ were interchangeable, $\Delta E^p = (\Delta E_c{}^{p} + \Delta E_{ic}{}^{p})$ would be independent of the path for any p, contradicting experimentally established results.

Lemma 10-3. Each of the two quantities $(\Delta E_c{}^{p_1} + \Delta E_c{}^{p_2})$, $(\Delta E_{ic}{}^{p_1} + \Delta E_{ic}{}^{p_2})$, is independent of the path.

PROOF. From the basic conversion equation the addition of those two quantities yields a function independent of the path, and from Lemma 10-2 it follows that none of the terms of the first quantity is mutually interchangeable with any of the terms of the second quantity. Therefore, by theorems 3-8 and 3-10 each of the two quantities must be independent of the path.

Now, a function Δz that is a sum of two functions Δx and Δy: $\Delta z = \Delta x + \Delta y$, is independent of the path iff either both Δx and Δy are independent of the path, or else they are mutually interchangeable. Applying this alternative to our problem, we are led to

Lemma 10-4. $\Delta E_{ic}{}^{p}$ is independent of the path.

Proof. It has been established that $(\Delta E_{ic}{}^{p_1} + \Delta E_{ic}{}^{p_2})$ is independent of the path. The issue at hand is to decide whether that sum is independent of the path because each term is independent of the path, or because the terms are mutually interchangeable but dependent on the path. The lemma asserts that the first case holds, and the assertion will be established by contradiction.

In fact, deny the conclusion by asserting that $\overline{\Delta E_{ic}}{}^{p_1} = \Delta E_{ic}{}^{p_1} + k$ and $\overline{\Delta E_{ic}}{}^{p_2} = \Delta E_{ic}{}^{p_2} + m$, where the dashed and the undashed quantities correspond to two different arbitrary paths. Because

$$\overline{\Delta E_{ic}}{}^{p_1} + \overline{\Delta E_{ic}}{}^{p_2} = \Delta E_{ic}{}^{p_1} + \Delta E_{ic}{}^{p_2},$$

it follows that $k + m = 0$: $k = -m$.

Now consider the following set of relations:

$$\Delta E = (\overline{\Delta E_c}{}^{p_1} + \overline{\Delta E_c}{}^{p_2}) + (\overline{\Delta E_{ic}}{}^{p_1} + \overline{\Delta E_{ic}}{}^{p_2})$$
$$= (\Delta E_c{}^{p_1} + \Delta E_c{}^{p_2}) + (\Delta E_{ic}{}^{p_1} + \Delta E_{ic}{}^{p_2}); \qquad (a)$$

$$\overline{\Delta E_c}{}^{p_1} + \overline{\Delta E_c}{}^{p_2} = \Delta E_c{}^{p_1} + \Delta E_c{}^{p_2}; \qquad (b)$$

$$\overline{\Delta E_{ic}}{}^{p_1} + \overline{\Delta E_{ic}}{}^{p_2} = \Delta E_{ic}{}^{p_1} + \Delta E_{ic}{}^{p_2}; \qquad (c)$$

$$\left.\begin{array}{l}\overline{\Delta E_{ic}}{}^{p_1} = \Delta E_{ic}{}^{p_1} + k \\ \overline{\Delta E_{ic}}{}^{p_2} = \Delta E_{ic}{}^{p_2} - k\end{array}\right\}. \qquad (d)$$

The set of relations $\{(a), (b), (c)\}$ has been established *without imposing any constraint on the possible value of k* and will be designated as set A. Relations (d) are hypothetical. The set $\{(a), (b), (c), (d)\}$ will be denoted as set B.

Introducing $\Delta E_{ic}{}^{p} = (\Delta E^{p}/p)p_0 + \Delta E_l{}^{p}$ and (d) into (c), we obtain

$$\triangle E^{p_1}\left[\frac{(\bar{p}_1)_0}{\bar{p}_1} - \frac{(p_1)_0}{p_1}\right] + \Delta E^{p_2}\left[\frac{(\bar{p}_2)_0}{\bar{p}_2} - \frac{(p_2)_0}{p_2}\right] + k\left[\frac{(\bar{p}_1)_0}{\bar{p}_1} - \frac{(\bar{p}_2)_0}{\bar{p}_2}\right]$$
$$+ (\overline{\Delta E_l}{}^{p_1} + \overline{\Delta E_l}{}^{p_2}) - (\Delta E_l{}^{p_1} + \Delta E_l{}^{p_2}) = 0. \quad (e)$$

Because in general $\overline{\Delta E_l}{}^{p_1} + \overline{\Delta E_l}{}^{p_2} \neq \Delta E_l{}^{p_1} + \Delta E_l{}^{p_2}$, to simplify writing we may assume the sum $(\Delta E_l{}^{p_1} + \Delta E_l{}^{p_2})$ to be negligible by comparison with $(\overline{\Delta E_l}{}^{p_1} + \overline{\Delta E_l}{}^{p_2})$, and this simply means that we are considering the undashed path as being much closer to reversibility than the dashed path;

this agreement will shorten the expressions without restricting the generality of the proof, for it will not enter in the demonstrative part of what follows.

In a similar way, substituting $\Delta E_c{}^p = \Delta E^p(1 - p_0/p) - \Delta E_l{}^p$ and (d) into (b) again yields equation (e), which now may be written

$$\sum_{i=1}^{2} E^{p_1}\left[\frac{(\bar{p}_i)_0}{\bar{p}_i} - \frac{(p_i)_0}{p_i}\right] + k\left[\frac{(\bar{p}_1)_0}{\bar{p}_1} - \frac{(\bar{p}_2)_0}{\bar{p}_2}\right] + (\overline{\Delta E_l}{}^{p_1} + \overline{\Delta E_l}{}^{p_2}) = 0. \quad \text{(f)}$$

Equation (f) clearly is a consequence of set B of relations.

By operating in a manner analogous to the above, but with the exclusion of (d), from set A of relations is deduced the equation

$$\sum_{i=1}^{2}\Delta E^{p_i}\left[\frac{(\bar{p}_i)_0}{\bar{p}_i} - \frac{(p_i)_0}{p_i}\right] + (\overline{\Delta E_l}{}^{p_1} + \overline{\Delta E_l}{}^{p_2}) = 0. \quad \text{(g)}$$

Equation (g) is a consequence of set A, with A = B − (d). But because B ⊃ A, it follows that B also implies (g). Consequently

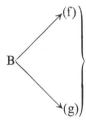

simultaneously for the two (dashed and undashed) processes.

But (f) and (g) can hold simultaneously if and only if

$$k\left[\frac{(\bar{p}_1)_0}{\bar{p}_1} - \frac{(\bar{p}_2)_0}{\bar{p}_2}\right] = 0$$

for *all* processes to which (f) and (g) apply. Because in general the bracketed expression will not be null, it follows that necessarily $k = 0$. Therefore $\overline{\Delta E_{ic}{}^p} = \Delta E_{ic}{}^p$, and $\Delta E_{ic}{}^p$ is a function of couples of states. The lemma has thus been demonstrated.

Now, from the definition of ΔP^{ap}, $\Delta E_{ic}{}^p = p_0\,\Delta P^{ap}$. Because p_0 is a fixed number (and thus independent of the path), by theorem 3-5 (and lemma 10-4) it follows that ΔP^{ap} must be independent of the path between states. Theorem 3-2 then asserts the existence of the associated function of state P^{ap}, defined to within a constant.

Corollary 10-1. $\Delta E_c{}^p$ is not independent of the path, but $\Delta E_c{}^{p_1}$ and $\Delta E_c{}^{p_2}$ are mutually interchangeable.

PROOF.   From experimental results it is known that ΔE^p is dependent on the path (illustrations are the experiments of Count Rumford and of

Joule), and by lemma 10-4, $\Delta E_{ic}{}^p$ is independent of the path. Then from $\Delta E^p = \Delta E_c{}^p + \Delta E_{ic}{}^p$ and theorem 3-8 (the basic state function theorem) it follows that $\Delta E_c{}^p$ cannot be independent of the path.

The second part of the corollary then is a consequence of lemma 10-3 and the basic state function theorem (theorem 3-10 being equally applicable in this context).

From the convertibility equation we have

$$
\Delta E_{ic}{}^p \Big]_{\mathcal{S},\mathfrak{I}}^b = \int_a^b \dot{E}_{ic}^p \, dt = p_0 \left[\int_a^b \frac{\dot{E}^p}{p} \Big]_{\mathcal{S},\mathfrak{I}} dt + \int_a^b \dot{P}_{\mathrm{irr}}^{ap} \, dt \right]_{\mathcal{S},\mathfrak{I}}
$$

$$
= p_0 \int_a^b \frac{\dot{E}^p + p\dot{P}_{\mathrm{irr}}^{ap}}{p} \, dt, \qquad (10\text{-}1)
$$

where $\dot{E}^p$ and $\dot{P}_{\mathrm{irr}}^{ap}$ are calculated along the *given* fixed process $\mathfrak{I}$ between the given fixed terminal states $\{a, b\}$ of the system $\mathcal{S}$.

Theorems 3-1 and 10-1 now provide us with another method for the calculation of $\Delta E_{ic}{}^p$: find any process $\mathfrak{I}'$ *between the same fixed* terminal states and determine $\Delta E_{ic}{}^p \Big]_{\mathcal{S},\mathfrak{I}'}^b$. By virtue of theorem 10-1 we know that

$$
\Delta E_{ic}{}^p \Big]_{\mathcal{S},\mathfrak{I}}^b = \Delta E_{ic}{}^p \Big]_{\mathcal{S},\mathfrak{I}'}^b .
$$

If the system is able to pass from state a to state b by a process that is sufficiently close, for the purposes of the investigation at hand, to a (theoretically) reversible process, we may calculate the coparameter increment quite simply:

$$
\Delta E_{ic}{}^p \Big]_{\mathcal{S},\mathfrak{I}}^b = \Delta E_{ic}{}^p \Big]_{\mathcal{S},\mathrm{rev}}^b = p_0 \int_a^b \frac{\dot{E}_{\mathrm{rev}}^p}{p} \, dt = p_0 \, \Delta P^{ap} \Big]_{\mathcal{S},\mathfrak{I}}^b . \qquad (10\text{-}2)
$$

It is evident that the mean-value theorems of the integral calculus will on occasions provide simplifications in the manipulation of expressions like (10-1) and (10-2).

When $p = T$ (temperature), the T-associated extensive parameter is called entropy in the literature and is symbolized by S. As a consequence of what has been demonstrated, S is a function of state and thus ΔS is independent of the path between states.

The following theorem identifies another coparameter of special interest.

Theorem 10-2. In a reversible process of compression or expansion between two fixed states, the increment of the pressure coparameter is given by the increment of volume of the system between the states.

PROOF. $\Delta P^{aP} = \dfrac{\Delta E^P_{\mathrm{rev}}}{P} = \dfrac{\Delta W_{\mathrm{rev}}}{P} = \dfrac{P\,\Delta V_{\mathrm{rev}}}{P} = \Delta V_{\mathrm{rev}}.$

This theorem has an immediate

Corollary 10-2. The P-coparameter has the dimensions of volume.

It must be carefully observed that $\Delta P^{aP} = \Delta V$ only under conditions of reversibility. However, denoting a fixed but arbitrary path by the symbol "arb", from $\Delta P^{aP}_{\mathrm{arb}} = \Delta P^{aP}_{\mathrm{rev}}$ it follows that $\Delta P^{aP}_{\mathrm{arb}} = \Delta V_{\mathrm{rev}}$ but in general $\Delta P^{aP}_{\mathrm{arb}} \neq \Delta V_{\mathrm{arb}}$ (naturally, $\Delta V_{\mathrm{arb}} \neq \Delta V_{\mathrm{rev}}$).

The Nota Bene in Chapter 6 applies in the context of the preceding corollary.

It has been seen that a coparameter, function of state, is associated with every intensive parameter. It is also known that the values of the intensive parameters corresponding to a state of the system are interrelated by what is called the equation of state of the system. The question immediately arises: are the coparameter values associated with a state of the system also mutually interrelated?

The preceding question will be answered affirmatively if we can establish that coparameter increments between two fixed but arbitrary states are mutually interrelated. In other words, if between states 1 and 2 we have coparameter increments $\Delta_1^2 P^{a p_1}$ and $\Delta_1^2 P^{a p_2}$, does there exist an invertible functional relation F such that $\Delta_1^2 P^{a p_2} = F(\Delta_1^2 P^{a p_1})$?

It has been established that ΔP^{ap} is independent of the path between states; hence, its value for the reversible path—even if only theoretically calculable—is equal to its value along any other path that may admit of implementation in the real. For the reversible process the value of ΔP^{ap} is given by $\Delta P^{ap} = \Delta E^p_{\mathrm{rev}}/p$. Therefore, since it is understood that all increments are being determined between the same terminal states, we have

$$\Delta P^{a p_1} = \frac{\Delta E^{p_1}_{\mathrm{rev}}}{p_1} \quad \text{and} \quad \Delta P^{a p_2} = \frac{\Delta E^{p_2}_{\mathrm{rev}}}{p_2}.$$

Now, the intensive parameters p_1 and p_2 are related by the equation of state of the system, and the quantities $\Delta E^{p_1}_{\mathrm{rev}}$ and $\Delta E^{p_2}_{\mathrm{rev}}$ are expressible in terms of each other by means of the first law of energy transfers and conversions—in fact, $\Delta E^{p_1} = A\,\Delta E^{p_2}$, where A is a constant (see theorem A-2). We can then demonstrate

Theorem 10-3. If the function $\dot{E}^{p_1}/p_1$ is integrable and the function $\dot{E}^{p_1}$ does not change sign within the interval $[t_1, t_2]$, and if also the equation of state of S establishes a linear functional relation (with generally variable coefficient c) between the intensive parameters p_1 and p_2, the coparameter increments between two states (corresponding to t_1 and t_2) are also related linearly.

PROOF.

$$\Delta P^{ap_1}_{[t_1,t_2]} = \int_{t_1}^{t_2} \dot{P}^{ap_1}\, dt = \int_{t_1}^{t_2} \frac{\dot{E}^{p_1}_{\text{rev}}}{p_1}\, dt = A\int_{t_1}^{t_2} \frac{\dot{E}^{p_2}_{\text{rev}}}{c(t)p_2}\, dt.$$

Naturally, $c(t)$ may also be a function of other intensive parameters distinct from p_1 and p_2. The functions $\dot{E}^{p_1}_{\text{rev}}$ and p_1 are both bounded within $[t_1, t_2]$ by physical considerations; therefore $\dot{E}^{p_2}_{\text{rev}}$, p_2, and c are also bounded. Furthermore, the function $\dot{E}^{p_2}_{\text{rev}}/p_2$ is integrable over $[t_1, t_2]$ because $\dot{E}^{p_1}_{\text{rev}}/p_1$ is integrable there; and, finally, $\dot{E}^{p_2}_{\text{rev}}$ does not change sign within $[t_1, t_2]$ because $\dot{E}^{p_2}_{\text{rev}} = (1/A)\dot{E}^{p_1}_{\text{rev}}$ where A is a constant. Therefore, by one of the mean-value theorems of the integral calculus (see, for example, [8], p. 366; [9], pp. 361-365) there exists a value $\bar{c}$, lying between the maximal and minimal values of $c(t)$ within $[t_1, t_2]$, such that

$$A\int_{t_1}^{t_2} \frac{\dot{E}^{p_2}_{\text{rev}}}{cp_2}\, dt = \frac{A}{\bar{c}} \int_{t_1}^{t_2} \frac{\dot{E}^{p_2}_{\text{rev}}}{p_2}\, dt.$$

Hence

$$\Delta P^{ap_1}_{[t_1,t_2]} = \frac{A}{\bar{c}} \Delta P^{ap_2}_{[t_1,t_2]}. \qquad (10\text{-}3)$$

As a simple illlustration of theorem 10-3 we may consider the case in which $p_1 = T$ (temperature), $p_2 = P$ (pressure), and the system is a portion of perfect gas undergoing reversible compression or expansion. Then $\Delta E^{p_1} = \Delta E^T = \Delta Q$, and $\Delta E^{p_2} = \Delta E^P = P\,\Delta V$. The only reason for the two idealizations is algorithmic simplicity: a perfect gas obeys a simple linear functional relation between the intensive parameters P and T; a reversible process provides us with a simple expression for ΔP^{aP} and $\Delta P^{aT} = \Delta S$.

From the equation of state of the system, $P = (nR/V)T$; and from the first law it follows that $\Delta Q/\Delta W = A$. Substituting,

$$\Delta P^{ap_2} = \Delta P^{aP} = \frac{\Delta E^P}{P} = \frac{\Delta W}{P} = \int_{t_1}^{t_2} \frac{\dot{Q}/A}{(nR/V)T}\, dt$$

$$= \frac{1}{nRA} \int_{t_1}^{t_2} V\frac{\dot{Q}}{T}\, dt = \left(\frac{\bar{V}}{nRA}\right)\int_{t_1}^{t_2} \frac{\dot{Q}}{T}\, dt$$

$$= \left(\frac{\bar{V}}{nRA}\right)\Delta S = \frac{\bar{V}}{nRA}\Delta P^{aT},$$

with $\bar{V}$ a value lying between the maximal and minimal values of V within the interval $[t_1, t_2]$.

Likewise

$$\Delta P^{aT} = \Delta S = \frac{\Delta Q}{T} = \frac{A \, \Delta W}{PV/nR} = nRA \int_{t_1}^{t_2} \frac{1}{V} \frac{\dot{W}}{P} \, dt$$

$$= \frac{nRA}{\bar{V}} \frac{\Delta W}{P} = \frac{nRA}{\bar{V}} \frac{\Delta E^P}{P} = \left(\frac{nRA}{\bar{V}} \right) \Delta P^{aP}$$

$$= \frac{nRA}{\bar{V}} \Delta V. \qquad (10\text{-}4)$$

Another, equivalent way of expressing relation (10-4) is given by

$$\Delta P^{aT} = \Delta S = nRA \int_{t_1}^{t_2} \frac{1}{VP} P\dot{V} \, dt = nRA \int_{V_1}^{V_2} \frac{dV}{V}$$

$$= nRA \ln \frac{V_2}{V_1}.$$

This form of the relation is well known (see, for example, [35], p. 161).

Nota Bene. Reversibility is *not* a condition in theorem 10-3. By virtue of theorem 10-1, however, an idealized (reversible) process could be used in demonstrating the thesis of Theorem 10-3, that thesis being valid for any process between two fixed but arbitrary states.

Expression (10-3) underlies the justification that may be given to the frequently used calculation of entropy changes for processes that are devoid of any heat transfer. As an illustration, consider the common case of the expansion through a throttle of a given quantity of gas. Ordinarily one calculates the entropy change between the given terminal states by expressing the "work of expansion" in terms of the "heat of expansion" ΔQ, and calculating the integral of the quotient $\Delta Q/T$ between the same terminal states. Actually in the process there may have been little or no heat transfer, depending on the conditions under, and the manner in, which the process was carried out. There certainly has been P-coparameter change, however. But equation (10-4) expresses that, for an ideal gas, an entropy change ΔS *is associated with* or *equivalent to* $(nRA/\bar{V}) \, \Delta P^{aP}$; if the gas is real but satisfies the conditions of theorem 10-3, equation (10-3), with the proper $\bar{c}$ value, gives us the relation between any two coparameter increments.

From what standpoint do we have the association or equivalence referred to above?

This question points to the deeper meaning of equation (10-3). To investigate this, let us start by rewriting (10-3) in more useful forms. A letter index will symbolize the state of the system, and the coefficient of the linear relation will be expressed by means of a letter with two number indices attached, each number corresponding to one of the two intensive parameters concerned. Then (10-3) becomes

$$\Delta P_{a,b}^{ap_1} = k_{12}\,\Delta P_{a,b}^{ap_2} = \Delta K \tag{10-5}$$

and

$$P_b^{ap_1} - k_{12}P_b^{ap_2} = P_a^{ap_1} - k_{12}P_a^{ap_2} \tag{10-6}$$

Remembering that P^{ap} is a function of state for any intensive parameter p, suppose that we have a system $\mathcal{S}$ the states of which, for the processes that are of interest and for the degree of approximation that is being considered as sufficient, can be described by $\{E, p_1, P^{ap_1}, p_2, P^{ap_2}\}$. Let us take an arbitrary state a as the initial state; system $\mathcal{S}$ in state a will be characterized by $\{E_a, p_{1a}, P_a^{ap_1}, P_{2a}, P_a^{ap_2}\}$, it being understood that p_{1a} and p_{2a}, being intensive parameters, may not be single numbers, but are numerical functions of δ-cells within $\mathcal{S}$. Likewise, another state called b will be characterized by $\{E_b, p_{1b}, P_b^{ap_1}, p_{2b}, P_b^{ap_2}\}$. Equation (10-5) then permits us to assert that

$$\{E_b,\, p_{1b},\, P_b^{ap_1},\, p_{2b},\, P_b^{ap_2}\}$$
$$= \{E_b,\, p_{1b},\, P_a^{ap_1} + \Delta P_{a,b}^{ap_1},\, p_{2b},\, P_a^{ap_2} + \Delta P_{a,b}^{ap_2}\}$$
$$= \{E_b,\, p_{1b},\, P_a^{ap_1} + k_{12}\,\Delta P_{a,b}^{ap_2},\, p_{2b},\, P_a^{ap_2} + \Delta P_{a,b}^{ap_2}\}.$$

To clarify let us consider a concrete illustration. Suppose that a gaseous system $\mathcal{S}$ is heated by ΔQ-transfer under conditions of constant volume. It its final state it will have a greater value of entropy, and—by virtue of the interpretation given in Chapter 6 to the coparameter increment—of the in-transfer $\Delta Q = \Delta E^T$ received by $\mathcal{S}$, a certain portion $\Delta E_{ic}^T = T_0\,\Delta S$ (where T_0 is the lowest available temperature in the environment $\mathcal{E}$) cannot be recovered by *using a temperature gradient*. Now, that in-transfer (ΔQ) under conditions of constant volume has increased the pressure of $\mathcal{S}$, and therefore the ΔQ-transfer is *associated with* a ΔE^P-transfer—or, equivalently, a ΔE^m-transfer (m standing for mass) of fluid being injected into $\mathcal{S}$ to raise the pressure within $\mathcal{S}$. Because $\mathcal{S}$ has now more energy and higher pressure, more output can be obtained from it by *using a pressure gradient* than could have been obtained before it received the ΔQ-input. But not all of the ΔE^P that is equivalent to the ΔQ-input is recoverable from $\mathcal{S}$; in fact a part $\Delta E_{ic}^P = P_0\,\Delta P^{aP}$ (where P_0 is the lowest available pressure in $\mathcal{E}$) will not be recoverable using a pressure gradient. If now we calculate the ΔE^P-transfer associated with the ΔQ-transfer into $\mathcal{S}$, and the correspondence in values between the temperature and the pressure in $\mathcal{S}$, and on that basis determine ΔP^{aP}

and $\Delta S = \Delta P^{aT}$, the two values thus determined will satisfy relation (10-5). Also, in the particular case of perfect gas and reversible process, (10-5) will assume the particular form of (10-4), the reversibility property, and the equation of state of the perfect gas, determining the form of the coefficient in (10-4).

In more general terms, just as an energy transfer ΔE^{p_1} corresponding to an intensive parameter p_1 may be associated with another energy transfer ΔE^{p_2} corresponding to intensive parameter p_2, so the potentiality for inconvertibility ΔP^{ap_1} that is inherent in the ΔE^{p_1}-transfer is associated with the potentiality for inconvertibility inherent in the ΔE^{p_2}-transfer. The magnitude of *actual* inconvertibility, however, will depend on the lowest available values of the parameters p_1 and p_2, and these are properties of $\mathcal{E}$, not of $\mathcal{S}$. That is the reason why, although a relation can be established between ΔP^{ap_1} and ΔP^{ap_2}, no relation can be established between $\Delta E_{ic}{}^{p_1}$ and $\Delta E_{ic}{}^{p_2}$, for the latter are functions of parameters of $\mathcal{E}$ (besides being also functions of parameters of $\mathcal{S}$).

Continuing the illustration, suppose that $\mathcal{S}$ now receives the same in-transfer ΔQ, but without the constraint of constant volume, its volume expanding as it receives the heat transfer. In its final state $\mathcal{S}$ will have a lower temperature, and in consequence—having received the same ΔQ as before—its ΔS will now be larger than formerly. Again, to the ΔQ so received will be associated a ΔE^P and a consequent increment in pressure within $\mathcal{S}$, but this increment will be less than in the original process (because the constant-volume limitation has now been lifted) and on occasion it may be zero. This smaller pressure within $\mathcal{S}$ makes more unlikely than formerly the recovery, *by means of a pressure gradient*, of much of the ΔE^P introduced; in fact, for equal P_0 in $\mathcal{E}$, the value of ΔP^{aP} will now be larger than before. The new values of ΔS and ΔP^{aP} (those corresponding to this new process under variable volume) will again satisfy equation (10-5).

A distinction must be observed between the two processes that have been used for illustration.

In the first process (at constant volume) there was only an in-transfer: $\Delta E^{Ti} = \Delta Q$, and with that in-transfer were associated coparameters P^{aT} and P^{aP} related by an equation of the form (10-5).

In the second process (with variable volume) there was an in-transfer ΔE^{Ti} and an out-transfer ΔE^{P_o}. With ΔE^{Ti} is associated $\Delta P_i{}^{aT} = \Delta S_i$, and with ΔE^{P_o} is associated $\Delta P_o{}^{aP}$. It being understood that all quantities refer to the same process, we may disregard for the sake of clearness in the application of (10-5) the symbols of the terminal states; then

$$\Delta P_i{}^{aT} = k_{TP}\,\Delta P_i{}^{aP}, \qquad \Delta P_o{}^{aP} = k_{PT}\,\Delta P_o{}^{aT},$$

and

$$\Delta P^{aT} = \Delta P_i^{aT} + \Delta P_o^{aT} = k_{TP} \Delta P_i^{aP} + \frac{1}{k_{PT}} \Delta P_o^{aP}$$

$$= k_{TP}(\Delta P_i^{aP} + \Delta P_o^{aP}). \tag{10-7}$$

In (10-7), the reversible part of ΔP_o^{aP} will be subtracted from ΔP_i^{aP}, because $\Delta P_{o\,\text{rev}}^{aP} = \Delta E_o^P/P$ and $\Delta E_o^P < 0$ (because ΔE_o^P is an out-transfer from S); that simply means that the reversible term of ΔP_o^{aP} is a coparameter outflow. The irreversible term of ΔP_o^{aP}, however, is positive and will be added to ΔP_i^{aP}.

What has been illustrated, for the case in which the intensive parameters P and T suffice to characterize the system and its transformations that are under consideration, extends without significant modification to situations which require for their characterization more than two intensive parameters (besides the energy and the associated extensive parameters).

Lemma 10-5.   Relation (10-5) expresses an equivalence relation between increments of coparameters.

PROOF.   (For equivalence relations and their properties see definition 3-5 and the paragraph that follows it.) The reflexive property is satisfied by the coefficient $k_{11} = 1$. The symmetric property is satisfied by the coefficients k_{ij} and $k_{ji} = 1/k_{ij}$, where i and j represent any symbols corresponding to intensive parameters. The transitive property is satisfied by the coefficients k_{ij}, k_{jl} and $k_{il} = k_{ij}k_{jl}$. In fact,

$$\Delta P^{ap_i} = k_{ij} \Delta P^{ap_j} = k_{ij}(k_{jl} \Delta P^{ap_l}) = k_{il} \Delta P^{ap_l}.$$

Theorem 10-4.   Under the conditions of theorem 10-3, to every process between fixed states corresponds an equivalence class of increments of coparameters, the class containing as many elements as distinct coparameters are needed for the characterization of the states of the process.

PROOF.   Immediate consequence of equation (10-5) and the preceding lemma.

From theorem 10-4 it follows that any one of the elements of the class may be used as *representative* of the class, precisely because the class is an *equivalence* class (consult, for example, [10], pp. 11–21, or [11], pp. 4–7).

During the last one hundred years P^{aT} (entropy) has been used as the sole representative of the equivalence class.

Theorem 10-5.   Given a general process involving any number n of distinct intensive parameters, the following relation holds:

$$\Delta P^{ap_j} = \Delta P_i^{ap_j} + \Delta P_o^{ap_j} = k_{p_j p_l} (\Delta P_i^{ap_l} + \Delta P_o^{ap_l}),$$

$$1 \le j \le n, \quad j \neq 1, \quad l = 1, 2, \ldots, j-1, j+1, \ldots, n.$$

PROOF.   Simple generalization of the demonstration of (10-7).

It is clear that the number of distinct coparameter values needed for the characterization of a *state* of the system (refer to the statement of theorem 10∹4) is equal to the number of intensive parameters that are needed, for each of these has its own associated extensive parameter (coparameter). But, on the other hand:

Theorem 10-6.   Given a fixed (but arbitrary) process, a *single* coparameter change suffices to characterize the *process*, as far as change in extensive quantities go.

PROOF.   Corollary of (10–5)—or theorem 10-5—and theorem 10-4.

11

Irreversible Production of the Coparameter: Internal Gradients— General Case

Thus far we have studied the coparameter production associated with unidimensional internal transfers, that sufficing for reaching the results obtained in Chapter 9. But, each p-cell being three-dimensional and having in general E^p-transfer across the whole or part of its boundary, it is seen that $\dot{E}^p$ need not (and in general will not) flow in the same direction everywhere. In fact, $\dot{E}^p$ and Δp are in reality *vector* functions of cell position and of time, and it is therefore expedient, especially in view of ulterior investigations, to obtain the expression for the coparameter production within a single cell, rather than at the junction of two p-cells (δ_p-sets). The additivity property of the coparameter then permits us to evaluate by addition the coparameter production within any system composed of p-cells. The expression for the $\dot{P}_{\text{irr}}^{ap}$ production (due to internal transfers) within a cell will be derived by using as a building block the expression for the coparameter production associated with unidimensional internal transfers.

Set up a cartesian (x, y, z) coordinate system in the physicochemical system $\mathcal{S}$, in which the $\dot{P}^{ap}$ production is to be studied. For algorithmic simplicity in the derivation suppose that the δ-sets are of cubic shape; it may easily be shown that this imposes no restriction on the results—in fact, the results obtained will be independent of the shape of the δ-sets used in the derivation.

The first observation to be made is that, unless one desires to impose from the start very restrictive hypotheses on the phenomena being studied, the processes of the differential calculus must be applied only

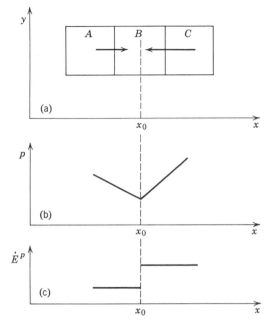

Figure 11-1   A particular form of $\dot{E}^p$-transfer internal to the system $S = (A \cup B \cup C)$.

with much circumspection. This is true in particular of Taylor's theorem, but is extensible to even the theorem of the mean of the differential calculus, which is valid under weaker hypothesis.*

The difficulty is that—*even when neglecting fluctuations*—the functions being handled may lack derivatives, and even possess discontinuities, at some critical points of their domain of definition.

Thus, by way of illustration, Figure 11-1a portrays three adjacent cells $\{A, B, C\}$ in linear succession, with a particular internal transfer within the system $S = (A \cup B \cup C)$, characterized by the functions p and $\dot{E}^p$ (as functions of x) shown in Figures 11-1b and 11-1c. Figure 11-2a represents the same system undergoing a different phenomenon, characterized by the functions p and $\dot{E}^p$ shown in Figures 11-2b and 11-2c. It is seen that, in both situations, the function $\dot{E}^p$ possesses a discontinuity (and therefore lacks a derivative) at point x_0, while the function p possesses a discontinuity in the first derivative at the same point x_0.

Notice that the linear property of the function p is an assumption in both cases (Figures 11-1b and 11-2b), as likewise the property of being

---

* In the literature it is easy to find an indiscriminate use of the processes of the differential calculus for problems similar in nature to the one that occupies our attention in this chapter.

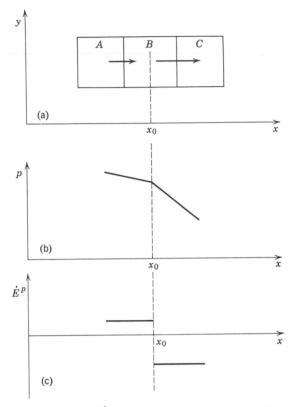

Figure 11-2   Another form of $\dot{E}^p$-transfer internal to the system $S = (A \cup B \cup C)$.

constant throughout intervals of the length of a cell is an assumed property of the function $\dot{E}^p$. In fact, all we know (from the meaning of δ_p-cell) is that the p-measuring instrument ("p-measuring" by definition) reads a certain value when it is inserted in the position of cell B (with, let us say, the midpoint of the instrument located on the x_0-line), and that it reads a different value when placed in cell A. The particular linear shape of the *point* functions shown in Figures 11-1b and 11-2b is an assumption. Furthermore, if fluctuations in the p-value were to be assumed for a point function $p = p(x)$, the derivative dp/dx would not be a monotone function of x.

Let the x-component of the $\dot{P}^{ap}$ production be analyzed, and because for the present we shall prescind from the other two components, the symbol $\dot{P}^{ap}$ will be used to represent the x-component of the rate of internal flow of the coparameter flow vector. The rate of E^p-transfer in the x-direction will in turn be symbolized by $\dot{E}^p$.

Neglecting friction for the moment, and assuming that the $\dot{E}^p$-transfer in the direction of any one of the three cartesian axes is *independent* of the p-gradients in the directions of the other two axes, from equation (8-1) we have

$$\underset{(A \to B)}{\dot{P}^{ap}} = \underset{(A \to B)}{\dot{E}^p} \frac{p_A - p_B}{p_A p_B} \tag{11-1}$$

and

$$\underset{(C \to B)}{\dot{P}^{ap}} = \underset{(C \to B)}{\dot{E}^p} \frac{p_C - p_B}{p_C p_B} = \underset{(B \to C)}{\dot{E}^p} \frac{p_B - p_C}{p_B p_C}. \tag{11-2}$$

Observe that the expression on the right side of (11-2), when applied to the situation depicted in Figure 11-1a, would have $(p_B - p_C)/p_B p_C < 0$, but also $\underset{(B \to C)}{\dot{E}^p} < 0$.

From lemma 2-2 (applied to P^{ap}) and the additivity property of $\dot{E}^p$ (see theorem A-5), it follows that

$$\underset{B}{\dot{P}^{ap}} = \underset{(A \to B)}{\dot{P}^{ap}} + \underset{(C \to B)}{\dot{P}^{ap}} = \frac{1}{p_B} \left[\frac{\underset{A \to B}{\dot{E}^p}(p_A - p_B)}{p_A} + \frac{\underset{C \to B}{\dot{E}^p}(p_C - p_B)}{p_C} \right]$$

$$= \frac{1}{p_B} \left[\underset{A \to B}{\dot{E}^p} \left(1 - \frac{p_B}{p_A} \right) + \underset{C \to B}{\dot{E}^p} \left(1 - \frac{p_B}{p_C} \right) \right] \tag{11-3}$$

Expression (11-3) yields $\underset{B}{\dot{P}^{ap}} = 0$ when $p_B = p_A = p_C$, as should be. On the other hand, it yields $\underset{B}{\dot{P}^{ap}}$ to be greater than any (finite) quantity when $p_B = 0$. This relation is also in accordance with the physical meaning attributed to the quantity P^{ap}, for if the system receiving the in-transfer ΔE^p remains at $p = 0$ in absolute scale, the whole in-transfer ΔE^p remains inconvertible (or non-retransferable) by means of a p-gradient, no matter what the lowest available p-value in the environment of the system may be (in our present context the system is cell B).

In expression (11-3), $\underset{(A \to B)}{\dot{E}^p}$ is the rate of in-transfer into B from cell A, while $\underset{(C \to B)}{\dot{E}^p}$ is the rate of in-transfer into B from cell C; their sum is therefore the *net rate of in-transfer* into cell B (along the x-axis, the only one being presently considered) and may be symbolized by $\underset{B}{\dot{E}^p}$.

Analogously, $\underset{(A \to B)}{\dot{P}^{ap}}$ is the rate of coparameter flow (into B) across the (A, B)-interface; $\underset{(C \to B)}{\dot{P}^{ap}}$ is the rate of coparameter flow (algebraically directed towards B) across the (B, C)-interface; their sum $\underset{B}{\dot{P}^{ap}}$ is the net rate of coparameter flow across the interfaces perpendicular to the x-axis, and algebraically directed towards B.

If the p-value between adjacent cells is considered to be a linear point function, and the length of a cell along the x-axis is denoted by Δx, then

$$p_A - p_B = \frac{d}{dx^-} \, p_{x_0} \, \Delta x, \tag{11-4a}$$

$$p_C - p_B = \frac{d}{dx^+} \, p_{x_0} \, \Delta x, \tag{11-4b}$$

where $(d/dx^-)p_{x_0}$ represents the left-side derivative of $p = p(x)$ at the point x_0; that is,

$$\frac{d}{dx^-} \, p_{x_0} = \lim_{\substack{x \to x_0 \\ x < x_0}} \frac{p_x - p_{x_0}}{x - x_0} \, ;$$

and analogously, $(d/dx^+)p_{x_0}$ represents the right-side derivative of $p = p(x)$ at x_0. Other notations to be used are

$$\frac{d}{dx^-} \, p_{x_0} = \frac{d}{dx^-} \, p_B \quad \text{and} \quad \frac{d}{dx^+} \, p_{x_0} = \frac{d}{dx^+} \, p_B.$$

Similarly we may define the symbols

$$\dot{E}^p_{B^-} = \dot{E}^p_{A \to B}, \qquad \dot{E}^p_{B^+} = \dot{E}^p_{C \to B}. \tag{11-5}$$

Substituting (11-4a), (11-4b), and (11-5) in the first of the expressions for $\dot{P}^{ap}_{B}$ in (11-3), we obtain

$$\dot{P}^{ap}_{B} = \frac{1}{p_B} \left[\frac{\dot{E}^p_{B^-} \left(\dfrac{d}{dx^-} \, p_B \, \Delta x \right)}{p_B + \dfrac{d}{dx^-} \, p_B \, \Delta x} + \frac{\dot{E}^p_{B^+} \left(\dfrac{d}{dx^+} \, p_B \, \Delta x \right)}{p_B + \dfrac{d}{dx^+} \, p_B \, \Delta x} \right] \tag{11-6}$$

Expression (11-6) is an equality when the p-gradients dp/dx are constant between adjacent cells (i.e., $p = p(x)$ is a linear point function). Otherwise (11-6) is only an approximation.

With the other two directions, y and z, there will be associated expressions exactly analogous to (11-3) and (11-6). From now on, for purposes of abbreviation and homogeneity, the symbol identifying the cell will be placed underneath the symbol of the quantity being predicated on the cell, and the component (along the axis) represented by a lower index. Furthermore, it is seen that $(p_A - p_B)$ is the measure of the p-gradient on the "left" boundary of the B-cell, while $(p_C - p_B)$ is the corresponding measure on the boundary on the right side of cell B. We shall therefore write

$$\Delta p_i \underset{B^-}{} = p_i \underset{A}{} - p_i \underset{B}{} = \frac{d}{dx_i^-} p_i \underset{B}{} \Delta x_i$$

for the ith component of the p-gradient on the left side of cell B, and $\Delta p_i \underset{B^+}{}$ will represent the corresponding quantity for the right side of cell B.

With the above conventions, the total $\dot{P}^{ap} \underset{B}{}$ accumulated in cell B is

$$\dot{P}^{ap} \underset{B}{} = \sum_{i=1}^{3} \frac{1}{p} \underset{B}{} \left[\frac{\dot{E}^{p} \underset{B^-}{} \left(\Delta p_i \underset{B^-}{} \right)}{p \underset{B}{} + \Delta p_i \underset{B^-}{}} + \frac{\dot{E}^{p} \underset{B^+}{} \left(\Delta p_i \underset{B^+}{} \right)}{p \underset{B}{} + \Delta p_i \underset{B^+}{}} \right]. \tag{11-7}$$

Equation (11-7) is valid on the assumption that the $\dot{E}^p$-transfer in each direction is independent of the p-gradients that are orthogonal to it, but it does not presuppose any particular functional relation for the p-quantity as a point function.

In the expression

$$\dot{P}^{ap} \underset{B}{} = \frac{1}{p} \underset{B}{} \left[\frac{\dot{E}^{p} \underset{B^-}{} \left(p \underset{A}{} - p \underset{B}{} \right)}{p \underset{A}{}} + \frac{\dot{E}^{p} \underset{B^+}{} \left(p \underset{C}{} - p \underset{B}{} \right)}{p \underset{C}{}} \right]$$

of equation (11-3), as well as in all the other expressions that have been derived equivalent to it, it is easily seen that the left side consists of a scalar quantity, while the right side consists of vectors multiplied componentwise. By defining the vectors

$$\dot{\mathbf{E}}^{p} \underset{B^-}{} \equiv \left\{ \dot{E}_i^{p} \underset{B^-}{}, \quad i = 1, 2, 3 \right\}, \qquad \dot{\mathbf{E}}^{p} \underset{B^+}{} \equiv \left\{ \dot{E}_i^{p} \underset{B^+}{}, \quad i = 1, 2, 3 \right\},$$

$$\Delta \mathbf{p} \underset{B^-}{} \equiv \left\{ \frac{1}{p} \underset{B}{} \frac{\Delta p_i \underset{B^-}{}}{p \underset{B}{} + \Delta p_i \underset{B^-}{}}, \quad i = 1, 2, 3 \right\}, \qquad \Delta \mathbf{p} \underset{B^+}{} \equiv \left\{ \frac{1}{p} \underset{B}{} \frac{\Delta p_i \underset{B^+}{}}{p \underset{B}{} + \Delta p_i \underset{B^+}{}} \right\},$$

with

$$\Delta \mathbf{p} \underset{B}{} = \Delta \mathbf{p} \underset{B^-}{} + \Delta \mathbf{p} \underset{B^+}{} \quad \text{and} \quad \dot{\mathbf{E}}^{p} \underset{B}{} = \dot{\mathbf{E}}^{p} \underset{B^-}{} + \dot{\mathbf{E}}^{p} \underset{B^+}{}$$

we may mathematically represent $\dot{P}^{ap} \underset{B}{}$ in the form of a particular scalar or ordered product of two set vectors (i.e., vectors associated with a set rather than with a point):

$$\dot{P}^{ap} \underset{B}{} \equiv \dot{\mathbf{E}}^{p} \underset{B}{} \cdot \Delta \mathbf{p} \underset{B}{} = \sum_{i=1}^{3} \dot{\mathbf{E}}_i^{p} \underset{B^-}{} \cdot \Delta \mathbf{p}_i \underset{B^-}{} \oplus \sum_{i=1}^{3} \dot{\mathbf{E}}_i^{p} \underset{B^+}{} \cdot \Delta \mathbf{p}_i \underset{B^+}{} \tag{11-8}$$

Regarding set tensors (and vectors) and ordered operations like the ordered multiplication used above, the reader may consult references [5] and [6], or preferably [49].

Now we are in a position to evaluate the rate of coparameter production over a system S composed of cubic cells. The first observation to be made is that a coparameter flow between cells internal to S corresponds to a coparameter *production* when regarded from the standpoint of the exchanges between S and $\mathcal{E}$, as has already been discussed in Chapter 8. In the present context, the coparameter production results from the fact that the coparameter outflow from one of the two adjacent cells has, in the numerator of its mathematical expression, the same arithmetical value as the numerator of the expression representing the coparameter inflow to the other cell, whereas the arithmetical values of their respective denominators differ. Thus,

$$\dot{P}^{ap}_{\to B} = \dot{E}^p_{\to B}\frac{1}{p_B} \quad \text{and} \quad \dot{P}^{ap}_{A\to} = \dot{E}^p_{A\to}\frac{1}{p_A},$$

with $\dot{E}^p_{\to B} = -\dot{E}^p_{A\to}$ and $p_A \neq p_B$, where $A\to$ symbolizes outflow from A, and $\to B$ denotes inflow into B. The above implies that $\left|\dot{P}^{ap}_{\to B}\right| \neq \left|\dot{P}^{ap}_{A\to}\right|$; therefore their algebraic addition will give rise to a quantity $\dot{P}^{ap}_{A\to B} \neq 0$. This quantity must be positive because, by the S.L. and G.G.L., $\left\{\dot{E}^p_{\to B} > 0,\ \dot{E}^p_{A\to} < 0\right\}$ is associated with $p_A > p_B$.

It is seen that the quantity $\dot{P}^{ap}_{A\to B} > 0$, associated with system $S = A \cup B$, arises as a result of a purely internal phenomenon (E^p-transfer from cell A of S to cell B of S) without entailing any modification in the environment of $S = A \cup B$. Therefore, internal coparameter flow brings about an increment in the coparameter value of the system without any decrement in the coparameter value of the environment. This is what is called coparameter production in S or interior to S.

In the context of the preceding we may experimentally confirm the interpretation of the coparameter increment given in Chapter 6.

Thus, consider system S consisting of two sections, A and B, and isolated from the environment $\mathcal{E}$ (see Figure 11-3). For simplicity suppose that both sections A and B have the same specific conductivity and capacity with respect to parameter p (this hypothesis not being in the least essential, of course). Assume that at the beginning $p_A = C + \delta$, $p_B = C - \delta$, and $p_{\mathcal{E}} = C$. Under these conditions, part of the energy in-transfer that brought S to its present state is convertible or recoverable, by using the p-gradient δ existing between section A of S, and $\mathcal{E}$. Now, maintaining S isolated, permit internal transfer between A and B until $p_A = p_B$. Then $p_A = p_B = C$. Such an internal transfer, as has been seen, brings the P^{ap} of S to a higher value. But under these new conditions (new state of S) there can be no retransfer back to $\mathcal{E}$ of the energy in-transfer that originally went into S. To increased coparameter value thus corresponds decreased potentiality for retransfer or conversion, as indicated in Chapter 6.

Equation (11-8) gives an expression for the coparameter production in cell B resulting from its energy exchange with adjacent cells A and C; therefore $\dot{P}^{ap}_{B}$ may be considered as generated within the system $A \cup B \cup C$—that system being, as far as the internal transfer is concerned, isolated from the rest of the universe.

A	S	B
p_A		p_B
$p_{\mathcal{E}}$	$\mathcal{E}$	$p_{\mathcal{E}}$

Figure 11-3 Diagram of the experimental setup described in the text shows that a decreased potentiality for retransfer or conversion corresponds to an increased comparameter value.

The preceding has the following consequence: if we apply any one of the above relations to calculate $\dot{P}^{ap}_{A}$, $\dot{P}^{ap}_{B}$, and $\dot{P}^{ap}_{C}$, the coparameter flows between A and B, as well as those between B and C, will be included twice. Now, if the system $A \cup B \cup C$ is isolated from the rest of the universe, cell A has coparameter flow only with cell B, and cell C has coparameter flow only with cell B; therefore, not only the coparameter flows associated with cell B, but also the coparameter flows associated with cells A and C, are being counted twice.

Now consider system S consisting of any geometrical spatial arrangement of disjoint cells, and let us employ the index k to identify the cells; we have demonstrated

Theorem 11-1. If every internal energy transfer is independent of gradients perpendicular to it, the rate of coparameter production in S is given by

$$\dot{P}^{ap}_{\text{irr}} = \frac{1}{2} \sum_{k \in S} \dot{\mathbf{E}}^{p}_{k} \cdot \Delta \mathbf{p}_{k}$$

$$= \frac{1}{2} \sum_{k \in S} \left(\sum_{i=1}^{3} \dot{\mathbf{E}}^{p_i}_{k^-} \cdot \Delta \mathbf{p}_{i}_{k^-} \oplus \sum_{i=1}^{3} \dot{\mathbf{E}}^{p}_{k^+} \cdot \Delta \mathbf{p}_{i}_{k^+} \right). \tag{11-9}$$

Observe that expression (11-9) does not include any coparameter increment in S that would be due to a coparameter flow from $\mathcal{E}$ to S; such a rate of coparameter flow would be added to (11-9) in order to obtain the total rate of coparameter increment in S (part of it due to flow from $\mathcal{E}$, and part due to production or generation within S). Further notice that, although there can be coparameter generation without simultaneous coparameter flow into S (the necessary and sufficient condition for this is that there be energy transfers internal to S while it is isolated from &), there cannot be a coparameter flow into S without the accompaniment of some coparameter production within S—this by virtue of the finite propagation hypothesis and theorem 9-2.

Theorem 9-3 and corollary 9-2 assert that there do not exist lossless, reversible processes in nature; in chapters 7 and 8 and in this chapter, a certain amount of theory has been developed for the quantitative evaluation of ΔP_{irr}^{ap} and therefore of $\Delta E_{irr}^{p} = \Delta P_{irr}^{ap} p_0$. The following inquiry now suggests itself: can there exist *purely irreversible* processes in nature?

Theorem 11-2. If $p_0 \neq A_0{}^p$, then there cannot exist purely irreversible processes in nature that involve a single intensive parameter. Processes involving more than one intensive parameter may be purely irreversible. In the case of two intensive parameters, a necessary condition for pure irreversibility is

$$\frac{\dot{E}^{p_1}}{\dot{E}^{p_2}} = -\frac{p_1}{(p_1)_0}\frac{(p_2)_0}{p_2}.$$

PROOF. For the first thesis of the theorem start with expression (5-3):

$$\dot{E}_{ic}{}^{p} = \dot{E}_{t}^{p} + \dot{E}_{irr}^{p} = \frac{\dot{E}^{p}}{p}p_0 + \dot{E}_{irr}^{p}.$$

The condition of pure irreversibility implies that $(\dot{E}^p/p)p_0 = 0$; in view of the hypothesis of the theorem that equality means that $\dot{E}^p = 0$ (for, naturally, the parameter p always has a finite value). The existence of the condition $\dot{E}^p = 0$ over any finite interval of time means the absence of the process during that time interval, since every process involves some kind of ΔE^p—either ΔE^q (in the case of conversion) or else in-transfer, out-transfer, or internal ΔE^p-transfer.

When several intensive parameters are involved,

$$\sum_{l=1}^{n}\dot{E}_{ic}{}^{p_l} = \sum_{l=1}^{n}\frac{\dot{E}^{p_l}}{p_l}(p_l)_0 + \sum_{l=1}^{n}\dot{E}_{irr}^{p_l},$$

and the condition of pure irreversibility gives

$$\frac{\dot{E}^{p_1}}{p_1}(p_1)_0 = -\sum_{l=2}^{n}\frac{\dot{E}^{p_l}}{p_l}(p_l)_0.$$

In the case of two intensive parameters this last condition becomes

$$\frac{\dot{E}^{p_1}}{\dot{E}^{p_2}} = - \frac{p_1}{(p_1)_0} \frac{(p_2)_0}{p_2} \, .$$

The last two theses of the theorem are thus demonstrated.

As an example, if $\dot{E}^{p_1}$ is in-transfer from $\mathcal{E}$ to $\mathcal{S}$, and $\dot{E}^{p_2}$ is out-transfer, and $p_1 = k(p_1)_0$, one can obtain a purely irreversible process by making $p_2 = k(p_2)_0$ and $|\dot{E}^{p_1}| = |\dot{E}^{p_2}|$. Satisfying those relations within a time interval Δt will provide a purely irreversible process during that interval.

It should be carefully observed that pure irreversibility ($\Delta E_t^{\,p} = 0$) does not mean pure inconvertibility: $\Delta E_c^{\,p} = 0$. Furthermore, in a purely irreversible process there is no net coparameter flow (the coparameter inflow equalling the coparameter outflow), but there is coparameter production. Thus,

$$\sum \Delta E_{ic}^{\;\;p_m} > 0$$

and

$$\sum_{m} \Delta E_c^{\;p_m} = \sum_{m} \Delta E^{p_m} - \sum_{m} \Delta E_{ic}^{\;\;p_m}.$$

Generally

$$\sum_{m} \Delta E^{p_m} \neq 0,$$

except in the case when there is only one intensive parameter p_m.

12

Criteria for Equilibrium

The second law asserts that a necessary condition for an energy transfer is the existence of a gradient of some intensive parameter, and the general gradient law affirms that, in the absence of constraints to the transfer, such a gradient is sufficient to produce the transfer.

For conversions that are not transfers, the conversion hypothesis predicates the necessity (and, in the absence of constraints, the sufficiency is likewise asserted) of a gradient of some quantity q associated to the system S. But, contrary to the S.L., the conversion hypothesis does not set forth any property or characteristic of the conversion parameter q—beyond stating, in the *definition* of gradient of q, that q is a strictly monotonic function of some other parameter s, with respect to which the gradient exists; s is the gradient parameter, q the conversion parameter.

It is evident that, if we are to be in a position to predict in specific situations whether or not a conversion will occur, and if so in what direction, we must be able to identify the conversion parameter and to calculate or measure its rate of change. This is essentially equivalent to saying that we must have available practical (calculable) criteria for predicting equilibrium.

Before proceeding with the necessary definitions, however, the following observations should be noticed.

An energy transfer takes place from δ-cell to δ-cell, and therefore it is to be expected that the gradient associated with the transfer should be the gradient of an intensive quantity that has different values at different δ-cells or parts of S.

On the other hand, as has been observed in Chapter 5, a conversion process may take place, either throughout the whole of the converter C (type A conversion) or in a localizable part of C (type B conversion). Conversions of type A occur when the conversion has for source the structure and nature of the matter of the converter itself. Thus, for example, the convertibility characteristics of C may be expressed in the structural constitution of the chemicals in C, or in the mathematical relation holding between the characterizing parameters of C.

A conversion of type B takes place in a localizable portion of C and is due to kinematic or dynamic relations of different parts of C with respect to each other. This, for example, is what happens when an automobile wheel turns over a road and there is frictional conversion into heat transfer and mechanical deformation.

As in the case of transfers, conversions of type B are associated with gradients of intensive quantities varying throughout C. These intensive parameters satisfy the second alternative of characteristic (c) of an intensive parameter (see definition 4-3).

Conversions of type A may be associated either with an extensive parameter (this is the most common situation) or with an intensive parameter having the same value throughout C at any one instant of time. These intensive parameters satisfy the first alternative of characteristic (c) of intensive parameters (see definition 4-3).

Similar considerations lead us to expect that, in a transfer or a conversion of type B, the gradient of the intensive quantity will be with respect to position in the system (these positions being the locations of the δ-cells). For conversions of type A the gradient parameter s will not be of the nature of a length, since it must be predicable of the whole system.

Definition 12-1. A system is in the state of *free equilibrium* iff, in the absence of constraints, the properties of the system are constant functions of time; it is in *steady state* iff the time rate of change of those properties that do not remain invariant is constant; it is in *non-steady state* iff it satisfies neither of the preceding two conditions.

The lack of variation of the·properties of S in the state of free equilibrium, and the constant time rates of change of the steady state, may be predicated of S only with reference to the precision of the measuring instruments being used. Thus, for example, a system in the state of free equilibrium for one observer may not be in that state for another observer.

When a non-steady state is followed by a steady state (of which the state of free equilibrium is a particular case), the non-steady state is then commonly called the *transient* or the transient state. The non-steady state is the special object of study of chemical kinetics and extensive parts of other branches of physics and chemistry.

A finer classification is brought about by introducing the following two principles for distinction:

α   Whether the processes (transfer or conversions) occur *in the interior* of the system or *between* the system and its surroundings. In view of this distinction, there are two kinds of constraints of interest: *boundary* and *internal* constraints.

β   Whether the phenomenon being studied subsists in the presence or in the absence of constraints (for example, whether transfer phenomena subsist in the presence or in the absence of constraints to the free flow of what is being transferred). From this follows

Definition 12-2.   If the properties of a system are constant functions of time in the presence of constraints, but at least one of the properties would change with time in the absence of constraints, then the system is said to be in *constrained equilibrium.*

Applying principles α and β of classification, the following possible states of a system are of special interest:

1. Free equilibrium with the surroundings.
2. Free internal equilibrium.
3. Constrained equilibrium with the surroundings.
4. Constrained internal equilibrium.
5. Steady state with the surroundings.
6. Internal steady state.
7. Non-steady state with the surroundings.
8. Internal non-steady state.

Evidently, states 1, 3, 5, and 7 have meaning only in relation to transfer phenomena. States 2, 4, 6, and 8 have meaning with reference to internal transfers (between subsystems) and to conversions.

A preliminary theorem:

Theorem 12-1.   A system that is not in equilibrium with its surroundings cannot be in internal equilibrium.

PROOF.   Immediate consequence of the finite propagation hypothesis (Chapter 9).

The criteria for equilibrium may be considered from two points of view.

A. That of the *universe of all systems of a certain well-defined type.* The equilibrium criteria then give means for distinguishing those elements (systems of the universe) that are in equilibrium—among all systems belonging to that universe at the particular instant of time under consideration.

B. That of the *history of a single system.* The equilibrium criteria then provide means for characterizing those instants (and periods of time) when the system under consideration is in a state of equilibrium.

The first point of view will be called the *universal*; the second one, the *historical*.

Now criteria will be established for the characterization of equilibria. These criteria will be expressed in terms of extensive parameters of the system and will apply to all kinds of conversions, including the particular conversions falling under the classification of transfers. The plausibility of this universality of the criteria expressed in terms of extensive parameters, considering that gradients associated with transfers must be gradients of an intensive parameter, stems from the fact that with each intensive parameter there is an associated extensive parameter.

Theorem 12-2. A system is in free internal equilibrium iff P^{ap} is at its maximum for every p and q.

PROOF. From theorem 12-1 it follows that, in the historical standpoint concerning equilibrium, the system S *in free internal equilibrium* (by hypothesis) must have constant energy. The hypothesis of free internal equilibrium and theorem 12-1 also demand that, for the universal standpoint in our study, the universe of systems being considered be characterized by the fact that every system of that universe has equal energy.

Consider now a system in which there is a p-gradient (any one). In the absence of constraints, the fundamental principle of energy transfer (S.L., first part) permits an internal E^p-transfer ΔE^p_{int}, the G.G.L. asserts its existence, and the second part of the S.L. specifies its direction. The $\dot{E}^p_{int}$ will exist as long as there is an internal Δp. But it has been demonstrated that $\dot{E}^p_{int} > 0$ implies $\dot{P}^{ap}_{irr} > 0$; therefore P^{ap} will increase as long as an isolated S is the seat of an internal transfer.

From definition 12-1, S will be in equilibrium when its properties are constant functions of time. By the G.G.L. and the preceding paragraph, this cannot happen unless there is no p-gradient in the interior of S. Under those conditions $\dot{E}^p_{int} = \dot{P}^{ap}_{irr} = 0$. Consequently P^{ap} will reach maximum at equilibrium—and only at equilibrium in the absence of constraints.

If instead of a transfer p-gradient the system possesses a conversion q-gradient, the conversion hypothesis (Chapter 5) and the law of degradation (Chapter 9), with a reasoning exactly analogous to the one above, lead us to the same conclusion: P^{aq} is a maximum at equilibrium.

The extension of the thesis to the case of several independent internal gradients is immediate. Theorem 12-2 provides us with a criterion that characterizes equilibrium, with reference to both transfers and conversions, in terms of extensive quantities. Moreover it is to be observed that the maximum predicated in the thesis of the theorem is a maximum from both the universal and the historical standpoint.

Theorem 12-2 may also be expressed as follows:

A system is in free internal equilibrium iff $\dot{P}^{ap} = 0$ and $\ddot{P}^{ap} < 0$ for every p and q.

Theorem 12-3. Under the conditions of theorem 10-3, and if the equation of state of S establishes a positive functional relation between p_1 and p_2, max P^{ap_1} implies max P^{ap_2} and vice versa.

PROOF.   Because the ratio $\Delta E^{p_1}/\Delta E^{p_2} > 0$, the thesis of the theorem is an immediate consequence of theorem 10-3.

Corollary 12-1.   If the hypotheses of theorem 12-3 are valid for any two of the intensive parameters characterizing the states of S, then S is in free internal equilibrium iff P^{ap} is at its maximum for any p (or q) of its characterizing internal parameters.

PROOF.   Corollary of theorems 12-2, 12-3, 10-4, and 10-5.

The simplification that corollary 12-1 introduces to the applications of the theory is considerable. The corollary may be stated in the following equivalent formulation:

If the hypotheses of theorem 12-3 are valid for any two of the intensive parameters characterizing the states of S, then S is in free internal equilibrium iff $\dot{P}^{ap} = 0$ and $\ddot{P}^{ap} < 0$ for any p or q of its characterizing internal parameters.

Theorem 12-4.   An isolated system is in constrained internal equilibrium when P^{ap} and P^{aq}, for every p and q, are at the maximum compatible with the existing constraints.

PROOF.   Immediate extension of the proof of theorem 12-2.

This theorem admits of a corollary exactly analogous to that of theorem 12-3; for brevity it will not be stated here.

Theorem 12-5.   Under conditions of constant P^{ap} and P^{aq}, for every p and q, a system is in free internal equilibrium iff its energy is a minimum.

PROOF.   Consider the universe of all possible systems in state A, all having identical $P_A{}^{ap}$ (and $P_A{}^{aq}$) for every p (and q) and E_A. Now apply to every system of this universe a transformation (different for each system) of a class characterized by the value of ΔP^{ap}; that is, in the new transformed states every system of the universe will have $P^{ap} = P_A{}^{ap} + \Delta P^{ap}$ (for every p and q) identical to every other system of the universe—although, in the new transformed states the systems of the universe may differ in every other respect (but P^{ap}). As consequence every member of the universe in the transformed state will also have the same $E_{ic}{}^p$, for they originally had identical E_A and have received equal $\Delta E_{ic}{}^p$ (p_0 is common to every system, being a property of $\mathcal{E}$). The systems will, therefore, differ only in the $\sum_i \Delta E_c{}^{p_i}$ that each of them has received (for brevity, we shall use p_i for both transfer and conversion parameters; for some values of i, p_i will stand for the parameter of a p-gradient, whereas, for other values of i, p_i will symbolize the parameter of a q-gradient).

Those systems that are in *free* internal equilibrium now must be such that the $\Delta E_c{}^{p_i}$ received by them during the specified preceding transformation will have been zero for every i. Otherwise, by virtue of corollary 10-1, and of the convertibility properties of $\Delta E_c{}^{p_i}$, there would be transfers and conversions within $\mathcal{S}$, thus denying the condition of free internal equilibrium. Hence $\sum_i \Delta E_c{}^{p_i} = 0$ and $\Delta E_c{}^{p_i} = 0$ for every i.

In the original state A all systems had equal energy E_A. During the process they received identical ΔP^{ap}, and the ones that after the process are in free internal equilibrium have received $\sum_i \Delta E_c{}^{p_i} = 0$. But $E = E_A + \sum_i \Delta E_c{}^{p_i} + \sum_i \Delta E_{ic}{}^{p_i}$, and $\sum_i \Delta E_{ic}{}^{p_i} = \sum_i (P^{ap_i} - P_A{}^{ap_i})(p_i)_0$. Because all systems had identical $P_A{}^{ap}$ before the process and have identical P^{ap} afterwards, it follows that $\sum_i \Delta E_{ic}{}^{p_i}$ is equal for all systems of the universe. Therefore, of all the systems having identical P^{ap}, those in free internal equilibrium have minimal energy.

Notice that this theorem cannot be demonstrated by reversing the ratio P^{ap}/E which is maximal for equilibrium according to theorem 12-2 and corollary 12-1. It is true that the reversal would yield minimal E/P^{ap}, but not under the condition of equal P^{ap} for every system of the universe.

Theorem 12-4 may be stated in the following equivalent form:

Under conditions of constant P^{ap} and P^{aq}, for every p and q, a system is in free internal equilibrium iff $\dot{E} = 0$ and $\ddot{E} > 0$.

Definition 12-3. A process is *spontaneous* in system $\mathcal{S}$ during interval of time $t_1 < t < t_2$ (where t_2 could be $+\infty$) iff it can and *does* take place in the absence of constraints, without energy in-transfer from $\mathcal{E}$ to $\mathcal{S}$ during the time interval $t_1 \leq t \leq t_2$.

Theorem 12-6. Under conditions of constant P^{ap} and in the absence of internal constraints, a spontaneous transfer process may occur only in a way that makes the energy of the system decrease.

PROOF. Consider system $\mathcal{S}$ as represented in Figure 12-1. Denote by ΔE^p an energy transfer between $\mathcal{S}$ and $\mathcal{E}$. In view of definition 12-3 and one of the hypotheses of the theorem, the external energy transfer ΔE^p cannot be from $\mathcal{E}$ to $\mathcal{S}$; the possibilities remain, however, that $\Delta E^p = 0$ or $\Delta E^p < 0$ (i.e., that it is an out-transfer from $\mathcal{S}$ to $\mathcal{E}$). The thesis of theorem 12-6 asserts that, under conditions of constant P^{ap}, it is the second possibility ($\Delta E^p < 0$) that holds, rather than the first ($\Delta E^p = 0$).

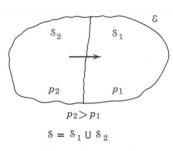

Figure 12-1 Basic system composed of two subsystems. S_1 and S_2 may be δ-cells.

If $\Delta E^p = 0$, there can be a transfer process only if there is an internal transfer, $\Delta E_1{}^p$, from some part S_2 of S to another part S_1. If $\Delta E^p \neq 0$, then necessarily $\Delta E^p < 0$, and we may assert

Lemma 12-1. In the absence of constraints to internal transfers, a system cannot remain in the quasi-static condition.

PROOF. If S is in the quasi-static condition and $\Delta E^p < 0$, there must be some cell of S (let us call it $S_{\delta 1}$) and a cell of ε (let us denote it by $S_{\delta 4}$) such that $\dot{E}_{14}{}^p > 0$. By the third assertion of the G.G.L., then $\dot{p}(S_1) < 0$. By the finite propagation hypothesis this $\dot{p}(S_1) < 0$ establishes a p-gradient internal to S (let us say between S_1 and S_2), and part I of the G.G.L. then guarantees the existence of an internal energy transfer $\dot{E}_{12}{}^p > 0$.

The lemma is equally valid if $\Delta E^p > 0$, using for the demonstration then part II of the G.G.L., followed by the finite propagation hypothesis and part I of the G.G.L. In this case S is in the quasi-static condition under condition α of definition 4-4b; the situation discussed in the preceding paragraph falls under condition β of definition 4-4b.

As a consequence of lemma 12-1 and of the preceding discussion, we see that, whether $\Delta E^p = 0$ or $\Delta E^p \neq 0$, the system will be the seat of an internal energy transfer—denote it by $\Delta E_1{}^p$. Then

$$\Delta P_S^{ap} = \frac{\Delta E^p}{p} + \Delta E_1{}^p \frac{p_2 - p_1}{p_1 p_2} + \Delta P_f{}^{ap},$$

and under conditions of constant $P_S{}^{ap}$:

$$-\frac{\Delta E^p}{p} = \Delta E_1{}^p \frac{p_2 - p_1}{p_1 p_2} + \Delta P_f{}^{ap}.$$

Now $\Delta E_1{}^p > 0$ and $(p_2 - p_1)/p_1 p_2 > 0$ (or, otherwise, $\Delta E_1{}^p < 0$ and $(p_2 - p_1)/p_1 p_2 < 0$), and $\Delta P_f{}^{ap} \not< 0$ by theorem 7-1. Therefore, because $p > 0$, necessarily $\Delta E^p < 0$. The theorem is thus demonstrated.

The following theorem will be stated without presenting its demonstration, since its verification is immediate in view of fundamental material already covered:

Theorem 12-7. In an isolated system free of internal constraints, a spontaneous process can occur only in a way that makes $P_S{}^{ap}$ increase.

Theorem 12-6 may be generalized as follows:

Theorem 12-8.   Under conditions of constant P^{ap}, a spontaneous process may occur only in a way that makes the energy of the system decrease.

PROOF.   For any process we have the relation

$$\Delta P_S{}^{ap} = \frac{\Delta E^p}{p} + \Delta P_{irr}^{ap},$$

and under conditions of constant $P_S{}^{ap}$, $\Delta E^p = -p\,\Delta P_{irr}^{ap}$. By the law of degradation (Chapter 9) $\Delta P_{irr}^{ap} > 0$ in every process in nature; $p > 0$ then implies that $\Delta E^p < 0$, and hence there is energy outflow from S to $\mathcal{E}$.

The advantage of separating the general statement of theorem 12-8 from its particular case in theorem 12-6 is that the latter will remain valid even if our understanding of the law of degradation were to be modified in the future.   Theorem 12-6 depends only on the S.L. and the G.G.L., which are generalizations more secure (in experience) than the law of degradation.

The necessity of the condition of constant coparameter value for the validity of the minimal energy criterion for equilibrium may obtain a more intuitive content from the following situation.   Take two systems S_1 and S_2 with equal E and P^{ap}.   Add, to the first, $\Delta E_1 = \Delta E_{1c} + \Delta E_{1\,ic}$ and, to the second, $\Delta E_2 = \Delta E_{2c} + \Delta E_{2\,ic}$, with $\Delta E_2 < \Delta E_1$, $\Delta E_{2c} > \Delta E_{1c}$ and $\Delta E_{2\,ic} < \Delta E_{1\,ic}$.

Now S_2 has less E than S_1, but it has more availability for transfers (internal or external) or conversions because the part of the ΔE_2 input that went into unavailable $\Delta E_{2\,ic}$ was less than the part of the ΔE_1 input that went into $\Delta E_{1\,ic}$. S_1 and S_2 started with equal E and P^{ap}, but at the end of their respective processes the one with *less E* (which is S_2) is *farther away from equilibrium* than the one with *more E* (which is S_1).   Naturally, the final P^{ap} values of the systems are not equal after the processes.

As an example illustrating that the state of equilibrium indeed demands maximal P^{ap} for constant E in the case $p = P$, consider the situation (Figure 12-2) in which a closed and isolated (constant E) vessel is only

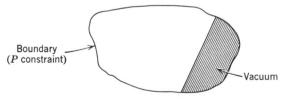

Figure 12-2   Gas entering an evacuated vessel. At equilibrium the gas will occupy the whole volume (ΔV maximal), and there will be no internal transfers (ΔP_{irr}^{ap} maximal).

partially occupied with gas. Experimentally this occurs when an evacuated vessel has just received a fixed amount of fluid injected, by man or by nature, from the outside. From experimental observations it is known that at equilibrium the fluid will occupy the whole volume, and this maximizes the term $P \Delta V/P$ in the expression

$$\Delta P^{ap} = \frac{P \Delta V}{P} + \Delta P^{ap}_{irr}.$$

Merely filling the whole volume will not bring about equilibrium, however. It is also known from experiment that at equilibrium there will not be any pressure gradient within the vessel, and consequently (Chapters 8 and 11) the term ΔP^{ap}_{irr} has reached its maximum. Therefore, if the system retains constant energy, when it attains equilibrium its P^{ap} value is at a maximum.

13

The Physicochemical Potentials*

It is deduced from the first law of energy transfers and conversions (Appendix A) that E, E_T, and U are functions of state. From that it follows that ΔE, ΔE_T, and ΔU are functions of couples of states and are consequently independent of the path or process followed by the system between states. Another way to mathematically express the same thing is to say that dE, dE_T, and dU are *perfect differentials*.

From the theory of differentials (see, for example, [8], pp. 268–280) we know that, if $\{X_i, i = 1, \ldots, n\}$ is a complete set of characterizing (generalized) parameters,

$$dE = \sum_{i=1}^{n} \frac{\partial E}{\partial X_i} \, dX_i, \tag{13-1}$$

and

$$\Delta E = \sum_{i=1}^{n} \frac{\partial E}{\partial X_i} \, \Delta X_i + \sum_{i=1}^{n} \epsilon_i \Delta X_i,$$

ϵ_i vanishing uniformly to a higher order than ΔX_i:

$$\lim_{\Delta X_i \to 0} \frac{\epsilon_i}{\Delta X_i} = 0.$$

It is evident that each of the terms $(\partial E/\partial X_i) \, dX_i$ and $(\partial E/\partial X_i) \, \Delta X_i$, for every i, must possess the properties of an extensive parameter, for so are dE and ΔE.

Convention. From now on we shall deal only with systems in which the intensive parameters can be considered to have constant values throughout the system.

---

* Readers not acquainted with the Legendre transformation, of which use will be made in this chapter, should read Appendix B as background material.

99

This agreement implies that in what follows we are prescinding from internal transfers, and limiting our attention to conversions and to interactions between S and $\mathcal{E}$.

In terms of the definition of intensive parameter (definition 4-3), the adopted convention simply means that, in the systems to be considered in the sequel, the first alternative of characteristic (c) of the definition holds: $p(S_1 \cup S_2) = p(S_1) = p(S_2)$, where p represents the intensive parameter, and S_1 and S_2 are any subsets of S.

Theorem 13-1.   If A is a property having constant value throughout S, and B is an extensive parameter of S, the product AB is also an extensive parameter of the system.

PROOF.   Observe that the theorem is not trivial because, although A is a constant during the time interval of concern, $B(S)$ may vary with time.

To demonstrate the additivity property consider $S = S_1 \cup S_2$, where S_1 and S_2 are disjoint. Then, indicating by $[AB]$ (S) the value of the quantity AB in S, we have

$$[AB](S) = A[B](S)$$
$$= A\{[B](S_1) + [B](S_2)\}$$
$$= [AB](S_1) + [AB](S_2).$$

The first equality above holds because A is a constant; the second equality is valid because B is an extensive parameter (and therefore additive); the third equality holds again because A is a constant.
To demonstrate the point continuity:

$$\lim_{\omega(S) \to 0} [AB](S) = \lim_{\omega(S) \to 0} A[B](S) = AO = 0.$$

The first equality holds because A is a constant; the second equality is valid because $[B](S)$ is point-continuous (being an extensive parameter).

Corollary.   If either of the factors $\{\partial E / \partial X_i, \ \Delta X_i\}$ is an intensive parameter and the other one is an extensive parameter, their product is an extensive parameter.

PROOF.   Immediate consequence of theorem 13-1 and the convention adopted.

As an example of the application of (13-1), in a reversible process $\dot{P}^{ap}_{rev} = \dot{E}^{p}_{rev}/p$, and, for $p = T$, $\dot{S}_{rev} = \dot{Q}_{rev}/T$. From this follows $\dot{Q}_{rev} = T\dot{S}_{rev}$ and $dQ_{rev} = T \, dS_{rev}$. Similarly, $\dot{V}_{rev} = \dot{W}_{rev}/P$ and $dW_{rev} = PdV_{rev}$. Then $dE = T \, dS + P \, dV$, which is of the form

$$dE = \sum_{i=1}^{2} \frac{\partial E}{\partial X_i} dX_i, \quad \text{with } X_1 = S \quad \text{and} \quad X_2 = V.$$

Here $\partial E/\partial X_i$ ($i = 1, 2$) represent intensive parameters, and X_i ($i = 1, 2$) extensive ones.

As another illustration of (13-1) consider the gravitational potential-energy term of the energy-balance equation:

$$\Delta E^g = \Delta \Omega_g = \frac{W}{g} \Delta h,$$

where W is the weight of S, and Δh is distance traveled along the line of force. Here $\partial E/\partial X = \partial \Omega_g/\partial h = W/g$, and $\Delta h = \Delta X$. In this case $\epsilon = 0$ because $\Delta \Omega_g$ is a linear function of Δh, and consequently $d\Omega_g = \Delta \Omega_g$. Notice that, contrary to the preceding example, here $\partial E/\partial X$ is the extensive parameter and $X = h$ the intensive one.

Gravitational potential-energy input or output (of converter) or transfer may also be of the form $\Delta \Omega_g = h(\Delta W/g)$, and both forms $[h(\Delta W/g)$ and $(W/g)\Delta h]$ may occur simultaneously, as indeed they do in all rocket flights.

As further illustration, if τ represents surface tension and $d\omega$ the variation in boundary surface of the system, then $\tau \, d\omega$ is the element of surface work of S. In this case τ is the intensive property and $d\omega$ the extensive property.

Based upon the preceding, E may be expressible as

$$E = E(X_1, \ldots, X_n),$$

or more shortly as

$$E = E(X_I).$$

By applying a Legendre transformation (see Appendix B), any one of the independent parameters X_i, $i = 1, \ldots, n$ (or several of them simultaneously), may be replaced by its conjugate $\partial E/\partial X_i$ (or by their conjugates if the transformation is applied to more than one independent variable) without altering the physicochemical phenomenon being mathematically described. [In the "language" of the parameters $\{E, X_i, i = 1, \ldots, n\}$, the phenomenon was described by the relation $E = E(X_I)$.] Each of the new dependent variables (Legendre transforms of E) thus obtained by means of the Legendre transformation will be called a *physicochemical potential*. The reason for the employment of this nomenclature is to be found in the analogy to be presently described.

In mechanics the conservative force is obtained by taking the derivative of the potential function with respect to the coordinate displacement along which the effect of the force is being considered, force and displacement being in this case the conjugate quantities. Analogously, taking the derivative of a physicochemical potential with respect to its associated independent variable, the conjugate of this independent variable will be obtained.

The truth of the preceding follows from the method of construction of the Legendre transform. In fact, if $E = E(X_I)$, the Legendre transform of E with respect to X_n is

$$L(E) = E - \frac{\partial E}{\partial X_n} X_n.$$

Now, in E, the only independent variables are $\{X_i, i = 1, \ldots, n\}$, while in $L(E)$ the independent variables are those of E, besides $\partial E/\partial X_n$ and X_n. Therefore

$$dL(E) = dE - d\left[\frac{\partial E}{\partial X_n} X_n\right]$$

$$= \sum_{i=1}^{n-1} \frac{\partial E}{\partial X_i} dX_i + \frac{\partial E}{\partial X_n} dX_n - \frac{\partial E}{\partial X_n} dX_n - X_n d\left(\frac{\partial E}{\partial X_n}\right)$$

$$= \sum_{i=1}^{n-1} \frac{\partial E}{\partial X_i} dX_i - X_n d\left(\frac{\partial E}{\partial X_n}\right).$$

It is seen that

$$\frac{\partial L(E)}{\partial(\partial E/\partial X_n)} = -X_n,$$

and hence, if X_n is considered as a "generalized force," $L(E)$ is its force potential with respect to the "generalized coordinate" $\partial E/\partial X_n$—just as E is the potential of $\partial E/\partial X_n$ with respect to the generalized coordinate X_n. In other words, with each potential are associated definite couples of generalized force and generalized coordinate.

The following presentation shows the anology in a succinct manner.

In mechanics:

$$P_1{}^2 = -\int_1^2 (F_x \, dx + F_y \, dy); \qquad \frac{\partial P}{\partial x} = -F_x, \quad \frac{\partial P}{\partial y} = -F_y.$$

In the theory of energy transfers and conversions:

$$\frac{\partial L(E)}{\partial(\partial E/\partial X_n)} = -X_n \qquad \begin{cases} L(E)\text{—generalized potential} \\[4pt] X_n\text{—generalized force} \\[4pt] \dfrac{\partial E}{\partial X_n} \text{—generalized coordinate} \\ \qquad \text{(distance)} \end{cases}$$

$$\underbrace{\qquad\qquad\qquad}_{\text{from}}$$

$$dL(E) = \left[\quad\quad\right] - X_n \, d\left(\frac{\partial E}{\partial X_n}\right).$$

Theorem 13-2. If X_i, for each i, is defined within an interval $a_i \leq X_i \leq b_i$, then $L(E)$ is a function of state.

PROOF. $L(E)$ will be a function of state if $dL(E)$ is an exact differential. From the hypothesis it follows that the set

$$\left\{ X_i, i = 1, \ldots, n - 1; \; \frac{\partial E}{\partial X_n} \right\}$$

is defined over an n-dimensional rectangle; by a well-known theorem (see, for example, [14], p. 303, Theorem V), $dL(E)$ will be an exact differential if

$$\frac{\partial(\partial E/\partial X_i)}{\partial X_j} = \frac{\partial(\partial E/\partial X_j)}{\partial X_i}$$

and

$$\frac{\partial(\partial E/\partial X_i)}{\partial(\partial E/\partial X_n)} = \frac{\partial X_n}{\partial X_i}$$

for $i, j = 1, \ldots, n - 1$. The first set of equalities follows from the fact that E is a function of state (and hence dE is an exact differential); the second set of equalities holds because, since $\{X_i, i = 1, \ldots, n\}$ forms a complete set of characterizing parameters,

$$\frac{\partial(\partial E/\partial X_i)}{\partial(\partial E/\partial X_n)} = \frac{\partial X_n}{\partial X_i} = 0.$$

Therefere $dL(E)$ is an exact differential; hence

$$\Delta L(E) = \int_a^b dL(E)$$

is independent of the path (see, for example, [15], pp. 354–365) and $L(E)$ is a function of state.

Examples of some very important physicochemical potentials are presented in Appendix D.

Appendix B

The Legendre Transformation

A general principle of learning is

Further insight is gained when an object of knowledge is examined from a different point of view.

Some important points of view and alternatives when studying a physicochemical problem are:

1. Local properties and global properties.
2. Representations in terms of vector fields (for example, force fields) and in terms of scalar fields (for example, potential fields).
3. Phenomenological theory and structural theory interpretations.
4. Action through a medium and action at a distance.
5. Physical interpretation (as for Newton's law of gravitation) and geometrical interpretation (as for Einstein's law of gravitation).
6. Algebraic, analytical, and geometric formulations of the mathematical formalism; also local and global (differential and integral) mathematical formulations.
7. Active and passive interpretations of the transformations and mappings.
8. Employment of different frames of reference; etc.

One of the ways of changing the reference frame in a physicomathematical problem consists in changing the coordinate system being employed in the formulation of the problem. The procedure used in this method of investigation is the following:

(a) Change the independent variables.

(b) Obtain the mathematical relation that will, in the new independent variables, represent the same geometrical configuration or physical phenomenon.

(c) Seek the geometrical or physical meaning of the new dependent variable and of the new relations.

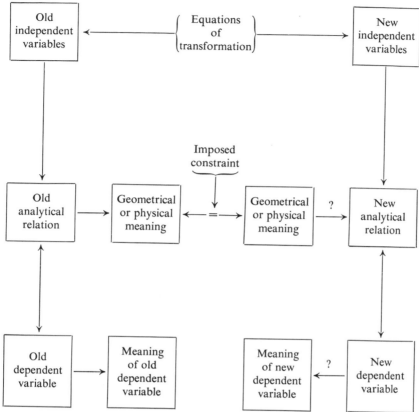

Figure B-1 Structure of the physicomathematical problem associated with a change of frame of reference.

Thus, if we have the relation $z = z(x, y)$ at hand, the first step means introducing the coordinate transformation $\begin{Bmatrix} x \to u \\ y \to v \end{Bmatrix}$. The second step leads to finding the function of $\{u, v\}$ that represents the same configuration or phenomenon that $z(x, y)$ represents. Suppose that $w = w(u, v)$ is such a function. Then in the last step the geometrical or physical meaning of the dependent variable w is investigated [obviously, steps (b) and (c) will quite often be performed simultaneously]. The *essential constraint* imposed on this process of research is that $w(u, v)$ must represent in the new independent variables the *same* geometrical configuration or physical phenomenon that $z(x, y)$ represented in the old independent variables $\{x, y\}$.

The procedure is shown schematically in Figure B-1. The two question marks in the chart indicate the two crucial sectors of the method.

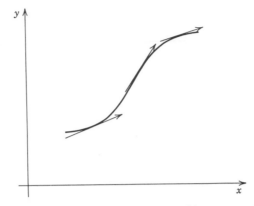

Figure B-2 Can a curve be characterized in terms of its tangents, instead of in terms of its point coordinates?

A particular coordinate transformation that has a long history of very useful service to science is the *Legendre transformation*, which is perhaps the simplest of the general kind that mathematicians call *contact transformations* (see, for example, [39], pp. 288 and 369; also [31]). In this transformation are studied the consequences of one or both of the following changes of independent variables:

$$x \to \frac{\partial z}{\partial x}, \qquad y \to \frac{\partial z}{\partial y}$$

(and similarly for the case of more than two independent variables). In other words, the Legendre transformation consists in taking as new independent variables the rate of change of the old dependent variable with respect to the old independent variables.

In geometry and kinematics the Legendre transformation changes point coordinates into line or Plücker coordinates (see, for example, [32], pp. 7–15, 291–315; [36], pp. 30, 34, 461–63; [37], pp. 217–225); then a curve, instead of being the locus of its points, becomes the envelope of its tangents. In mechanics the Legendre transformation changes the Lagrangian formulation into the Hamiltonian formulation (see, for example, [33], pp. 20–21) and into the formulation of Routh. In every case there result new conceptual and algorithmic instruments for further research and applications. In this appendix is presented the motivation and outline of the derivation of the Legendre transformation, which is applied in Chapters 13 and 15 and in Appendix D.

It is advisable to first study the problem involving only one independent variable, because in that case we have to handle only two variables (dependent and independent) and such a situation permits seeking a geometrical interpretation in the two-dimensional plane. The geometrical interpretation suggests to the intuition means for solving the analytical problem, and the analytical solution is then easily generalized to *n* degrees of freedom.

Geometrical Interpretation of the Problem (see Figure B-2): to *characterize* a curve, instead of in terms of the point coordinates *x* and *y*, in terms of another set of coordinates, of which set one of the elements is the quantity $p = dy/dx$.

We have therefore the schematic representation of the problem (see Figure B-3). The analytical problem consists in finding the function $?(p)$,

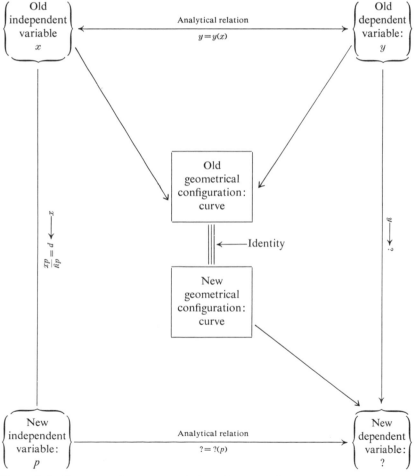

Figure B-3 Structure of the geometrical problem associated with a change of independent variables. The identity of the old to the new geometrical configuration is a constraint imposed upon the analytical solution $y = ?(p)$ to the problem.

of the independent variable p, that satisfies the identity in the diagram. This identity is a constraint upon the analytical solution of the problem. Associated with this analytical solution there is a geometrical problem: to find the geometrical meaning of the new dependent variable represented in the diagram by the symbol ?

Nota Bene.   Geometry is being used now as an aid in developing the method. In the applications of the Legendre transformation to be made in Appendix D, the interpretation for the new dependent variable will be sought in the realms of physics and physical chemistry, not in geometry.

If a geometrical configuration is characterized by one equation in two variables (i.e., by a relation between two sets of numbers), this means that the geometrical domain in question (characterized by that equation) is a one-dimensional subspace embedded in a two-dimensional space. Such a configuration is commonly called a curve.

Now $(dy/dx)_{x_0} = y_{x_0}' = p_{x_0}$ is a number characterizing—in the $\{x, y\}$ frame of reference—the tangent to the curve corresponding to the value of x_0 of the independent variable. But characterizing the tangent is not equivalent to characterizing the curve at the value x_0 of x. In fact, there can be an infinity of curves having identical y_{x_0}' (see Figure B-4).

It is quite clear that any geometrical configuration in two-dimensional space requires a system of reference composed of two variables. Our next step then must be to find another quantity that, in conjunction with y', will serve to characterize (individualize) curves in two-dimensional space, that is, to find a quantity that, together with y', will form an

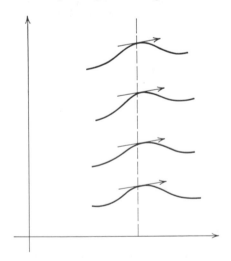

Figure B-4   There is an infinity of curves having the same set of tangents.

adequate framework for the characterization of configurations in two-dimensional space. That quantity must fulfill the following two requirements:

1. It must be independent of y', for otherwise the two quantities would already be bound by a *fixed* relation, and they could not then be used to individualize *different* curves by the imposition of different analytical relations upon the two variables.

2. It must be expressible in terms of x and y (as y' itself is also expressible in terms of x and y), for one frame of reference must be expressible in terms of the other. Indeed, a mathematical frame of reference is like a "language" (in terms of which things are represented), and any one language must be expressible in terms of another language (whether of sounds or of signs).

Our problem now is seen to consist in establishing a transformation of coordinate systems or frames of reference under the following two conditions:

(a) One of the coordinate systems is the $\{x, y\}$ frame of reference.

(b) The other coordinate system has, for one of its elements (coordinates), the quantity y'.

(The problem is essentially the same as that confronting a linguist who is given a certain language and is asked to construct an *equivalent* language under some stipulation; for example, the second language could be constrained to consist of only certain types of signs or to specifically include certain signs. This stipulation on the second language would correspond, in the analogy, to the fact that one of the elements—coordinates—of the second reference frame has already been specified: y'.)

To find the second element or component of the reference frame let us examine again the graphical illustration of a curve (see Figure B-5).

It has been seen that the y' component of the new coordinate system cannot, by itself, distinguish between two curves that, at x_0, have the same slope y_{x_0}' but are displaced vertically one above the other. In consequence, our objective has been attained if we find another component that serves to distinguish tangent lines having identical y'-values at x_0, for two components or coordinates suffice to characterize each unit element (or unit tangent) of the curve in two-dimensional space (i.e., such an element has two degrees of freedom).

In other words, the second element of the new coordinate system must serve to characterize the *vertical displacement of unit tangents* having identical y' at x_0. Requirement 2 then adds that this second element must be expressible in terms of x and y.

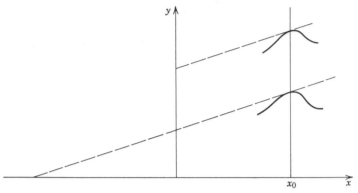

Figure B-5 Two parallel tangents can be distinguished by their intersections with the *x*-axis or with the *y*-axis.

From an examination of Figure B-5 it is immediately seen that *the intersection of the line of slope y'* (tangent to the curve) *with either the y-axis or the x-axis satisfies the above two demands.*

To illustrate, denote by q the intersection of the line given by y' with the *y*-axis. Then (see Figure B-6), the curve can be equally well

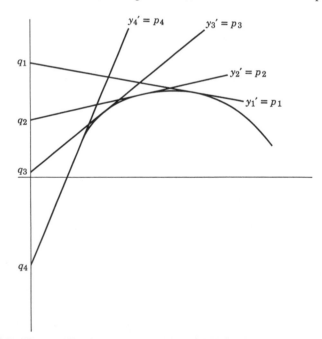

Figure B-6 The combination {slope of tangent, intersection of tangent with *y*-axis} characterizes the curve as well as the point coordinates of the curve.

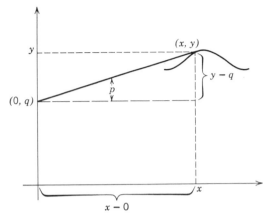

Figure B-7 Diagram to establish relation between the point coordinates $\{x, y\}$ and the slope-intersection coordinates $\{p, q\}$.

characterized by the relation $y = y(x)$, assigning one number from the y-set to every x-value of the curve, or by a relation of the form $y' = y'(q)$ or $q = q(y')$, assigning a correspondence between q-values and y'-values. To each q-y'-correspondence belongs a curve and vice versa.

The next step consists in establishing an analytical expression for q in terms of x and y; that is, to continue our "dictionary" in the direction $\{x, y\} \rightarrow \{p, q\}$, the "dictionary" having as first entry the "translation" $p = dy/dx = y'$. Later the "dictionary" must be established in the opposite direction: $\{p, q\} \rightarrow \{x, y\}$—how to find x and y on the basis of p and q. It is evident that a transformation of coordinate system is but the mathematical counterpart of a two-way bilingual dictionary.

What remains is fairly formal.

From Figure B-7 it is seen that $p = (y - q)/(x - 0)$, and thus

$$q = y - px. \tag{a}$$

In (a), q is called the Legendre transform of y; if we denote it by $L(y)$, (a) would be rewritten as

$$L(y) = y - \frac{dy}{dx} x. \tag{a}$$

By differentiating

$$y = y(x) \tag{b}$$

we obtain

$$p = p(x). \tag{c}$$

Eliminating x and y from (a). (b), and (c), the relations

$$\left. \begin{aligned} q &= q(p) \\ p &= p(q) \end{aligned} \right\} \tag{d}$$

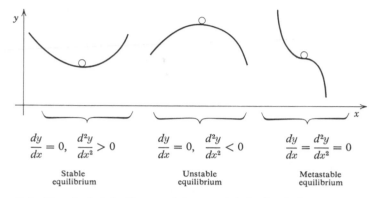

$$\frac{dy}{dx} = 0, \quad \frac{d^2y}{dx^2} > 0 \qquad \frac{dy}{dx} = 0, \quad \frac{d^2y}{dx^2} < 0 \qquad \frac{dy}{dx} \quad \frac{d^2y}{dx^2} = 0$$

Stable   Unstable   Metastable
equilibrium   equilibrium   equilibrium

Figure B-8   The physical significance of the second derivative d^2y/dx^2, from mechanics.

are obtained. This elimination is possible as long as p and x are not independent, for in such a case relation (c) does not exist. Moreover, if p is independent of x,

$$p' = \frac{dp}{dx} = \frac{d^2y}{dx^2} = 0.$$

The geometrical significance of the relation $d^2y/dx^2 = 0$ may be observed from Figure B-8. A small mechanical ball has been placed at each of the points for which $dy/dx = 0$, and the terminology used in the science of mechanics to denote the three corresponding situations from the viewpoint of stability of equilibrium has also been included in the figure. Observe that the equilibrium defined and discussed in Chapter 12 corresponds to the type called stable, for in it

$$\frac{dE}{dt} = 0 \quad \text{and} \quad \frac{d^2E}{dt^2} > 0;$$

however, questions of stability are not our concern, either in Chapter 12 or in this appendix.

It remains for us to fill the "dictionary" in the opposite direction. To do this, we derive (a) with respect to any suitable parameter (t or x, etc.), obtaining

$$\frac{dq}{dt} = \frac{dy}{dt} - p\frac{dx}{dt} - x\frac{dp}{dt}.$$

But because $p = dy/dx$, it follows that

$$\frac{dy}{dt} = \frac{dy}{dx}\frac{dx}{dt} = p\frac{dx}{dt}$$

if t is a universal parameter. Hence

$$\frac{dq}{dt} = -x\frac{dp}{dt} \quad \text{and} \quad -x = \frac{dq}{dp}. \tag{e}$$

Eliminating p and q from (a), (d), and (e), we obtain anew the relation $y = y(x)$.

From the preceding it follows that

$$y = xp + q \tag{f}$$

yields y as the inverse Legendre transform of q.

The following table of correspondences may therefore be established:

$$x \longrightarrow p = \frac{dy}{dx}$$

$$y \longrightarrow q = L(y)_x = y - px$$

$$p \longrightarrow x = -\frac{dq}{dp}$$

$$q \longrightarrow y = q + xp = L^{-1}(q)_p$$

The quantities p and x are called the *conjugate variables*, and $q = L(y)_x$ is the Legendre transform of y with respect to x, while $y = L^{-1}(q)_p$ is the inverse Legendre transform of q with respect to p.

We have thus derived the expressions for the direct and the inverse Legendre transform for the simple geometrical configuration of a curve embedded in two-dimensional Euclidean space. An exactly similar study can be carried out for other geometrical configurations embedded in spaces of larger numbers of dimensions; it suffices to note that the number of variables (independent plus dependent) must equal the number of (geometrical) degrees of freedom or dimensions of the embedding space, while each equation between those variables corresponds to a constraint, each constraint thus eliminating one degree of freedom.

To illustrate the preceding consider a surface in three-dimensional space, and let it be analytically represented by $z = z(x, y)$. From this relation follow

$$\dot{z} = \frac{\partial z}{\partial x}\dot{x} + \frac{\partial z}{\partial y}\dot{y}$$

and the differential

$$dz = \frac{\partial z}{\partial x}dx + \frac{\partial z}{\partial y}dy.$$

In such expressions the variable x is the conjugate of $X = \partial z/\partial x$, and the conjugate of y is $Y = \partial z/\partial y$. Let it be desired to obtain the Legendre transform of z with respect to y. This transform is the function

$$L(z)_y = f\left(Y = \frac{\partial z}{\partial y}, x\right)$$

that analytically represents the same surface as the original analytical relation $z = z(x, y)$.

From the chart on p. 113 it is seen that the Legendre transform (new dependent variable) is obtained by subtracting from the old dependent variable the product of the conjugate variables; therefore

$$L(z)_y = z - yY.$$

It follows that

$$dL(z)_y = dz - y\,dY - Y\,dy = X\,dx + Y\,dy - y\,dY - Y\,dy$$
$$= X\,dx - y\,dY,$$

and

$$\frac{\partial}{\partial x} L(z)_y = X = \frac{\partial z}{\partial x},$$

while

$$\frac{\partial}{\partial Y} L(z)_y = -y.$$

If the Legendre transform with respect to both independent variables is desired, the same procedure is applied to each one. Thus,

$$L(z)_{x,y} = z - xX - yY,$$

giving

$$dL(z)_{x,y} = -x\,dX - y\,dY,$$

with

$$\frac{\partial}{\partial X} L(z)_{x,y} = -x$$

and

$$\frac{\partial}{\partial Y} L(z)_{x,y} = -y.$$

Besides the expressions for the Legendre transforms, we have derived the expressions for their differentials (or, what is equivalent, for their derivatives) because we are interested in the applications of the method of the Legendre transformation to physicochemical phenomena (see Chapters 14 and 15), and in these we have to consider changes and rates of transfer. Thus, if z stands for the energy E, we are obviously interested in the expressions for ΔE and $\dot{E}$, since it is these, and not E, that are directly or indirectly measured, and in terms of which we may be able to understand and make predictions concerning the future course of the phenomenon. Therefore, we are interested in also having at hand expressions for the rates of change of the various Legendre transforms of $z = E$.

For those acquainted with the elements of analytical mechanics, the Legendre transform may become a more familiar instrument if it is here shown how, with its use, the Lagrangian equations of motion are transformed into the Hamiltonian equations.

The problem of the Legendre transformation, for a single variable, may be synthesized for this purpose as follows:

Given: $f(x, y, t)$,
To find: $g(x, z, t)$ such that $z = \partial f/\partial y$ and $\partial g/\partial z = y$.
Solution: $g(x, z, t) = yz - f(x, y, t)$.

Let us now obtain the Legendre transform of the Lagrangian function $L = L(q_1, \ldots, q_n, \dot{q}_1, \ldots, \dot{q}_n, t)$, applying it to the variables $\dot{q}$. That is, $\dot{q}_k \to p_k = L/\dot{q}_k$, for all values of k.

In the context of the abstract formulation of the Legendre transformation problem given above, $\dot{q}_k = y$, $p_k = z$, and $L = f$.

The transform of L will then be

$$H = \sum_k \dot{q}_k p_k - L, \qquad \text{with } H = H(q_1, p_1, q_2, p_2, \ldots, t).$$

The function H is called the *Hamiltonian function.*

Now, the total differential of the Hamiltonian is given by

$$dH = \sum_k \dot{q}_k \, dp_k + \sum_k p_k \, d\dot{q}_k - \sum_k \frac{\partial L}{\partial q_k} \, dq_k - \sum_k \frac{\partial L}{\partial \dot{q}_k} \, d\dot{q}_k - \frac{\partial L}{\partial t} \, dt.$$

Because $p_k = \partial L/\partial \dot{q}_k$, the total differential reduces to

$$dH = \sum_k \dot{q}_k \, dp_k - \sum_k \frac{\partial L}{\partial q_k} \, dq_k - \frac{\partial L}{\partial t} \, dt.$$

From this it follows that

$$\frac{\partial H}{\partial p_k} = \dot{q}_k \quad \text{and} \quad \left(\frac{\partial H}{\partial q_k}\right)_p = -\left(\frac{\partial L}{\partial q_k}\right)_{\dot{q}}.$$

But from the Lagrangian equation of motion

$$\frac{d}{dt}\frac{\partial L}{\partial \dot{q}_k} - \frac{\partial L}{\partial q_k} = 0$$

it follows that

$$\dot{p}_k = \frac{d}{dt}\frac{\partial L}{\partial \dot{q}_k} = \frac{\partial L}{\partial q_k}.$$

In consequence $\dot{q}_k = -(\partial H/\partial q_k)$.

The set of equations

$$\begin{cases} \dot{q}_k = \dfrac{\partial H}{\partial p_k} \\[2mm] \dot{p}_k = -\dfrac{\partial H}{\partial q_k} \end{cases}, \quad k = 1, \ldots, n$$

are called *Hamilton's equations of motion*. They are differential equations of the first order, whereas Lagrange's equations are of the second order.

14

The Fundamental Physicochemical Equation

The convertibility equation together with the energy conservation equation (first law; see Appendix A) gives the basic conversion (and transfer) equation

$$\dot{E} = \dot{E}^{p_1} + \dot{E}^{p_2} = \dot{E}_c{}^{p_1} + \dot{E}_c{}^{p_2} + \dot{E}_{ic}{}^{p_1} + \dot{E}_{ic}{}^{p_2},$$

with $\dot{E}_{ic}{}^{p} = p_0\dot{P}^{ap}$ and $\dot{P}^{ap} = (\dot{E}^p/p) + \dot{P}^{ap}_{irr}$ for both $p = p_1$ and $p = p_2$.
From the last equation is deduced

$$\dot{E}^p = p\dot{P}^{ap} - p\dot{P}^{ap}_{irr}.$$

Substituting in the basic conversion equation,

$$\dot{E} = \dot{E}^{p_1} + \dot{E}^{p_2} = p_1\dot{P}^{ap_1} + p_2\dot{P}^{ap_2} - p_1\dot{P}^{ap_1}_{irr} - p_2\dot{P}^{ap_2}_{irr}. \qquad (14\text{-}1)$$

Because E and P^{ap} are functions of state, equation (14-1) leads to

$$dE = p_1\, dP^{ap_1} + p_2\, dP^{ap_2} - p_1\, \delta P^{ax_1}_{irr} - p_2\, \delta P^{ap_2}_{irr} \qquad (14\text{-}2)$$

with

$$p_1 = \frac{\partial E}{\partial P^{ap_1}} = -\frac{\partial E}{\partial P^{ap_1}_{irr}} \quad \text{and} \quad p_2 = \frac{\partial E}{\partial P^{ap_2}} = -\frac{\partial E}{\partial P^{ap_2}_{irr}}. \qquad (14\text{-}3)$$

Naturally, δP^{ap}_{irr} is not a function independent of the path (Chapters 7, 8, and 11).

At first sight it might seem that equations (14-3) contain an inconsistency, for to form the expressions in the center we use the ratio of two functions (ΔE and ΔP^{ap}) independent of the path, whereas to form their right sides we employ the ratio of a function independent of the path (ΔE) to a function dependent on the path: ΔP^{ap}_{irr}. The inconsistency, however, is only apparent, for on passing to the limit the path is reduced to a single state, and the distinction between dependence and independence of path is eliminated. That the passage to limit $\Delta P^{ap} \to 0$ implies reduction of the path to a single state follows from the fact that P^{ap} is a function of state and ΔP^{ap} a function of couples of states. That the passage to limit $\Delta P^{ap}_{\mathrm{irr}} \to 0$ has the same implication follows because, by the law of degradation, $\Delta P^{ap}_{\mathrm{irr}} > 0$ for every process in nature; therefore, $\lim \Delta P^{ap}_{\mathrm{irr}} = 0$ means the absence of process, and thus that passage to limit mathematically isolates a state. This is as it should be, for the left sides of (14-3), p_1 and p_2, may be considered as being functions of state by virtue of the convention adopted in Chapter 13.

Because $\dot{E}^p = p(\dot{P}^{ap} - \dot{P}^{ap}_{\mathrm{irr}}) = p\dot{P}^{ap}_{\mathrm{rev}} = p\dot{P}_t{}^{ap}$, it also follows that, for the (idealized) reversible processes:

$$p_1 = \frac{\partial E}{\partial P^{ap_1}} \overset{\mathrm{rev}}{\equiv} \frac{\partial E}{\partial P_t^{ap_1}} \quad \text{and} \quad p_2 = \frac{\partial E}{\partial P^{ap_2}} \overset{\mathrm{rev}}{\equiv} \frac{\partial E}{\partial P_t^{ap_2}}.$$

Theorem 14-1. For given values of the intensive parameters and for processes that may be considered as being sufficiently close to reversibility,

$$E = E(P^{ap_1}, P^{ap_2}) \tag{14-4}$$

that is, E is a function of a complete set of extensive characterizing parameters, all of which are functions of state.

PROOF.   Consequence of (14-1) and (14-2).

Equation (14-4) will be called the *fundamental physicochemical equation* for *reversible* processes.

In cases in which irreversibility is a non-negligible phenomenon (and herein by far our greater interest lies) equations (14-1) and (14-2) cannot be integrated to give an equation analogous to (14-4), with $P^{ap_1}_{\mathrm{irr}}$ and $P^{ap_2}_{\mathrm{irr}}$ included among the characterizing parameters, because $\Delta P^{ap}_{\mathrm{irr}}$ and $\delta P^{ap}_{\mathrm{irr}}$ are not functions of couples of states. $\Delta P^{ap}_{\mathrm{irr}}$ is predicable of a definite process (path) between two states, but P^{ap}_{irr} is not in a similar relation with respect to the states of the system: there is no univalent function from the states of the system to values of P^{ap}_{irr}.

However, by introducing the symbols $\delta E^{p_1}_{\mathrm{irr}} = p_1 \, \delta P^{ap_1}_{\mathrm{irr}}$ and $\delta E^{p_2}_{\mathrm{irr}} = p_2 \, \delta P^{ap_2}_{\mathrm{irr}}$, equation (14-2) may be written as

$$dE = p_1 \, dP^{ap_1} + p_2 \, dP^{ap_2} - \delta E^{p_1}_{\mathrm{irr}} - \delta E^{p_2}_{\mathrm{irr}}. \tag{14-5}$$

Theorem 14-2. $\delta E^{p_1}_{\mathrm{irr}}$ and $\delta E^{p_2}_{\mathrm{irr}}$ are not functions of couples of states, but they are interchangeable.

PROOF. $\delta E^p_{\mathrm{irr}}$, for any p, is not a function of couples of states because $\delta E^p_{\mathrm{irr}} = p \, \delta P^{ap}_{\mathrm{irr}}$, p being a constant for the system by virtue of the convention adopted in Chapter 13, and $\delta P^{ap}_{\mathrm{irr}}$ being dependent on path; by theorem 3-8 then, δE^p_{irr} is dependent on the path. For the second thesis of the theorem, because dE, $p_1 \, dP^{a p_1}$, and $p_2 \, dP^{a p_2}$ are all three functions of couples of states, from theorem 3-8 it follows that $(\delta E^{p_1}_{\text{irr}} + \delta E^2_{\text{irr}})$ must also be a function of couples of states; by theorem 3-10 (or by lemma 10-1) the terms $\delta E^{p_1}_{\text{irr}}$ and $\delta E^{p_2}_{\text{irr}}$ must then be interchangeable.

Corollary 14-1. $\delta E^{p_1}_{\text{irr}} + \delta E^{p_2}_{\text{irr}} = dE_{\text{irr}}$, and E_{irr} is a function of state.

PROOF.   From theorem 14-2, definition 3-9, and theorem 3-2.

Assumption. E_{irr}, the function of state associated with dE_{irr}, is a linear function of an extensive parameter R. Under this assumption we may write

$$dE_{\text{irr}} = A \, dR \qquad (14\text{-}6)$$

with

$$A = \frac{d}{dR}(E_{\text{irr}}). \qquad (14\text{-}7)$$

Equation (14-2) then becomes

$$dE = p_1 \, dP^{a p_1} + p_2 \, dP^{a p_2} - dE_{\text{irr}} = p_1 \, dP^{a p_1} + p_2 \, dP^{a p_2} - A \, dR$$

$$(14\text{-}8)$$

with

$$p_1 = \frac{\partial E}{\partial P^{a p_1}}, \quad p_2 = \frac{\partial E}{\partial P^{a p_2}}, \quad \text{and} \quad A = -\frac{\partial E}{\partial R}. \qquad (24\text{-}9)$$

Theorem 14-3.   For given values of the intensive parameters and under assumption (14-6), the *fundamental physicochemical equation of the system*, valid for real (irreversible) processes, is of the form $E = E(P^{a p_1}, P^{a p_2}, R)$, every parameter being extensive and a function of state.

PROOF.   Immediate consequence of (14-8).

Nota Bene.   The extension of theorem 14-3 and of the whole substance of this chapter to systems having more than three degrees of freedom is a straightforward matter; it is only for notational simplicity that the preceding material has been presented in the context of system and process requiring three degrees of freedom.

From (14-8) and (14-9) can be deduced the physical meaning that may be attributed to A and R. Examining those expressions in the light of the material discussed in Chapter 13, it is seen that R may be considered to be a generalized coordinate and A a generalized force. In view of (14-6) and (14-8), R is that generalized parameter that measures the *degree of progress of the irreversible process*, while A is the coefficient that measures the *effect that the progress (or advance) of the process has upon the degree of irreversibility that the process has achieved.*

Observe what has been accomplished. A system is known to have two characterizing parameters which, were the system to undergo exclusively ideal (reversible) transformations, would form a *complete* set of characterizing parameters. But a complete set of characterizing parameters *becomes an incomplete* set of such parameters on passing from the ideal to the real—in other words, the real has more degrees of freedom than the ideal.

Now, the fact that

$$\int \dot{E}_{irr}\, dt = \int_{t_1}^{t_2} (\dot{E}_{irr}^{p_1} + \dot{E}_{irr}^{p}) \, dt = \int_{t_1}^{t_2} (p_1 \dot{P}_{irr}^{ap_1} + p_2 \dot{P}_{irr}^{ap_2}) \, dt$$

is independent of the path means that E_{irr} suffices to characterize the passage from the ideal to the real. By a known general methodological principle (lemma 3-1; for more detail see [38]) any strictly monotonic function of E_{irr} (and R is one such function) will serve equally well to attain the same characterization. With the decomposition of ΔE_{irr} into $A\,\Delta R$, every term of (14-8) is expressed in the same form.

It is clear that, in practice, it suffices to choose as R any parameter that serves to measure—that is, is in one-to-one correspondence with—the degree of progress of the (real, irreversible) process. Naturally, the parameter R that is most adequate for one kind of process may not necessarily be as adequate for another type of transformation in nature. As an illustration of one such parameter R, in Appendix C it is shown that the quantity there defined as the "degree of advance or progress of the reaction" is an adequate parameter to measure the degree of progress of the irreversible processes called chemical reactions. For processes of an entirely different nature, a different quantity must be used for R.

The characterizing parameters of S may all be labeled by the same letter and distinguished among themselves by an index thus: $X_i, i = 1, \ldots, n$ (for the case of n degrees of freedom). The fundamental physicochemical equation may then be written as $E = E(X_1, \ldots, X_n)$, and equation (14-8) acquires the form

$$dE = \sum_{i=1}^{n} \frac{\partial E}{\partial X_i} \, dX_i, \qquad (14\text{-}10)$$

every parameter $X_i, i = 1, \ldots, n$, being extensive and a function of state.

15

General Conditions for Equilibrium

The Legendre transform gives us the means to express one and the same physicochemical phenomenon or process in terms of relations between different, though related, sets of variables. It is therefore desirable to extend the conditions for equilibrium that have been derived in Chapter 12, where these conditions are expressed in terms of E and P^{ap}, to conditions for equilibrium that are expressed in terms of the Legendre transforms of the primitive quantities. A variety of different but equivalent formulations of the conditions for equilibrium will permit application of the formulation that is most suitable for the situation at hand.

Notation. $L(E)_{X_n}$ will symbolize the Legendre transform of E with respect to X_n, where X_n is any one of the characterizing parameters in the physicochemical equation of S; refer to equations (14-10).

Theorem 15-1. Under conditions of constant $\partial E/\partial X_n$, a necessary and sufficient condition for equilibrium is that

$$\frac{d}{dt} L(E)_{X_n} = 0 \quad \text{and} \quad \frac{d^2}{dt^2} L(E)_{X_n} > 0.$$

That is, for $\partial E/\partial X_n = $ constant, equilibrium corresponds to a minimum value of $L(E)_{X_n}$, and a spontaneous process can proceed only in such a way that $\Delta L(E)_{X_n} < 0$.

PROOF. The condition $\partial E/\partial X_n = $ constant, applied to the expression $L(E)_{X_n} = E - (\partial E/\partial X_n)X_n$, implies the relation

$$\frac{d}{dt} L(E)_{X_n} = \dot{E} - \frac{\partial E}{\partial X_n} \dot{X}_n. \tag{15-1}$$

Proof of Necessity. By definition 12-1, at equilibrium $\dot{X}_n = 0$ and $\ddot{X}_n = 0$, and it has been demonstrated (theorems 12-5, 12-6, and 12-8) that a necessary and sufficient condition for equilibrium, for constant values of coparameters, is that E be a minimum ($\dot{E} = 0$, $\ddot{E} > 0$). Therefore

$$\frac{d}{dt} L(E)_{X_n} = \dot{E} - \frac{\partial E}{\partial X_n} \dot{X}_n$$

at equilibrium becomes $(d/dt)L(E)_{X_n} = 0$. Also, when $(\partial E/\partial X_n) =$ constant,

$$\frac{d^2}{dt^2} L(E)_{X_n} = \ddot{E} - \frac{\partial E}{\partial X_n} \ddot{X}_n. \tag{15-2}$$

Therefore at equilibrium necessarily $(d^2/dt^2)L(E)_{X_n} > 0$.

Proof of Sufficiency. By contradiction; suppose that the stated conditions are compatible with lack of equilibrium.

The condition $(d/dt)L(E)_{X_n} = 0$ on (15-1) implies that

$$\dot{E} = \frac{\partial E}{\partial X_n} \dot{X}_n. \tag{15-3}$$

In (15-3), X_n is an arbitrary characterizing parameter, since the thesis of the theorem is asserted for any value of i in the fundamental equation $E = E(X_1, \ldots, X_i, \ldots, X_n)$. Deny equilibrium, and thus $\dot{X}_i \neq 0$ for at least one value of the index i. Then from (15-3) it follows that $\dot{E}$ might not be a uniform (single-valued) function—as demanded by physical reality—for in general $\partial E/\partial X_i \neq 0$, and $\partial E/\partial X_i$ will have different values for different indices i. On the other hand, $\dot{X}_i = 0$ for every i implies $\dot{E} = 0$ as a unique value for $\dot{E}$.

Finally, the condition $(d^2/dt^2)L(E)_{X_n} > 0$ on (15-2) implies $\ddot{E} > (\partial E/\partial X_n)\ddot{X}_n$. But for constant values of the coparameter, $\ddot{X}_n = 0$, since $E = E(P^{a\,p_i}, i = 1, \ldots, n) = E(X_i, i = 1, \ldots, n)$. Therefore $\ddot{E} > 0$ suffices to satisfy the inequality. But $\ddot{E} > 0$ is precisely (theorems 12-5, 12-6, and 12-8) the second sufficiency condition for equilibrium under condition of constant coparameters. The theorem is therefore demonstrated.

16

Processes in the Neighborhood of Absolute Zero Value of an Intensive Parameter

It is to be expected that processes depending on gradients of intensive parameters, whether for transfers or for conversions, will display special properties when either or both of the values p_0, p, of the transfer or conversion parameter approach the absolute zero value $A_0{}^p$. The study of this behaviour will be the task of the present chapter, and in it we shall remain, for transfer processes, under the convention adopted in Chapter 13 regarding the invariability of the values of the intensive parameters under δ-cell displacements throughout S.

Suppose first that S or C receives a single parameter input ΔE^p; from the convertibility equation,

$$\Delta E^p = \Delta E_c{}^p + \Delta E_{ic}{}^p = \Delta E_c{}^p + \Delta P^{ap} p_0 = \Delta E_c{}^p + \frac{\Delta E^p}{p}\, p_0 + \Delta E^p_{\mathrm{irr}},$$

it follows that $p_0 \to A_0{}^p$ implies $\Delta E^p_{\mathrm{irr}} = \Delta P^{ap}_{\mathrm{irr}} p_0 \to 0$, $\Delta E_{ic}{}^p \to 0$, and thus $\Delta E_c{}^p \to \Delta E^p$. These limiting relations remain valid whether p represents a transfer or a conversion parameter, and we have thus obtained a generalization of the first thesis of theorem 5-1:

Theorem 16-1. The limiting relation $p_0 \to A_0{}^p$ necessarily implies the limiting relation $\Delta E_c{}^p \to \Delta E^p$, and the inequality $p_0 > A_0{}^p$ implies $\Delta E^p_{ic} > 0$.

PROOF OF THE SECOND THESIS OF THE THEOREM: Since $\Delta P^{ap} = (\Delta E^p/p) + \Delta P^{ap}_{\mathrm{irr}}$, and $\Delta E_c{}^p > 0$ for inputs and $p_0 > A_0{}^p$ by hypothesis, the thesis follows from the convertibility equation and theorem 9-1 (for transfer processes), and from the convertibility equation and the law of degradation (for conversions).

Theorem 16-2. If in a single-parameter process the condition

$$\lim (p/p_0) = 1$$

holds, then also $\lim \dot{E}_c^p < 0$.

PROOF. Because $\dot{E}_{irr}^{ap} > 0$, the convertibility equation $\dot{E}^p = \dot{E}_c^p + (\dot{E}^p/p)p_0 + \dot{E}_{irr}^p$ under the condition $\lim (p/p_0) = 1$ implies

$$\lim \dot{E}_c^p = \lim \dot{E}^p\left(1 - \frac{p_0}{p}\right) - \dot{E}_{irr}^p = 0 - \dot{E}_{irr}^p < 0.$$

This result is as would be expected on the basis of qualitative physical reasoning. In fact, of any energy input ΔE^p in-transferred into $\mathcal{S}$ under the condition $p = p_0$, no part can be recovered by using a p-gradient, and, furthermore, the energy loss ΔE_{irr}^p would have to be compensated by withdrawing from $\mathcal{S}$ convertible (usable) energy that is not part of the input ΔE^p being considered but was introduced into $\mathcal{S}$ previously. But this energy withdrawal from $\mathcal{S}$ cannot be realized by means of a p-gradient, for there is none; therefore:

Corollary 16-1. It is impossible, by means of a single-parameter process, to reach the condition $\lim p = p_0$.

Corollary 16-2. It is impossible, by means of a single-parameter process, to reach the absolute zero value for that parameter.

PROOF. Consequence of corollary 16-1 when $p_0 = A_0^p$.

Consider now a two-parameter process, the first parameter being a conversion parameter (and also the in-transfer parameter into $\mathcal{C}$), and the second parameter corresponding to the conversion product and out-transfer from $\mathcal{S}$. Let us denote these parameters by q and p, respectively.

The convertibility equation applied to the conversion gives

$$\Delta E^q = \Delta E_c^q + \frac{\Delta E^q}{q} q_0 + \Delta E_{irr}^q, \qquad (16\text{-}1)$$

where ΔE^q is the input to $\mathcal{C}$ and ΔE_c^q is its conversion output—and input to the out-transfer from $\mathcal{S}$. Applying the convertibility equation to this out-transfer,

$$-\Delta E_c^q = -\Delta E^p = -\Delta E_c^p - \frac{\Delta E^p}{p} p_0 + \Delta E_{irr}^p. \qquad (16\text{-}2)$$

Making a net input-output balance on S,

$$\Delta E^q - \Delta E^p = \frac{\Delta E^q}{q}q_0 - \Delta E_c^{\ p} - \frac{\Delta E_c^{\ q}}{p}p_0 + (\Delta E_{\text{irr}}^q + \Delta E_{\text{irr}}^p). \quad (16\text{-}3)$$

Of the terms on the right of (16-3), the first one is proportional to the coparameter flow from $\mathcal{E}$ to S; the second represents convertible energy leaving S; the third one is proportional to the coparameter flow from S to $\mathcal{E}$; the terms in parentheses represent the irreversible losses in both processes.

The problem now at hand is: can $p \to A_0^{\ p}$ in finite time? It must be remembered that p is the p-value at which the out-transfer takes place, and also the p-value within S. We are now assuming that $p_0 > A_0^{\ p}$, and that, with the aid of the conversion, we are trying to attain the first absolute zero value in history.

From physical considerations it follows that the quantities $|\Delta E^q|$ and $|\Delta E^p|$ are finite over a finite time interval. As a consequence the left side of (16-3) is a finite (bounded) quantity, and from (16-1) it is deduced that $|\Delta E_c^{\ q}|$ is also bounded.

As $p \to A_0^{\ p}$, the term $-(\Delta E_c^{\ q}/p)p_0 \to -\infty$, since $|\Delta E_c^{\ q}|$ is bounded. Because $|\Delta E_{\text{irr}}^q| < |\Delta E^q|$ and $|\Delta E_{\text{irr}}^p| < |\Delta E^p|$ (Chapters 7, 8, and 11) the term in parentheses in (16-3) is also bounded, and thus the preceding would have as a consequence that the term $(\Delta E^q/q)q_0 \to +\infty$. But this is impossible. In fact, we have $0 < q_0$, for the reverse would mean that a first absolute-zero value, $A_0^{\ q}$, had already been reached. Because there always exists a number M such that $q < M$, it follows that $(E^q/q)q_0 \to +\infty$ would necessitate $\Delta E^q \to +\infty$, contradicting the boundedness of the input to the converter. The following theorem has therefore been demonstrated.

Theorem 16-3. By means of a process consisting of a conversion and an out-transfer it is impossible in finite time to reach the absolute zero value of the out-transfer parameter.

Theorem 16-4. In a process consisting of a conversion and an out-transfer, if q is the conversion parameter and p the out-transfer parameter, then

$$\lim_{p \to A_0^{\ p}} \frac{\partial}{\partial p} \dot{E}^q = +\infty.$$

PROOF. Consider ΔE^q, the input to the converter, as a non-decreasing function of time. Because the quantum behavior of nature is not the object of our study, the quantities p_0 and $\dot{E}_c^{\ q}$ can be considered to be continuous functions of time t and of p over the interval $A_0^{\ p} + \epsilon \leq p \leq p_1$, where ϵ is an arbitrary quantity and p_1 is the initial value of p at the start of the process. Then there exists a number M_1, function of p_1 and ϵ, such that

$$\frac{(p_0 \, \Delta E_c{}^q)}{p} = M_1 \frac{1}{p} = Z.$$

Moreover, $\lim\limits_{p \to A_0{}^p} -(\partial/\partial p)Z = +\infty$ because $\Delta p < 0$. (Naturally, the passage to the limit $p \to A_0{}^p$ implies $\epsilon \to 0$, for ϵ must be subject to the condition $A_0{}^p + \epsilon < p$.)

For reasons analogous to those above there also exist numbers M_2 and M_3, functions of ϵ, such that [see equation (16-3)], $\dot{E}^q = M_2 - Z + M_3$. Therefore,

$$\lim_{p \to A_0{}^p} \frac{\partial}{\partial p} \dot{E}^q = \lim_{p \to A_0{}^p} \frac{\partial}{\partial p}(M_2 - Z + M_3) = +\infty.$$

Corollary 16-3. In a process consisting of a conversion and an out-transfer, if q is the conversion parameter and p the out-transfer parameter, and if $\dot{E}^q$, $(\partial \dot{E}^q/\partial p)$, and $(\partial/\partial p)\,\dot{E}^q$ are continuous within the domain $\{A_0{}^p + \epsilon \le p \le p_1, t(A_0{}^p + \epsilon) \le t \le t(p_1)\}$, where ϵ is an arbitrary quantity, then

$$\lim_{p \to A_0{}^p} \frac{d}{dt}\left(\frac{\partial \dot{E}^q}{\partial p}\right) = +\infty.$$

PROOF.   Immediate consequence of theorem 16-4 and the well-known conditions for the equality of the order of differentiating (see, for example, [8], p. 267).

The conditions expressed in corollary 16-3 are not the least stringent that are known for the reversal in the order of differentiation (see, for example, [8], pp. 265–267, or [16], pp. 165–172, as well as [17], pp. 146–151).

Theorem 16-5. In the absence of states of negative energy, a process consisting of a conversion and an out-transfer, where q is the conversion parameter and p the out-transfer parameter, has the property that $\lim\limits_{p \to A_0{}^p} P^{ap} = 0.$

PROOF.   The coparameter is a function of state; hence, if $P_f{}^{ap}$ and $P_i{}^{ap}$, respectively, denote the values of P^{ap} at the final and the initial states of the process, then

$$P_f{}^{pa} = P_i{}^{ap} + \Delta P^{ap}(i, f) \quad \text{and} \quad \lim_{p \to A_0{}^p} P_f{}^{ap} = P_i{}^{ap} + \lim_{p \to A_0{}^p} \Delta P^{ap}(i, f).$$

Now, $P_i{}^{ap}$ is a fixed finite quantity, and

$$\Delta P^{ap}(i, f) = -\frac{\Delta E^p}{p} + \Delta P^{ap}_{irr} = -\frac{\Delta E_c{}^q}{p} + \Delta P^{ap}_{irr}.$$

The quantity $\Delta P_{\mathrm{irr}}^{ap}$ is positive and also bounded because $|\Delta P_{\mathrm{irr}}^{ap} p_0| = |\Delta E_{\mathrm{irr}}^p| < |\Delta E^p|$ and both p_0 and $|\Delta E^p|$ are finite. Therefore there exist positive numbers B_1 and B_2 such that

$$\lim_{p \to A_0{}^p} P^{ap} = \lim_{p \to A_0{}^p} P_f{}^{ap} = B_1 + \lim_{p \to A_0{}^p} \left(-\frac{\Delta E_c{}^q}{p} \right) + B_2.$$

It has been seen in the demonstration of theorem 16-4 that

$$\lim_{p \to A_0{}^p} \left(-\frac{\Delta E_c{}^q}{p} p_0 \right) < -D,$$

no matter how large the positive quantity D may be, and in consequence the term $-(\Delta E_c{}^q/p)$ eventually will (as $p \to A_0{}^p$) deplete the coparameter quantity $B_1 + B_2$. That $P^{ap} \nless 0$ follows from the physical meaning of the coparameter (Chapter 6) and the law of degradation (Chapter 9); thus, since the coparameter is a measure of the potentiality for inconvertibility of the energy E stored in the system (which has been introduced into S by means of successive energy in-transfers ΔE^p throughout the history of the system), and since there are no reversible processes—that is, with every energy input into S is introduced a positive amount of potentiality for inconvertibility—a net negative coparameter value would mean that the state to which it corresponds is a state of negative energy.

Theorem 16-6. In the absence of states of negative energy and under the conditions of theorem 10-3, if p is the out-transfer parameter and g is any intensive parameter different from p, then $\lim_{p \to A_0{}^p} (\partial P^{ag}/\partial g) = 0$ under conditions permitting the reversal of the order of limiting processes.

PROOF. Because the conditions of theorem 10-3 are satisfied, we may apply equations (10-5) and (10-6) to our problem; using the index b to identify any arbitrary but fixed base state, we obtain

$$P^{ag} = (P_b{}^{ag} - k_{gp} P_b{}^{ap}) + k_{gp} P^{ap} \tag{16-4}$$

In (16-4), $P_b{}^{ag}$ and $P_b{}^{ap}$ are fixed numbers corresponding to state b, while P^{ap} and P^{ag} are functions of the (final) state of the system. Passing to the limit,

$$\lim_{p \to A_0{}^p} \frac{\partial P^{ag}}{\partial g} = \lim_{p \to A_0{}^p} \frac{\partial}{\partial g} (P_b{}^{ag} - k_{gp} P_b{}^{ap}) + \lim_{p \to A_0{}^p} \frac{\partial}{\partial g} (k_{gp} P^{ap}). \tag{16-5}$$

The first limit on the right side of (16-5) vanishes because $P_b{}^{ag}$ and $P_b{}^{ap}$ in the expression within the parentheses are fixed numbers, since any coparameter is a function of state.

Under conditions permitting the reversal of the order of limiting processes,

$$\lim_{p \to A_0{}^p} \lim_{\Delta g \to 0} \frac{\Delta(k_{gp}P^{ap})}{\Delta g} = \lim_{\Delta g \to 0} \lim_{p \to A_0{}^p} \frac{\Delta(k_{gp}P^{ap})}{\Delta g}.$$

The quantity Δg is independent of p, the quantity k_{gp} is bounded above and below, and $\lim_{p \to A_0{}^p} P^{ap} = 0$ by theorem 16-5. Therefore the second term on the right side of (16-5) also vanishes, and $\lim_{p \to A_0{}^p} (\partial P^{ag}/\partial g) = 0$ as affirmed by the thesis of the theorem.

For necessary and sufficient conditions under which reversal of the order of passing to the limits is permissible, the reader may consult, for example, [30], pp. 408–414. Uniformity is a sufficient, though not necessary, condition for reversal of limiting processes, and it is easy to verify that this condition is satisfied by almost every macroscopic physical process of physical interest (at least, it is verified by the models that are presently being used to represent theoretically these physical processes).

Observe that, because the convertibility equation has been employed in demonstrating all the theorems and corollaries of this chapter, these theorems and corollaries are to be considered valid (at least, in the absence of other, less demanding, demonstrations) only under the conditions assumed in the derivation of the convertibility equation. These assumptions have not been explicitly included in the statements of the hypotheses of the theorems and corollaries because they are common to the whole theory presented (see Chapters 4 and 5). It is easy to see, however, that the two linearity assumptions introduced in Chapter 5 may be relaxed considerably (for example, by substituting in their place the power function with any fixed positive exponent) without affecting the validity of the theorems in this chapter.

Theorem 16-3 and corollary 16-2, when applied to the case in which $p = T$ (temperature), reduce to the third law of thermodynamics as formulated by Fowler and Guggenheim in [18], pp. 224 ff, and by Klein in [29], p. 14. Theorem 16-5, also in the case of $p = T$, covers the most common formulation of the third law of thermodynamics (see, for example, [19], Chapter 6; [20], p. 810; [21], p. 43). Finally, theorem 16-6, also when $p = T$, includes as special case the first formulation of the third law of thermodynamics given by Klein in [29], p. 14.

As illustrations of the theorems and corollaries deduced in this chapter for phenomena other than those corresponding to $p = T$, we may consider two possible methods for the reduction of pressure to as close to perfect vacuum ($A_0{}^p$) as possible.

The first method would use an exclusively P-transfer phenomenon. Assume an environment ε with $p_0 = P_0 = A_0{}^p$ (or as near to $A_0{}^p$ as possible) and place $\mathcal{S}$, with pressure P, in contact with $\mathcal{E}$. Corollaries 16-1 and 16-2 then assert that $P(\mathcal{S})$ will never—that is, in finite time—reach $P_0 = A_0{}^P = A_0{}^p$.

As a second possible method we may use a conversion-transfer process employing some kind of mechanical or electromechanical equipment to pump fluid from $\mathcal{S}$ to $\mathcal{E}$. Theorem 16-3 in this case asserts that it will be impossible to reach perfect vacuum in a finite time by means of the conversion–out-transfer contraption. Theorem 16-4 and corollary 16-3 in essence state that, the closer we are to absolute zero, the costlier it becomes to lower the pressure by one more unit; that is, the closer we are to a perfect vacuum, the more input (pumping) is required to lower the pressure by a unit (of pressure). Theorem 16-5 affirms that, when the system reaches perfect vacuum, the potentiality for inconvertibility of the total net $\sum \Delta E^P$ that $\mathcal{S}$ has stored up to that moment is null.

All the preceding applications of the deductions of the theory are in agreement with experimental observations.

It would seem at first sight that gravitational energy does not obey deductions of the theory. Indeed, in gravitational phenomena we may consider $p = h$ as the distance from the attracting body, and it would seem possible to attain $A_0{}^h$, that is, by reaching with the attracted body the gravitational center (mass center) of the attracting body.

A closer examination of the phenomena, however, shows that we are not dealing here with an out-transfer parameter p, or seeking an *absolute* zero value of h, that is, an h-value that is zero *for all gravitational phenomena* in the *whole part of the universe* in which the postulates of our theory have significance and validity.

The phenomenon of gravitational attraction of two (or more) bodies is an energy *conversion within* the system (the whole of which in this case is also the converter: $\mathcal{S} = \mathcal{C}$) composed of the bodies that enter into the gravitational phenomenon being studied. The conversion may be between kinetic energy of motion and gravitational energy of attraction (as in the earth-moon system), or it may be between gravitational energy and some kind of physicochemical energy (as in some geological phenomena), or it may be of some other kind—but in every case it is a process internal to $\mathcal{S}$, and of the nature of a conversion rather than of an internal transfer.

In consequence of the preceding, the zero of the intensive parameter associated with gravity-potential energy conversion is only a *local* zero, local to the system being considered. The zero h-value for the system comprised of the earth and a pebble somewhere on the surface of the earth or in its atmosphere is entirely different from the zero h-value for the system comprised of the Andromeda galaxy and one of its stars, and both of these are entirely different from the zero h-value for the system comprised of the sun, its planets, and their satellites. The conversion being a phenomenon purely internal to S, the zero value in each case will depend on S—will be a function of S.

The *absolute* zero value of an intensive parameter, on the contrary, is a *global* zero value—a property, not of S, but *of the universe U* comprised of S and $\mathcal{E}$.

17

The Process Velocity
and the Affinity Function.
The Direction of Time.

In Chapter 14 were postulated the extensive parameter R, a measure of the degree of progress of the irreversible process, and the coefficient $A = (d/dR)(E_{irr})$; it was there shown that the quantities E_{irr} and R are functions of state. In this chapter we shall study the functions R and A and their properties in the neighborhood of a state of equilibrium.

Nomenclature. The coefficient A of dR in the fundamental physico-chemical equation will be called the *affinity* of the process. We have $A = -(\partial E/\partial R)$.

In cases in which the process is a chemical reaction, $R = \lambda$ (see Appendix C) and A is called the *chemical affinity*. Then, naturally, $A = -(\partial E/\partial \lambda)$.

Note. The chemical affinity defined above is the chemical affinity concept as introduced by Th. de Donder (see, for example, [34]). Another concept of chemical affinity introduced previously by Van't Hoff (see, for example, [35], p. 177) is still in common use.

Theorem 17-1. The affinity A is a function of state.

PROOF. From $dE = \sum_i p_i \, dP^{a p_i} - A \, dR$, $A = -(\partial E/\partial R)$, considering that both sides of an equality must have the same properties.

From Chapter 14, equation (14-5) and corollary 14-1,

$$dE = \sum_i p_i \, dP^{a p_i} - \sum_i \delta E_{irr}^{p_i} = \sum_i p_i \, dP^{a p_i} - dE_{irr},$$

131

with $dE_{irr}/dR = A$, and dE_{irr} being a function of couples of states. On the other hand, if there is only one value of i, $\delta E^p = p\,dP^{ap} - p\,\delta P^{ap}_{irr} = p\,dP^{ap} - \delta E^p_{irr}$, with δE^p_{irr} dependent on the path of the process.

Naturally, in a lossless (ideal, reversible) process, $\delta E^p_{irr} = 0$.

Because it is only seldom that a physicochemical process can be characterized by a single degree of freedom, we are more interested in studying the properties of the fundamental physicochemical equation than those of the expression for δE^p.

From $dE_{irr} = A\,dR$ we obtain

$$\frac{dE_{irr}}{dt} = \lim_{\Delta t \to 0} \frac{1}{\Delta t}(A\,\Delta R) = A\,\frac{dR}{dt},$$

and thus

$$E_{irr} = \int_{\mathfrak{F}\,t_1}^{t_2} A(R)\dot{R}\,dt,$$

the integral being calculated from instant t_1 to instant t_2 along path (process) $\mathfrak{F}$. Because A is a function of state, it is a function of R, as the system transforms from one state to another. Furthermore, because dE_{irr} is a function of couples of states,

$$\int_{\mathfrak{F}_1\,t(\alpha)}^{t(\beta)} A\dot{R}\,dt = \int_{\mathfrak{F}_2\,t(\alpha)}^{t(\beta)} A\dot{R}\,dt = E_{irr}(\beta) - E_{irr}(\alpha),$$

for any two arbitrary processes between the same coterminal states α and β. The same cannot be said of δE^p and δE^p_{irr}, of course.

Nomenclature. The quantity $dR/dt = v$ will be called the *process velocity*.

Lemma 17-1. In real macroscopic processes, and outside of states of equilibrium, the quantities A, ΔR, and v must all have the same sign.

PROOF. The law of degradation (Chapter 9) asserts that $dE_{irr} > 0$ for all real (and macroscopic) processes; as a consequence, A and v must always have the same sign, for $\dot{E}_{irr} = Av$. Furthermore, in all real macroscopic processes by convention $\Delta t > 0$; therefore, since $v = \lim_{\Delta t \to 0}(\Delta R/\Delta t)$, necessarily ΔR and v must have the same sign.

Theorem 17-2. In the ideal, limiting case of a reversible process, the process velocity is zero. More exactly: $\lim_{\dot{E}_{irr} \to 0} v = 0$.

PROOF. In the ideal, limiting case of reversibility $\dot{E}_{irr} = 0$; because A, a function of state, in general will not equal 0 it follows that $v = 0$ for reversible processes. This is as it should be, for a reversible process

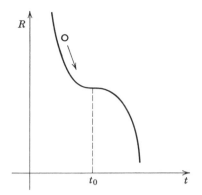

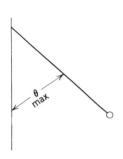

Figure 17-1 Mechanical system illustrating that the condition $v = (dR/dt)_{t_0} = 0$ is *not* sufficient for equilibrium.

Figure 17-2 Another mechanical illustration of the fact that zero velocity is not sufficient for equilibrium.

demands an "infinitely slow" rate, as follows from the material in Chapter 9 (see, for example, [35], pp. 34, 95, 150).

Nota Bene. From definition 12-1 it follows that in a state of equilibrium necessarily $\dot{R} = 0$, and therefore $\dot{E}_{irr} = 0$. Under these conditions we cannot infer that the quantities A and v must have the same sign, as the thesis of lemma 17-1 asserts, for zero can be the limiting value of both positive and negative quantities, that is, it can be the limiting value of quantities that are products of factors of the same sign, as well as of quantities that are products of factors of opposite signs.

It would be erroneous to infer that $v = 0$ is a *sufficient* condition for equilibrium. The correctness of this admonition can be seen in Figure 17-1. In it

$$v_{t_0} = \frac{dR}{dt}\bigg]_{t_0} = 0,$$

but the ball will not be in equilibrium at instant t_0, according to definition 12-1. As another illustration consider the pendular phenomena (Figure 17-2). When the pendulum is in its position of maximal displacement, its velocity is null, but it is not in a state of equilibrium.

In general, while $\lim_{\dot{E} \to 0} v = 0$, it is not true that $\lim_{v \to 0} \dot{E} = 0$. Thus:

Theorem 17-3. Under constant P^{ap} (for every p), the set of conditions $\{v = 0, A \neq 0\}$ is not sufficient for equilibrium.

PROOF. Deny the thesis of the theorem. From the relation $dE = \sum_i p_i \, dP^{ap_i} - A \, dR$ it follows that $\{v = 0, A \neq 0\}$ imply $A = -(\partial E/\partial R) \neq 0$. Lemma 17-1 asserts that, in the deleted neighborhood of equilibrium (*not* at exactly the state of equilibrium)*, the quantities A, v, and ΔR have the same sign. Therefore, to an advance of the process, breaking the assumed equilibrium, would correspond either $\dot{R} > 0$ and $A > 0$, or $\dot{R} < 0$ and $A < 0$; in both cases the relation $A = -(\partial E/\partial R) = -(\dot{E}/\dot{R})$ will imply that $\dot{E} < 0$ ($\Delta E < 0$)—a decrease in the energy of the system. By theorem 12-5 this contradicts the assumption that the system was originally in equilibrium.

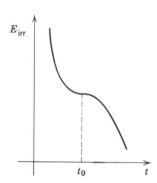

Observe that it is not valid to infer equilibrium from the condition $A = 0$ on the basis that this condition implies $\dot{E}_{irr} = 0$. In fact, the condition $v = 0$ also implies $\dot{E}_{irr} = 0$, and the preceding illustrations and theorem demonstrate that equilibrium is not a necessary consequence of those conditions. In fact, the condition $\dot{E}_{irr} = 0$ is fulfilled at every point of inflection of the curve E_{irr} versus t (see Figure 17-3), but these points do not correspond to states of stability. To see this observe that, from $\dot{E} = \sum_i p_i \dot{P}^{ap_i} - \dot{E}_{irr}$, for constant values of P^{ap_i} it follows that $\dot{E} = -\dot{E}_{irr}$. But under those conditions (constant P^{ap_i}) theorem 12-5 asserts that a necessary and sufficient condition for free internal equilibrium is that $\dot{E} = 0$ and $\ddot{E} > 0$. As a consequence of the equality $\dot{E} = -\dot{E}_{irr}$ we then have

Figure 17-3   At t_0 the quantity $\dot{E}_{irr} = 0$, but that point is not one of stable equilibrium.

Theorem 17-4.   If P^{ap_i} is a constant for every i, a necessary and sufficient condition for free internal equilibrium is that $\dot{E}_{irr} = 0$ and $\ddot{E}_{irr} < 0$.

The following may be asserted concerning the properties of A in the neighborhood of equilibrium.

Theorem 17-5.   If P^{ap_i} is constant for every i, the system will be in a state of free internal equilibrium if $(\partial A/\partial R) < 0$ and either one of the two following sets of relations holds:

$$\{\ddot{R} > 0, A < 0\} \quad \text{or} \quad \{\ddot{R} < 0, A > 0\}\text{—i.e., } \ddot{R}A < 0.$$

PROOF.   From $\dot{E} = \sum_i p_i \dot{P}^{ap_i} - A\dot{R}$ and $\dot{E}_{irr} = A\dot{R}$ it follows that, for constant P^{ap_i},

$$\ddot{E} = -\ddot{E}_{irr} = -A\ddot{R} - (\dot{R})^2 \frac{\partial A}{\partial R}.$$

---

* A deleted neighborhood of a point x is a neighborhood of that point with the point x itself excluded.

The thesis of the theorem is a consequence of the application to that equality of the thesis of theorem 12-5 or that of theorem 17-4.

Theorem 17-6. If $P^{a_{p_i}}$ is constant for every i, the system will be in a state of free internal equilibrium iff $\partial A/\partial R < -A\ddot{R}/(\dot{R})^2$.

PROOF. From $\ddot{E} = -A\ddot{R} - (\dot{R})^2(\partial A/\partial R) > 0$ it follows immediately that

$$A\ddot{R} + (\dot{R})^2 \frac{\partial A}{\partial R} < 0 \quad \text{and} \quad \frac{\partial A}{\partial R} < \frac{-A\ddot{R}}{(\dot{R})^2}.$$

Observe that, while theorem 17-5 is a corollary of theorem 17-6, the latter is applicable to a much wider class of situations than the former. Among other implications, theorem 17-6 asserts that, for constant $P^{a_{p_i}}$, if $\partial A/\partial R > 0$, then necessarily $A\ddot{R} < 0$.

Theorem 17-7. If $P^{a_{p_i}}$ is a constant for every i, and if quantum effects are negligible, the system is in some deleted neighborhood of a state of free internal equilibrium iff either one of the two following sets of relations hold:

$$\{\dot{R} < 0, \dot{A} > 0\} \quad \text{or} \quad \{\dot{R} > 0, \dot{A} < 0\}\text{—i.e., } (\dot{R}\dot{A} < 0).$$

PROOF. If quantum effects are negligible, $\partial^2 E/\partial t\,\partial R = \partial^2 E/\partial R\,\partial t$. But

$$\frac{\partial^2 E}{\partial t\,\partial R} = -\dot{A}, \quad \text{and} \quad \frac{\partial}{\partial R}\dot{E} = \dot{E}\frac{dt}{dR} = \frac{\dot{E}}{\dot{R}}.$$

The last set of equalities has meaning only in a deleted neighborhood of equilibrium, because at the state of equilibrium $\dot{R} = 0$ and the ratio becomes unbounded. Therefore, $\dot{A} = -(\dot{E}/\dot{R})$, valid in a deleted neighborhood. The thesis of the theorem then follows from application of the condition $\ddot{E} > 0$ (theorem 12-5) to that equality.

Nota Bene. The condition $\ddot{E} > 0$ was demonstrated in theorem 12-5 to apply to the state of equilibrium, and it has been applied above to states in the neighborhood of the state of equilibrium. The justification for this is found in a theorem that asserts that, if a continuous function has a certain sign at a point, it possesses the same sign in some neighborhood of that point (and, of course, in every other neighborhood contained in that first one). For demonstration of that theorem see, for example, [8] pp. 214–215; or [15], p. 40. The assumption that $\ddot{E}$ is continuous is here made on the basis of the hypothesis that quantum effects are negligible.

Corollary 17-1. Under the conditions of theorem 17-7, either one of the two following sets of relations is a necessary and sufficient condition for

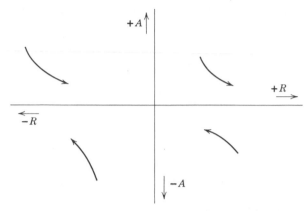

Figure 17-4 Graphical illustration of the sufficiency condition for free internal equilibrium expressed analytically by theorem 17-5: $(\partial A/\partial R) < 0$ *and* $\ddot{R}A < 0$ (P^{av}, constant for every i).

the system to be in some deleted neighborhood of equilibrium:

$$\{A < 0, \dot{A} > 0\} \quad \text{or} \quad \{A > 0, \dot{A} < 0\}\text{—i.e., } (A\dot{A} < 0).$$

PROOF.   Application of lemma 17-1 to the thesis of theorem 17-7.

It should be observed that, based upon the relation $A = -(\partial E/\partial R)$, the affinity could receive the interpretation of a generalized force, with respect to E as generalized potential and R as generalized distance (refer to the discussion in Chapter 13). From the negative sign of that relation, and from $A = \dot{E}_{\text{irr}}/\dot{R} = \partial E_{\text{irr}}/\partial R$, the affinity could be interpreted as a generalized force that, at each state of the system, is proportional to the tendency for irreversibility that the system has in that state. For this reason, the affinity function *measures*, at each particular state, *the tendency or force of the system to keep going or to move along the process in question*, while this movement or advance is measured by R. In the light of this understanding of the meaning of A, the relation $\dot{E}_{\text{irr}} = A\dot{R}$ may be seen to contain within itself the finite propagation hypothesis, the law of degradation, and theorems 9-2 and 9-3 (with corollary 9-2), as well as theorem 17-2.

A graphical illustration of the sufficiency condition for free internal equilibrium expressed analytically in theorem 17-5 is shown in Figure 17-4. The two upper trajectories correspond to the set of conditions $\{\partial A/\partial R < 0, A > 0, \ddot{R} < 0\}$; the two lower trajectories, to the alternative set of conditions $\{\partial A/\partial R < 0, A < 0, \ddot{R} > 0\}$. Observe that in both cases $|A|$ is a monotonically decreasing function of R.

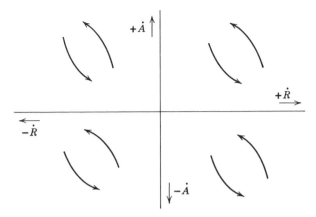

Figure 17-5 Graphical representation of the condition $\dot{R}\dot{A} < 0$, which is necessary and sufficient for a deleted neighborhood of free internal equilibrium ($P^{a}{}_{pi}$ constants).

A similar kind of diagram, but with the trajectories represented in terms of the parameter t, serves to illustrate graphically the necessary and sufficient conditions for a deleted neighborhood of equilibrium, as analytically stated in theorem 17-7; see Figure 17-5. The trajectories with arrows pointing to the right of the reader correspond to the set of conditions $\{\dot{R} > 0, \dot{A} < 0\}$; the trajectories with arrows pointing to the left correspond to the set of conditions $\{\dot{R} < 0, \dot{A} > 0\}$.

The graphical representation of the thesis of corollary 17-1 is shown in Figure 17-6. The trajectories in the upper half of the diagram correspond

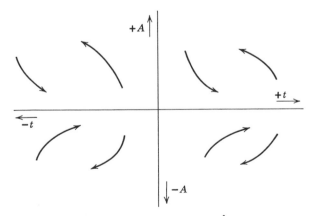

Figure 17-6 Graphical illustration of the condition $A\dot{A} < 0$, which is necessary and sufficient for a deleted neighborhood of equilibrium ($P^{a}{}_{pi}$ constants).

to the set of conditions $\{A > 0, \dot{A} < 0\}$; the trajectories in the lower half illustrate the set of conditions $\{A < 0, \dot{A} > 0\}$.

Observe that theorem 17-7 and corollary 17-1, stating necessary and sufficient conditions for the deleted neighborhood of the state of equilibrium, do not imply the necessity for $|A|$ to be a monotonically decreasing function of t if we include under consideration processes proceeding along the negative direction of time. This is in contrast to theorem 17-5, which implies the monotonically decreasing property of $|A|$ with reference to R irrespective of the sign of R. Theorem 17-7 and corollary 17-1 therefore provide a criterion for discerning, under the hypotheses of the theorem, the *positive sense of time:* it is *given by decreasing absolute values of the affinity function.*

Nota Bene. The (generally accepted) agreement that real macroscopic processes coincide with $\Delta t > 0$ was employed in lemma 17-1 to demonstrate that $v = \dot{R}$ and ΔR possess the same sign; it was not used to show that A and $\dot{R}$ have the same sign. This part of the lemma (that A and $\dot{R}$ possess the same sign for real processes) was used in passing from theorem 17-7 to corollary 17-1, from which the above criterion for the positive sense of time was derived. The inference is valid because in the demonstration of theorem 17-7 and corollary 17-1 no hypothesis that would exclude either sign of Δt was used.

The law of degradation supports the equality of sign of A and $\dot{R}$ and the inference of corollary 17-1, but this law would not provide as convenient a criterion for distinguishing the directions of time. In fact, the law of degradation is a generalization of the thesis of theorem 8-1. The thesis of that theorem remains unchanged if the direction of time is reversed and simultaneously the direction of positive *internal* energy transfer is also reversed. Energy transfers internal to a system can often be very difficult to study experimentally to determine its directions of flow, and these directions can be very complicated in their over-all patterns (see Chapter 11). The criterion in terms of the absolute value of the affinity function is free of those objections, since it is applicable to energy transfers of the system as a whole with the environment, and it is formulated in terms of absolute values.

18

Systems Far from Equilibrium.
Negative Absolute Values
of the Intensive Parameter

In this chapter we shall investigate some first consequences that ensue when a system is "far" from equilibrium. Such a study is possible because we have a hand in the results of our preceding work several characterizations of the equilibrium condition and of neighborhoods of equilibrium, as well as conditions for approach to equilibrium. Denying those characterizations, we shall investigate what consequences follow from the denial.

Because of the changing nature of the phenomena to be studied, it will be convenient to have available the following explicit clarification of an expression to be used in the sequel.

Nomenclature. We shall say that system $\mathcal{S}$ *ultimately acquires property* Q iff there exists an instant t_0 of time such that, for $t \geq t_0$, system $\mathcal{S}$ possesses property Q.

Notice that the expression "$\mathcal{S}$ ultimately acquires property Q" indicates not only the acquisition of property Q by system $\mathcal{S}$, but also the retention of the property (at least for the remainder of the period of concern in the study of the phenomenon.)

A system may be disturbed from a state of free equilibrium in many ways. For ease of expression we shall for the present group several of those different ways into a special class, as shown by the following:

Nomenclature. We shall say that system $\mathcal{S}$ is *receding from equilibrium* iff (1) $\dot{E}(\mathcal{S}) > k > 0$ *and* (2) there exists some parameter p such that $\dot{p}(\mathcal{S}) > l > 0$.

The reason for specifying $\dot{E}(S) > k > 0$ instead of simply $\dot{E}(S) > 0$ is to discard the asymptotic case in which $\dot{E}(S) > 0$ but $\dot{E}(S) \to 0$. The same reason applies to the use of the number $l > 0$ in the condition $\dot{p}(S) > l > 0$.

Later on (definition 18-1) the expression "receding from equilibrium" will be made more precise, and other classes of processes also defined. For the present, however, the identification of recession from equilibrium given above is sufficient.

The word "recession" as used here may be interpreted in the sense of recession from an originally given state of equilibrium. But that interpretation is not essential. We may equally well suppose that the system was in some state in which at least one of the two conditions specified above for recession from equilibrium did not hold, from which state the system then passed to one of recession from equilibrium (as such a condition is defined here).

The recession of S from equilibrium may have its origin in two different types of processes:

A. A net energy transfer from $\mathcal{E}$ to S, that is, a retransfer phenomenon with

$$|\Delta E^{po}| < |\Delta E^{pi}|.$$

B. An energy input from $\mathcal{E}$ to S, followed by a conversion internal to S (the converter C being either part of S or the whole of S).

Either one or both of those two conditions must be considered as subsisting during any interval Δt of time during which S is under study.

Because the relation $C \subset S$ includes $C = S$ as a special case, we shall consider the former in our study. Our point of departure will be the basic conversion equation

$$dE = p_1 \, dP^{ap_1} + p_2 \, dP^{ap_2} - \delta E_{\text{irr}}^{p_1} - \delta E_{\text{irr}}^{p_2}$$

$$= p_1 \, dP^{ap_1} + p_2 \, dP^{ap_2} - dE_{\text{irr}}$$

$$= p_1 \, dP^{ap_1} + p_2 \, dP^{ap_2} - A \, dR$$

established in Chapter 14.

In a retransfer process (case A above), $p_1 = p_2$.

In the transfer-conversion process (case B above) we shall assume that the process is free of parasitic conversions (i.e., the conversion is ideal), and we shall apply the basic conversion equation *to the converter* instead of to the system. Applying our study to C instead of to S means that we can dispense with the parameter pi of the in-transfer to S, equate therefore $\dot{E}^{pi} = \dot{E}$, consider $\dot{E}$ as the input rate to C, and handle a single parameter: the conversion parameter.

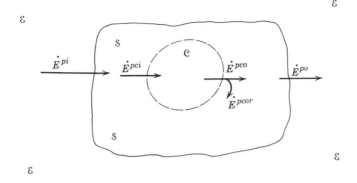

Figure 18-1   Schematic of combination transfer-conversion-transfer process.

A combination of both processes, A and B, is the transfer-conversion-transfer process, illustrated in Figure 18-1. The last part of this process may be considered as a retransfer process, with $\dot{E}^{pco}$ as rate of input and $\dot{E}^{po}$ as rate of output. In fact, this corresponds to considering a new system: that part of S that operates between C and $\mathcal{E}$. In this case we can likewise limit ourselves to a single parameter: that characterizing the output of C. This process therefore will also be included in our study, as a special type of retransfer process. In it, $\dot{E}^{pco} > 0$ and $\dot{E}^{pco} > \dot{E}^{po}$.

For the two phenomena, the retransfer process in S and the ideal conversion in C, the basic conversion equation for systems receding from equilibrium will then take the form

$$\dot{E} = p\dot{P}^{ap} - A\dot{R} > k > 0$$

with

$$A = -\frac{\partial E}{\partial R} = \frac{dE_{\text{irr}}}{dR}.$$

The second derivative of the rate of energy in-transfer (to S or to C) is

$$\ddot{E} = \frac{d}{dt}(p\dot{P}^{ap}) - \frac{d}{dt}\left(\frac{dE_{\text{irr}}}{dR}\dot{R}\right) \tag{18-1}$$

with

$$\frac{d}{dt}\left(\frac{dE_{\text{irr}}}{dR}\dot{R}\right) = \dot{A}\dot{R} + A\ddot{R}. \tag{18-2}$$

On the basis of physical considerations, the P^{ap} values associated with S can be taken to be a single-valued function of the time t. This function can be used as a foundation to study the dynamic (and hence also the equilibrium) history of S, employing the historical point of view on equilibrium, as explained in Chapter 12.

Now for each value of P^{ap} in S consider the universe of all systems having that same value of P^{ap}. Because of the transitivity property of the functional relation, a universe of systems will be placed in correspondence with each value of t, each such universe being characterized by a value of P^{ap}. Naturally, the possibility is open that two or more different values of t may have in correspondence the same value of P^{ap} and therefore also the same universe of systems. It will later be demonstrated that such a theoretical possibility cannot take place under the present conditions of our study (recession from equilibrium), for it will be shown that $\dot{P}^{ap} > 0$ under these conditions, and therefore P^{ap} increases monotonically with time.

With the preceding arrangement we have combined the historical and the universal points of view in the study of equilibrium and also in the study of the dynamics of systems.

Theorems 17-5 and 17-7 and corollary 17-1 are applicable to each universe of systems associated with a value of the parameter t. From the theorems it follows that, *in each such universe*, the systems that are away from a neighborhood of equilibrium are those in which the following necessary conditions hold:

$$A\ddot{R} > 0, \qquad A\dot{R} > 0, \qquad A\dot{A} > 0.$$

Applying that to equation (18-2), there follows

Lemma 18-1. A necessary condition for a system to be away from a neighborhood of equilibrium is that

$$\frac{d}{dt}\left(\frac{dE_{\text{irr}}}{dR}\dot{R}\right) = \frac{d}{dt}(A\dot{R}) > 0.$$

The first term of (18-1) in expanded form is

$$\frac{d}{dt}(p\dot{P}^{ap}) = \dot{p}\dot{P}^{ap} + p\ddot{P}^{ap}. \tag{18-3}$$

By virtue of theorems 7-1, 8-1, 9-1, and 9-2 and the law of degradation, $\dot{P}^{ap}_{\text{irr}} > 0$ for all real processes. For both kinds of processes with which we are concerned, $\dot{E} > k > 0$. Because of the results of Chapter 16, $p > A_0{}^p$. Hence

$$\dot{P}_t{}^{ap} = \frac{\dot{E}^p}{p} = \frac{\dot{E}}{p} > 0,$$

and consequently

$$\dot{P}_t{}^{ap} + \dot{P}_l{}^{ap} = \dot{P}^{ap} > 0.$$

Now consider S as a subsystem of $\mathfrak{U} = S \cup \mathcal{E}$. Denoting by $\dot{E}(\mathcal{E}, S)$ the rate of energy transfer from $\mathcal{E}$ to S (or that from $\mathcal{C}$ to S), and by $\dot{E}(S, \mathcal{E})$ the rate of energy out-transfer from S to $\mathcal{E}$, we can express our fundamental supposition of net energy in-transfer as $\dot{E}(\mathcal{E}, S) > \dot{E}(S, \mathcal{E})$.

Referring to definition 4-4b, we may consider $S = (S_{\delta 1} \cup S_{\delta 2})$ and $\mathcal{E} = (S_{\delta 3} \cup S_{\delta 4})$. If then we subtract the quantity $\dot{E}(S, \mathcal{E})$ from both sides of the inequality $\dot{E}(\mathcal{E}, S) > \dot{E}(S, \mathcal{E})$ and from the quantity $\dot{E}(S, \mathcal{E})$ itself—and these two subtractions correspond to but a translation of scale—we find that S in the retransfer process (type A process, as denoted above) is a quasi-static subsystem of $\mathfrak{U}$ by satisfying condition α of definition 4-4b.

On the other hand, putting $(S_{\delta 1} \cup S_{\delta 2}) = \mathcal{C}$ places the transfer-conversion process (type B) also under condition α of definition 4-4b.

Part III of the G.G.L. then asserts that $\dot{p}(S) > 0$—or $\dot{p}(\mathcal{C}) > 0$—for the two types of processes with which we are concerned.

Nota Bene. The two types of processes now being studied are definitely of a dynamic nature, for we are negating the characterizations of equilibrium and of approach to equilibrium. But what we have called a quasi-static condition is a special formulation of a much more general dynamic condition—indeed, lemma 12-1 asserts that, in the absence of internal constraints, the quasi-static condition originates an internal energy transfer in S. Actually, the two conditions, dynamic and quasi-static, may be looked at as *related by a change of scale.* As an alternative method of approach we could postulate that, in a dynamic process in which there is a net $\dot{E}(S) > 0$, we necessarily have $\dot{p}(S) > 0$. As a third alternative, we could use lemma 12-1 to establish the implication.

As a consequence of the preceding we have

Theorem 18-1. In systems away from a neighborhood of equilibrium, and having a net energy in-transfer, both $\dot{P}^{ap} > 0$ and $\dot{p} > 0$.

The first term of (18-3) thus is positive.

Observe that to demonstrate the first thesis of theorem 18-1, both hypotheses were needed, but to demonstrate the second thesis only the second hypothesis was used (and the assumption that p has a uniform value throughout S). This last demonstration means that the second condition for a system to be receding from equilibrium is a consequence of the first. This demonstration can also be easily extended to the case in which the parameter p is not uniform throughout S—the extension being accomplished by subdivision and passage to the limit.

Now we have three situations to consider: $\ddot{E} < 0$, $\ddot{E} = 0$, and $\ddot{E} > 0$. They yield, respectively, the following relations:

$$\ddot{E} = \dot{p}\dot{P}^{ap} + p\ddot{P}^{ap} - \frac{d}{dt}(A\dot{R}) < 0;$$

$$\ddot{E} = \dot{p}\dot{P}^{ap} + p\ddot{P}^{ap} - \frac{d}{dt}(A\dot{R}) = 0;$$

$$\ddot{E} = \dot{p}\dot{P}^{ap} + p\ddot{P}^{ap} - \frac{d}{dt}(A\dot{R}) > 0.$$

Because $\dot{p}\dot{P}^{ap} > 0$ and $(d/dt)(A\dot{R}) > 0$, these relations imply the following set of inequalities:

$$\ddot{E} < 0 \Rightarrow \begin{cases} \text{either} \quad p\ddot{P}^{ap} < 0 \\ \text{or} \qquad 0 < p\ddot{P}^{ap} < \frac{d}{dt}(A\dot{R}) - \dot{p}\dot{P}^{ap}; \end{cases} \qquad (18\text{-}4)$$

$$\ddot{E} = 0 \Rightarrow p\ddot{P}^{ap} = \frac{d}{dt}(A\dot{R}) - \dot{p}\dot{P}^{ap}; \qquad (18\text{-}5)$$

$$\ddot{E} > 0 \Rightarrow \begin{cases} \text{either} \quad p\ddot{P}^{ap} > 0 \\ \text{or} \qquad 0 > p\ddot{P}^{ap} > \frac{d}{dt}(A\dot{R}) - \dot{p}\dot{P}^{ap}. \end{cases} \qquad (18\text{-}6)$$

From $\dot{P}^{ap} = (\dot{E}^p/p) + \dot{P}_l{}^{ap}$ we get

$$\ddot{P}^{ap} = \frac{\ddot{E}^p}{p} - \frac{\dot{E}^p\dot{p}}{p^2} + \ddot{P}_l{}^{ap}. \qquad (18\text{-}7)$$

Our study will now be limited by the following

Assumption. Frictional dissipation and secondary internal gradients will be taken to be negligible in the considerations of this chapter.

This assumption is not significantly limiting, although it does rule out some cases of mechanical motions, as well as situations of significant turbulence within S. But most of our results will remain valid even when frictional dissipation is not negligible, because the coparameter production due to frictional dissipation is positive. Similar remarks apply to secondary internal gradients: carrying them in our formulae and deductions would burden the work without contributing anything of importance to the results.

From the expressions derived in Chapter 11 for the general case of irreversible production of coparameter due to internal gradients, it is seen that such expressions are of the same *form* as the simpler ones of Chapter 8.

In fact, the basic difference between the two expressions is that the more general one is three-dimensional and vectorial, whereas the simpler one is unidimensional and scalar. Because in the sequel we shall be concerned with consequences that follow from the *form* of the expression and with those that follow from the *relative values* of quantities, but shall not be concerned with exact numerical calculations, the simpler expression of coparameter production will suffice for our purposes.

The assumption that has been adopted, together with the considerations of the preceding paragraph, permits us to write

$$\dot{P}_l^{\,ap} = \dot{E}_1^{\,p} \frac{\Delta p}{p^2} \tag{18-8}$$

as the form for the rate of coparameter production in the boundary of a couple of adjacent cells ($\dot{E}_1^{\,p}$ being the energy transfer between them), or for the rate of coparameter production in a single cell (with Δp as the p-gradient within the cell, and $\dot{E}_1^{\,p}$ the net algebraic transfer into the cell).

If the system has length l (and, as remarked above, without loss of generality we may consider only one-dimensional systems), expression (18-8) takes the form

$$\dot{P}_l^{\,ap} = \int_0^l \frac{\dot{E}_1^{\,p}}{p^2} \frac{dp}{ds} \, ds, \tag{18-8a}$$

where s is the symbol denoting distance, and l is the total length of the system.

Expression (18-8) may be applied to the whole system in two ways. One of them is to consider S as consisting of a single cell. The other way results from the triple application of the theorem of the mean of the integral calculus (see, for example, [9], pp. 361–365) to expression (18-8a).

We shall adopt the second method. Expression (18-8) may then be written as

$$\dot{P}_l^{\,ap} = \dot{E}_{1m}^{\,p} \frac{\Delta_m p}{p_m^{\,2}} . \tag{18-8b}$$

In this expression, $\Delta_m p$ stands for some value intermediate between the maximal and the minimal that the function takes for any couple of adjacent cells within S. Corresponding interpretations are given to the other symbols of the expression.

The mean value $\dot{E}_{1m}^{\,p}$ in expression (18-8b) in general will not be equal to the value $\dot{E}^p = \dot{E}$ at which inputs to S or to C take place, nor will p_m be equal to the p-value of the input. However, the ratios $(\dot{E}^p - \dot{E}_{1m}^{\,p})/\dot{E}^p$ and $(p - p_m)/p$ are monotone decreasing functions of $\dot{E}^p$ and p, respectively. We shall assume that their values ultimately become small enough that we can make $\dot{E}_{1m}{}^p/\dot{E}^p \approx 1$ and $p_m/p \approx 1$ for sufficiently high values of $\dot{E}^p$ and p, respectively. This mathematical supposition will simplify calculations greatly without significantly reducing the domain of applicability of the results.

Observe also that, from physical considerations, $\dot{p}/p$ ultimately acquires the property of being monotone non-increasing; in fact,

$$\lim_{p \to \infty} \frac{\dot{p}}{p} = 0. \tag{18-9}$$

From (18-8b),

$$\ddot{P}_i{}^{ap} = \ddot{E}_{1m}{}^p\left(\frac{\Delta_m p}{p_m{}^2}\right) + \dot{E}_{1m}{}^p\left[\frac{(d/dt)(\Delta_m p)}{p_m{}^2} - \frac{2\Delta_m p}{p_m{}^3}\right]. \tag{18-10}$$

Substituting (18-10) in (18-7) and making the identifications $p_m/p = 1$ and $\dot{E}_{1m}{}^p/\dot{E}^p = 1$, we obtain

$$\ddot{P}^{ap} = \frac{\ddot{E}^p}{p}\left(1 + \frac{\Delta_m p}{p}\right) - \frac{\dot{E}^p}{p^2}\left[\dot{p} - \frac{d}{dt}(\Delta_m p) + \frac{2\Delta_m p}{p}\right]. \tag{18-11}$$

We shall be interested in those processes in which p has reached values sufficiently high so that ultimately $\Delta_m p \ll p$. The substitution $p_m/p = 1$ is mathematically equivalent to accepting $\lim_{p \to \infty} (\Delta_m p/p) = 0$. Physically this means that the velocity of transfer propagation in the interior of S permits interior transfer rate to be approximately equal to input transfer rate. The relation $\lim_{p \to \infty} (\Delta_m p/p) > 1 \gg 0$ would not permit us to equate the mean value of interior transfer rate to the rate of input to the system. The relation $\lim_{p \to \infty} (\Delta_m p/p) = 0$ is also compatible with our restriction to processes in which frictional dissipation and secondary internal gradients are negligible.

On the basis of the asymptotic relation $\lim_{p \to \infty} (\Delta_m p/p) = 0$ and of theorem 18-1, we have

$$\lim_{p \to \infty} \frac{2\Delta_m p/p}{\dot{p}} = 2 \lim \frac{\Delta_m p}{p} \lim \frac{1}{\dot{p}} = 0.$$

We shall use this limiting relation to simplify (18-11).

At this point we shall introduce important nomenclature in the form of

Definition 18-1. A system will be said to be *distant from equilibrium* iff the following conditions are satisfied:

α The condition of lemma 18-1 is satisfied.

β The approximation $\Delta_m p/p \approx 0$ falls within the degree of accuracy with which the system is being studied.

If in addition the condition

$$\gamma \quad \dot{E}^p > k > 0 \quad \text{and} \quad \dot{p} > l > 0$$

holds, we shall say that $\mathcal{S}$ is *receding from equilibrium*.

On the other hand, $\mathcal{S}$ will be said to be *returning towards equilibrium*, while still distant from equilibrium, iff in addition to α and β the following condition holds:

$$\gamma' \quad \dot{E}^p < k < 0 \quad \text{and} \quad \dot{p} < l < 0.$$

The preceding paragraphs then have demonstrated

Theorem 18-2. In systems distant from equilibrium, if frictional dissipation and secondary internal gradients are negligible, the following relation is obeyed:

$$p\ddot{p}^{ap} = \dot{E}^p - \frac{\dot{E}^p}{p}\left[\dot{p} - \frac{d}{dt}(\Delta_m p)\right]. \tag{18-12}$$

Here we may also state that, although the consideration of non-negligible secondary internal gradients would complicate equation (18-12), its structural form would not be substantially altered.

We have seen that $\dot{E}^p$, p, and $\dot{p}$ are all positive. The value p in (18-12) is that value of the intensive parameter at which $\dot{E}^p$ is received into $\mathcal{S}$ (i.e., the value $p_\mathcal{B}$ at the boundary $\mathcal{B}$ of $\mathcal{S}$), or it may be some value of p intermediate between the p-value $p_\mathcal{B}$ at $\mathcal{B}$ and the value p_m in (18-8b) (since we are taking $(p_\mathcal{B} - p_m)/p_\mathcal{B}$ to be smaller than the degree of accuracy of our study). The symbol $\dot{p}$, which originated in (18-3), has then the corresponding significance.

Using the mean-value theorem of the differential calculus (see, for example, [15], p. 43, or [30], p. 357), we can write

$$\frac{d}{dt}\Delta_m p = \frac{d}{dt}\left(\frac{dp}{ds}\right)_m \Delta s,$$

where Δs is the length of $\mathcal{S}$. Inverting the order of derivation (for conditions permitting this see, for example, [8], pp. 262–268), we obtain

$$\frac{d}{dt}\Delta_m p = \frac{d}{ds}\dot{p}_m \Delta s.$$

If $[\dot{p} - (d/dt)\Delta_m p] = [\dot{p} - (d/ds)\dot{p}_m \Delta s] < 0$, this would imply $\dot{p}_{\delta A} < 0$ at some δ-cell δA interior to $\mathcal{S}$. In view of the fact that secondary internal gradients are assumed to be negligible, the existence of a δA such that $\dot{p}_{\delta A} < 0$ would violate part III of the G.G.L. The same conclusion will be reached by considering $\mathcal{S}$ as a single cell.

Therefore we have

Theorem 18-3.   In systems receding from equilibrium, if the conditions of theorem 18-2 are satisfied, then $\dot{E}^p$, p, $\dot{p}$, and $[\dot{p} - (d/dt)\,\Delta_m p]$ are all positive.

Now, when $\ddot{E} < 0$—refer to (18-4)—from (18-12) it follows that necessarily $\ddot{P}^{ap} < 0$, because $p\ddot{P}^{ap}$ is then the algebraic sum of two negative numbers, and $p > 0$. This agrees with the first alternative in (18-4): $p\ddot{P}^{ap} < 0$.

The second alternative of (18-4), $0 < p\ddot{P}^{ap} < (d/dt)(A\dot{R}) - \dot{p}\dot{P}^{ap}$, requires that p and $\ddot{P}^{ap}$ possess the same sign.

It is obviously impossible that $\{p > 0,\ \ddot{P}^{ap} > 0\}$, in virtue of (18-12) and the condition $\dot{E}^p < 0$.

The combination $\{p < 0,\ \ddot{P}^{ap} < 0\}$ will be *mathematically* compatible with both (18-4) and (18-12) as long as the conditions

$$0 < p\ddot{P}^{ap} < \frac{d}{dt}(A\dot{R}) - \dot{p}\dot{P}^{ap} \quad \text{and} \quad \frac{\ddot{E}}{\dot{E}} > \frac{\dot{p} - (d/dt)\Delta_m p}{p}$$

are satisfied. We shall now show

Theorem 18-4.   The inequalities

$$0 < p\ddot{P}^{ap} < \frac{d}{dt}(A\dot{R}) - \dot{p}\dot{P}^{ap} \quad \text{and} \quad \frac{\ddot{E}}{\dot{E}} > \frac{\dot{p} - (d/dt)\Delta_m p}{p}$$

are mathematically compatible with the set of conditions $\{p < 0,\ \ddot{P}^{ap} < 0\}$.

PROOF.   An examination of the proofs of theorems 17-5 and 17-7 shows that the sign of the quantity p does not enter into the demonstrations (nor does it enter into that of corollary 17-1), and hence we can extend the thesis of lemma 18-1 as follows:

Lemma 18-1a.   A necessary condition for a system to be away from a neighborhood of equilibrium is that

$$\frac{d}{dt}\left(\frac{dE_{\text{irr}}}{dR}\,\dot{R}\right) = \frac{d}{dt}(A\dot{R}) > 0,$$

the condition holding for both positive and negative values of p.

In the second term $(-\dot{p}\dot{P}^{ap})$ of the first inequality of theorem 18-4, its first factor $\dot{p} > 0$. Because of (18-8b), the second factor

$$\dot{P}^{ap} = \dot{P}_t^{ap} + \dot{P}_l^{ap} = \frac{\dot{E}^p}{p} + \dot{E}_1^{\ p}\,\frac{\Delta_m p}{p_m^{\ 2}},$$

with $\dot{E}^p \geq \dot{E}_1{}^p > 0$. The ratio p_m/p, for positive values of p, was taken as sufficiently close to unity to satisfy the accuracy of our study. The arguments adduced for this can be extended to the case of negative p-values. Therefore we may write $\dot{P}^{ap} \leq (\dot{E}/p)[1 + (\Delta_m p/p)]$.

If the quantity $\Delta_m p < 0$, then evidently $(\dot{E}/p)[1 + (\Delta_m p/p)] < 0$. If $\Delta_m p > 0$, we still have $\Delta_m p < |p|$ and hence $[1 + (\Delta_m p/p)] > 0$, leading to $(\dot{E}/p)[1 + (\Delta_m p/p)] < 0$ for negative values of p. In consequence $\dot{P}^{ap} \leq (\dot{E}/p)[1 + (\Delta_m p/p)] < 0$, and $(-\dot{p}\dot{P}^{ap}) > 0$ for negative p-values.

Nota Bene. Observe that $\dot{p} > 0$ because $\mathcal{S}$ is receding from equilibrium.

The first inequality of theorem 18-4, $0 < p\ddot{P}^{ap} < (d/dt)(A\dot{R}) - \dot{p}\dot{P}^{ap}$, has therefore been shown to be valid for negative values of p.

The second inequality of the theorem,

$$\frac{\ddot{E}}{\dot{E}} > \frac{\dot{p} - (d/dt)\Delta_m p}{p},$$

is consistent for $p < 0$ because then both sides of the inequality are negative, since $\dot{E} > 0$, $\ddot{E} < 0$, $\dot{p} > 0$, and $[\dot{p} - (d/dt)\Delta_m p] > 0$.

This completes the proof of theorem 18-4, and we may state

Corollary 18-1. The conditions $\{p < 0, \ddot{P}^{ap} < 0\}$ are mathematically compatible with the second alternative of (18-4) and with (18-12).

The combination $\{p < 0, \ddot{P}^{ap} < 0\}$ therefore leads to no mathematical inconsistency. What may be its physical significance?

In exploring that inquiry the first questions will be: would negative values of p be "higher" or "lower" than positive values of p? Indeed, what criterion can be adopted for ordering the values of p?

The criterion that will be selected for this purpose is based upon the second part of the second law of energy transfers; that is, we shall stipulate

Definition 18-2. Denote by p_2 the p-value at S_2 and by p_1 the p-value at S_1; then $p_2 > p_1$ iff the direction of E^p-transfer is from S_2 towards S_1.

Observe that the order relation introduced by definition 18-2 satisfies the conditions of a partial ordering (see [11], p. 187). That is, (1) $p_1 > p_2$ and $p_2 > p_1$ imply $p_1 = p_2$, and (2) $p_1 > p_2$ and $p_2 > p_3$ imply $p_1 > p_3$. The second property (transitivity) is satisfied by the directions of E^p-transfers between δ_p-cells, as is known from experimental physics. Definition 18-2 in fact establishes an order isomorphism between p-values and equivalence classes of cells. Two cells, S_a and S_b, are equivalent iff, in the absence of constraint, there is no E^p-transfer between them when in contact. Then, by definition 18-2, $p_a = p_b$. The absence of E^p-transfer may be considered as the mutual neutralization of two transfers equal in magnitude and opposite in directions. With this convention, the E^p-transfers also satisfy the first condition of a partial ordering.

Now consider the isolated system $S = S \cup S'$, with subsystem S' at positive p-value p', and subsystem S with negative value of p. Assume for the moment that negative p-values are lower than positive p-values according to the criterion of definition 18-2. Furthermore, let the place of S in $S = S \cup S'$ be taken by any one system from $(\mathfrak{U} - S')$, where $\mathfrak{U}$ is the universe of all real systems, and S' is a fixed system of very low positive p (i.e., p close to $A_0{}^p$).

Given any fixed S placed in $S = S \cup S'$ by parts I and II of the G.G.L. (no constraint existing to energy transfer between S and S') there will be an energy transfer such that p' decreases and p increases. Now, among all the systems in $(\mathfrak{U} - S')$ there will be at least one (denote it by S_0) such that, when placed in contact with S', both $p(S')$ and $p(S_0)$ approach $A_0{}^p$ to within the same degree of approximation, although, naturally, from different directions.

Now take from $(\mathfrak{U} - S')$ any system S_a at $p(S_a) < p(S_0)$ such that, when placed in contact with S_0, the final p-value of $(S_0 \cup S_a)$ is $p(S_0 \cup S_a) \leq \frac{1}{2}p(S_0)$. Form $S = S_a \cup S'$. There are two possibilities: either the final $p(S_a \cup S')$ is lower than $A_0{}^p$, or $p(S_a \cup S') > A_0{}^p$.

The first alternative is excluded by the results of Chapter 16. If the second alternative were to hold, the law of conservation of energy would be violated. In fact, because $p(S_a \cup S') > A_0{}^p$, and because $p(S') \to A_0{}^p$ when S' was placed in contact with S_0, it follows that the out-transfer from S' to S_0 is not smaller than the out-transfer from S' to S_a—this being a consequence of the G.G.L. On the other hand, S_a would have received an energy input at least double that which would have been received by S_0—this following from the relations $p(S_a) < p(S_0)$, $p(S_0 \cup S_a) \leq \frac{1}{2}p(S_0)$, $p(S_a \cup S') > A_0{}^p$, and because $p(S_0) < A_0{}^p$ when S_0 was placed in contact with S' (again applying the G.G.L. to these relations).

Observe that there is a third conceivable possibility in the preceding situation: that $p(S')$ approaches $A_0{}^p$ from above, and $p(S_a)$, while rising, remains at a final value such that the energy received by S_a is equal to the energy that S_0 received when placed in contact with S'. This final value of $p(S_a)$ must be lower than the final value attained by $p(S_0)$ when placed in contact with S', because $p(S_0 \cup S_a) \leq \frac{1}{2}p(S_0)$. There would thus be a gradient $p(S') - p(S_a) \gg 0$ without a further energy transfer and the corresponding reduction of the p-gradient. Parts I and II of the G.G.L. would thus be violated.

The assumption that negative values of p are lower than positive values in the sense of definition 18-2 has been shown to contradict the

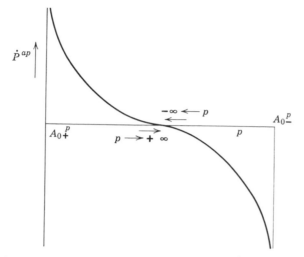

Figure 18-2   Shape of the functional relation between $\dot{P}^{ap}$ and p. Not to scale.

fundamental laws of the science. No such contradiction exists if positive p-values are taken to be lower than negative ones. This last ordering will therefore be adopted for the values of the intensive parameter p.

The ordering of the p-values is not yet finished, however. The ordering criterion adopted in the preceding paragraph permits two specific linear orderings: $\{A_{0+}{}^{p}, +\infty, A_{0-}{}^{p}, -\infty\}$ and $\{A_{0+}{}^{p}, +\infty, -\infty. A_{0-}{}^{p}\}$, where $A_{0+}{}^{p}$ denotes absolute zero p-value approached through positive p-values, and $A_{0-}{}^{p}$ denotes absolute zero p-value approached through negative p-values.

The choice of specific linear ordering of the p-values will also be based on physical considerations. If the first alternative, $\{A_{0+}{}^{p}, +\infty, A_{0-}{}^{p}, -\infty\}$, were adopted, the rate of coparameter change, as a function of p, would suffer a discontinuity in the transition from $p \to \infty$ to $p \to A_{0-}{}^{p}$. Furthermore, the rate $\dot{P}^{ap}$ would be required to actually *attain* an infinite value *in the interior* of the domain of p over which it is defined, and this in turn implies that the accompanying discontinuity in $\dot{P}^{ap}$ would be infinite in absolute magnitude. Those observations are immediate consequences of the expression

$$\dot{P}^{ap} = \frac{\dot{E}^{p}}{p} + \dot{E}_{1}{}^{p}\frac{\Delta_{m}p}{P_{m}{}^{2}}.$$

The second alternative, $\{A_{0+}{}^{p}, +\infty, -\infty. A_{0-}{}^{p}\}$, is free of the preceding objections, and it gives a $\dot{P}^{ap}$ versus p curve of the shape shown in Figure 18-2. Figure 18-3 then shows the type of curve that represents the functional relation between P^{ap} and p.

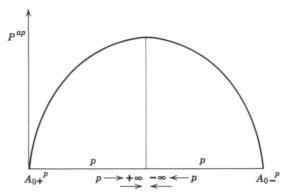

Figure 18-3   Shape of the functional relation between P^{ap} and p. Not to scale.

The following characteristics of the curves are worthy of observation:

1. The change in sign of $\dot{P}^{ap}$ as it passes from positive to negative values of p.

2. $\lim\limits_{p \to +\infty} \dot{P}^{ap} = 0$ and $\lim\limits_{p \to -\infty} \dot{P}^{ap} = 0$.

3. $\lim\limits_{p \to A_{0+}{}^{p}} \dot{P}^{ap} = +\infty$ and $\lim\limits_{p \to A_{0-}{}^{p}} \dot{P}^{ap} = -\infty$.

Observation 3 is related to theorem 16-4.

The curves of Figures 18-2 and 18-3 in reality should not be symmetrical about the midpoint $(+\infty, -\infty)$ of the domain of values of p, even if $\dot{E}^{p}$ were constant over the whole p-domain. In fact, if $\dot{E}^{p}$ were constant over the whole domain of p, the first term on the right of the expression

$$\dot{P}^{ap} = \frac{\dot{E}^{p}}{p} + \dot{E}_{1}{}^{p}\frac{\Delta_{m}p}{p_{m}{}^{2}}$$

would give a function symmetrical about the midpoint of the p-domain, and of opposite signs on opposite sides of that midpoint. But the second term of the expression is positive over the whole domain and hence distorts the symmetry of the first term. The curves of Figures 18-2 and 18-3 should thus be seen as only approximative illustrations that give an idea of the functional variations involved.

In view of the preceding we may state

Theorem 18-5.   The values of the intensive parameter p follow the scale of increasing values:

$$A_{0+}{}^{p}, +\infty, -\infty, A_{0-}{}^{p}.$$

From the S.L., the G.G.L., and theorem 18-5, there follows

Corollary 18-2. Negative values of p may be attained only in systems for which

$$\lim_{p \to +\infty} \frac{dE^p}{dp} = 0.$$

PROOF. If $\lim_{p \to +\infty} (dE^p/dp) > 0$, then $E^p \to +\infty$ as $p \to +\infty$. Under the condition of finiteness of available energy input, the S.L. and the G.G.L. finish the proof of the corollary.

Part III of the G.G.L. asserts that, in a quasi-static system, to $\dot E^p > 0$ corresponds $\dot p > 0$. In consequence, the functional relation between $E(\mathcal{S})$ and p is monotone increasing (see Figure 18-4 for a typical and general case of such a functional relation).

Now we have the following situation:

1. The curve P^{ap} versus p is monotone increasing in the interval $(A_{0+}{}^p, +\infty)$.
2. The same curve is monotone decreasing over the interval $(-\infty, A_{0-}{}^p)$.
3. The curve p versus $E(\mathcal{S})$ is monotone increasing over the whole domain.

Now, a change of independent variable effected by means of a monotone function does not alter the *sign* of the slope of the original function. That is, a monotone increasing function of a monotone increasing function yields a monotone increasing function as composite function; and a monotone decreasing function of a monotone increasing function gives as composite a monotone decreasing function.

The preceding implies that the functional relation between P^{ap} and $E(\mathcal{S})$ will be represented by a curve of the same type as P^{ap} versus p; see Figure 18-5 for an illustration.

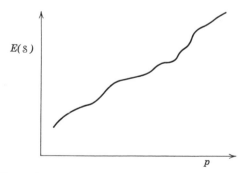

Figure 18-4 Illustration of a monotonically increasing relation between $E(\mathcal{S})$ and p.

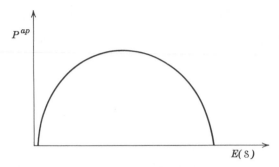

Figure 18-5 Shape of the functional relation between $E(8)$ and P^{ap}. Not to scale.

The fact that negative p-values are higher than positive p-values has an immediate physical significance in terms of definition 18-2—a significance in terms of direction of energy transfer. But a most important question arises: *in terms of the interpretation assigned to the coparameter increment* (Chapter 6), what is the physical significance of the fact that negative p-values are higher than positive p-values?

To investigate this question let us first analyze the rate of coparameter production for negative values of p. Consider $8 = S_1 \cup S_2$, in which S_1 and S_2 have p-values p_1 and p_2 such that $-\infty < p_2 < p_1 < A_{0-}{}^p$. There will be an E^p-transfer from S_1 to S_2, such that $\dot{E}_1{}^p < 0$ and $\dot{E}_2{}^p = -\dot{E}_1{}^p$, where $\dot{E}_2{}^p$ is the rate of input into S_2 and $\dot{E}_1{}^p$ is the rate of output from S_1.

Under the assumption of negligible frictional dissipation and negligible secondary internal energy-transfers, the rate of coparameter production will be given by

$$\dot{P}_i{}^{ap} = \frac{\dot{E}_1{}^p}{p_1} + \frac{\dot{E}_2{}^p}{p_2} = \dot{E}_1{}^p\left(\frac{p_2 - p_1}{p_2 p_1}\right) = \dot{E}_2{}^p\left(\frac{p_1 - p_2}{p_1 p_2}\right).$$

Because $\dot{E}_1{}^p < 0$ and $(p_2 - p_1)/p_2 p_1 < 0$, and because $\dot{E}_2{}^p > 0$ and $(p_1 - p_2)/p_1 p_2 > 0$, it follows that the rate of coparameter production $\dot{P}_i{}^{ap} > 0$ for negative values of p.

Consider now the same system, but with $A_{0+}{}^p < p_2 < +\infty$ and $-\infty < p_1 < A_{0-}{}^p$. Then $(p_2 - p_1)$ is positive whereas $\dot{E}_1{}^p$ and $p_2 p_1$ are negative, giving again $\dot{P}_i{}^{ap} > 0$. The same result follows from the fact that $(p_1 - p_2)$ and $p_1 p_2$ are negative whereas $\dot{E}_2{}^p$ is positive.

The positivity of $\dot{P}_i{}^{ap}$ has been demonstrated to result from the existence of primary internal (to 8) p-gradients, with their consequent internal energy transfers. Variations within those internal p-gradients and E^p-transfers give rise to secondary internal p-gradients, with their consequent secondary internal E^p-transfers. These secondary internal p-gradients are generally multidirectional. The rate of coparameter production resulting from these secondary internal p-gradients again follows a law of the form of (18-8) or its equivalent expressions, (18-8a) and (18-8b). But it was from the form of this law alone that the positivity of $\dot{P}_t^{\,ap}$ was derived for the case of primary internal p-gradients. The derivation therefore remains valid for secondary internal p-gradients, since these follow a law of the same form.

Thus we have established

Theorem 18-6. $\dot{P}_t^{\,ap} > 0$ in every process, independently of the signs of the values of the intensive parameter.

Now let us turn our attention to the coparameter flow for negative values of p.

If S receives an input rate $\dot{E}^p$ from $\mathcal{E}$, we have $\dot{P}_t^{\,ap} = \dot{E}^p/p$. In the case of positive p, for $S:\dot{P}_t^{\,ap}(S) = (\dot{E}^p/p) > 0$, while for $\mathcal{E}:\dot{P}_t^{\,ap}(\mathcal{E}) = (\dot{E}^p/p) < 0$. The first represents a positive rate of coparameter flow into S; the second, a rate of coparameter outflow from $\mathcal{E}$.

When p is negative, $\dot{P}_t^{\,ap}(S) < 0$, while $\dot{P}_t^{\,ap}(\mathcal{E}) > 0$.

On the other hand, when the system is returning towards equilibrium and S has an output rate $\dot{E}^p$ to $\mathcal{E}$, every sign is reversed in the preceding, for $\dot{E}^p(S) < 0$ in such a situation.

Thus we have

Theorem 18-7. Table 18-1 presents the *direction of coparameter flow* as it depends upon the characteristics of the process.

Now we return to our original inquiry: with reference to the rate of coparameter increase, what is the physical significance of the fact that negative p-values are higher than positive p-values? That significance cannot be found in the context of $\dot{P}_t^{\,ap}$, because $\dot{P}_t^{\,ap} > 0$ independently of the sign of p.

In Chapter 6 it was stated that, if ΔP^{ap} is associated with a ΔE^p received by S, that ΔP^{ap} is a measure of the potentiality for inconvertibility that

Table 18-1

p-Value at Boundary of S and $\mathcal{E}$	System Receding from Equilibrium	System Returning towards Equilibrium
Positive	From $\mathcal{E}$ to S $\dot{P}_t^{\,ap}(S) > 0$	From S to $\mathcal{E}$ $\dot{P}_t^{\,ap}(S) < 0$
Negative	From S to $\mathcal{E}$ $\dot{P}_t^{\,ap}(S) < 0$	From $\mathcal{E}$ to S $\dot{P}_t^{\,ap}(S) > 0$

accompanies ΔE^p. The higher ΔP^{ap} is, the smaller the part of ΔE^p that is recoverable from S, for equal values of p_0 (the lowest p-values available to establish the gradient for the recovery).

Consider now a ΔE^p received by S at negative p-values, and to avoid unnecessary complications suppose that the $\dot{P}_i{}^{ap}$ of the process is negligible. This will not detract from the generality of our resulting interpretation, since $\dot{P}_i{}^{ap} > 0$ independently of the sign of p.

After receiving the ΔE^p at negative p-value, the system will be in a final state of higher energy and lower coparameter value (see Table 18-1). Consequently, given the same *positive* p_0 in the environment of S, not only the whole of the ΔE^p received is recoverable (retransferable or, more generally, convertible) but also a portion of the energy that S had in its initial state (before receiving ΔE^p) has now become convertible.

This follows from $\Delta E^p = \Delta E_c{}^p + \Delta E_{ic}{}^p = \Delta E_c{}^p + \Delta P^{ap} p_0$. If $\Delta P^{ap} < 0$ and $p_0 > 0$, then $\Delta E_c{}^p > \Delta E^p$. On the other hand, if p_0 is negative and $\Delta P^{ap} < 0$, then $\Delta E_c{}^p < \Delta E^p$.

Therefore

Theorem 18-8. A $0 < \Delta E^p < \infty$ input to S at negative p-values is accompanied by $\Delta E_c{}^p > \Delta E^p$ if p_0 is positive and $\Delta P_i{}^{ap}$ is negligible; it is accompanied by $\Delta E^p > \Delta E_c{}^p$ if p_0 is negative.

Naturally, if there is going to be any convertibility at all when p_0 is negative, it is necessary that $-\infty < p_0 < p < A_{0-}{}^p$, where p is the p-value of the input. This is a consequence of definition 18-2; otherwise no p-gradient would be available for the convertibility.

The thesis of theorem 18-8 (see also the second paragraph before the theorem) is consistent with our previously established conception of the coparameter change.

In fact, consider positive p_0 and imagine a ΔE^p input to S at $p = +\infty$. Then, because we are neglecting $\dot{P}_i{}^{ap}$, it turns out that $\Delta P^{ap} = \Delta P_i{}^{ap} = \Delta E^p / p = 0$ whenever $\Delta E^p < \infty$. Hence $\Delta E_c{}^p = \Delta E^p$. This was to be expected: *an input that would establish an infinite gradient would also be fully recoverable.*

If the ΔE^p input is at $-\infty < p$, the gradient consists of two parts: $\{p$ to $-\infty$, and $+\infty$ to $p_0\}$. The second part by itself gives us a $\Delta E_c{}^p$ in the system that equals the ΔE^p input to it. But by virtue of part I of the G.G.L., in passing through the gradient $(p, -\infty)$ the system will also put out an energy transfer, and that energy output will be *part of the energy inputs that S formerly received.*

Negative values of an intensive parameter were obtained experimentally for the first time, for $p = T$, by Purcell and Pound [40] in experiments studying the properties of systems of nuclear spins in very pure crystals of lithium fluoride. Theoretical interpretations of negative values of p, again for the case $p = T$, may be found in reference [41] and [42]. Those interpretations are quite different from each other and also from our treatment of the same problem.

Relations (18-4), (18-5), and (18-6) may now be modified for negative values of p.

In fact, in the demonstration of theorem 18-4 it was shown that $\dot{P}^{ap} < 0$. Indeed, $\dot{P}_t^{ap} < 0$, $\dot{P}_l^{ap} > 0$, and $|\dot{P}_t^{ap}| > |\dot{P}_l^{ap}|$ for negative p-values. Hence $\dot{p}\dot{P}^{ap} < 0$, since $\dot{p} > 0$. Finally, because of lemma 18-1a, we have that $(d/dt)(A\dot{R}) - \dot{p}\dot{P}^{ap} > 0$.

But from (18-1) it follows that $p\ddot{P}^{ap} = \ddot{E} + (d/dt)(A\dot{R}) - \dot{p}\dot{P}^{ap}$. Therefore

Theorem 18-9. The following relations hold for systems receding from equilibrium at negative values of p:

$$\text{For } \ddot{E} < 0: \quad p\ddot{P}^{ap} \gtrless 0 \quad \text{according as}$$

$$\left. |\ddot{E}| \lessgtr \left| \frac{d}{dt}(A\dot{R}) - \dot{p}\dot{P}^{ap} \right| ; \right\} \tag{18-4'}$$

$$\text{For } \ddot{E} = 0: \quad p\ddot{P}^{ap} > 0; \tag{18-5'}$$

$$\text{For } \ddot{E} > 0: \quad p\ddot{P}^{ap} > 0. \tag{18-6'}$$

Observe that (18-4'), (18-5'), and (18-6') give in general more precise information than the corresponding inequalities, (18-4), (18-5), and (18-6). that hold for positive values of p.

We have already deduced the results shown in Table 18-2.

The last possible combinations with $\ddot{E} < 0$ remain to be considered:

$$\{\ddot{E} < 0, \text{ negative } p, \dot{P}^{ap} < 0, \ddot{P}^{ap} > 0\}$$

Table 18-2

Quantities	Compatibility
$\ddot{E} < 0$, p positive $\dot{P}^{ap} > 0$, $\ddot{P}^{ap} < 0$	Compatible with both (18-4) and (18-12)
$\ddot{E} < 0$, p positive $\dot{P}^{ap} > 0$, $\ddot{P}^{ap} > 0$	Incompatible with (18-12)
$\ddot{E} < 0$, p negative $\dot{P}^{ap} < 0$, $\ddot{P}^{ap} < 0$	Compatible with both (18-4') and (18-12)

and

$$\{\dot{E} < 0,\ \text{negative } p,\ \dot{P}^{ap} < 0,\ \ddot{P}^{ap} = 0\}.$$

It is easy to see that the first of these theoretical possibilities is compatible with both (18-4′) and (18-12). In fact, when applied to (18-12), this combination yields

$$\frac{\ddot{E}}{\dot{E}} < \frac{\dot{p} - (d/dt)(\Delta_m p)}{p}$$

with both sides negative quantities. On the other hand, applied to (18-4′), it gives

$$|\ddot{E}| > \left| \frac{d}{dt}(A\dot{R}) - \dot{p}\dot{P}^{ap} \right|.$$

The second combination $\{\ddot{E} < 0,\ \text{negative } p,\ \dot{P}^{ap} < 0,\ \ddot{P}^{ap} = 0\}$ is compatible with (18-4′), on condition that $|\ddot{E}| = |(d/dt)(A\dot{R}) - \dot{p}\dot{P}^{ap}|$, and with (18-12), because then $\ddot{E}^p = (\dot{E}^p/p)[\dot{p} - (d/dt)(\Delta_m p)]$, and both sides of this equation are negative.

The condition $\ddot{E} < 0$ therefore yields a functional relation P^{ap} versus t of the form illustrated in Figure 18-6 and with the characteristics shown in Table 18-3.

Because $\dot{E}_c{}^p = \dot{E}^p - \dot{E}_{ic}{}^p = \dot{E}^p - \dot{P}^{ap}p_0$, for a fixed p_0 the curves showing the variability of $\int_{t_0}^{t} \dot{E}^p\, dt$ with time and the variability of $\int_{t_0}^{t} \dot{E}_c{}^p\, dt$ with time follow patterns like those shown in Figure 18-6. In that figure, t_0 is an arbitrary but fixed initial instant.

In a more exact graph, the abscissa point at which p changes from

Table 18-3   System Receding from Equilibrium

Case: $\ddot{E}^p < 0$

p-Value	$\ddot{P}^{ap}$	Conditions
Positive	Negative	None necessary
Negative	Negative	$|\ddot{E}| < \left|\dfrac{d}{dt}(A\dot{R}) - \dot{p}\dot{P}^{ap}\right|$
	Zero	$\ddot{E} = \dfrac{d}{dt}(A\dot{R}) - \dot{p}\dot{P}^{ap}$
	Positive	$|\ddot{E}| > \left|\dfrac{d}{dt}(A\dot{R}) - \dot{p}\dot{P}^{ap}\right|$

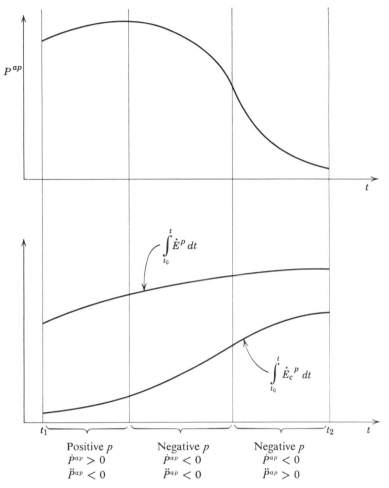

Figure 18-6 Relative shapes of the variations of P^{ap}, and of input and output, as functions of time, for system receding from equilibrium and with $\ddot{E} < 0$ (p_0 positive). Not to scale.

positive to negative would not coincide with the point at which $\dot{P}^{ap}$ passes from positive to negative. The first point should be slightly to the left of the second because $\dot{P}^{ap} = \dot{P}_t{}^{ap} + \dot{P}_l{}^{ap}$ does not become negative the moment that $\dot{P}_t{}^{ap}$ does (i.e., when p becomes negative), but only when $|\dot{P}_t{}^{ap}| > \dot{P}_l{}^{ap} > 0$.

We shall now consider the case $\ddot{E} = 0$.

From (18-12) and theorem 18-3 it follows that $p\ddot{P}^{ap} < 0$ whenever $p > 0$, and this in turn implies $\ddot{P}^{ap} < 0$. The inequality $p\ddot{P}^{ap} < 0$ and lemma 18-1a, applied to (18-5), yield $0 < (d/dt)(A\dot{R}) < p\dot{P}^{ap}$.

For negative values of p, equation (18-12) gives $p\ddot{P}^{ap} > 0$ and thus again $\ddot{P}^{ap} < 0$. This, applied to (18-5), yields $(d/dt)(A\dot{R}) > p\dot{P}^{ap}$. Lemma 18-1a asserts that $(d/dt)(A\dot{R}) > 0$, while theorem 18-7 implies that $p\dot{P}^{ap} < 0$; both of these conditions are compatible with the relation $(d/dt)(A\dot{R}) > p\dot{P}^{ap}$.

It is consistent with the interpretation of $\dot{R}$ as the process velocity, and with the interpretation that has been given to P^{ap} (over the whole domain of values of p), that for positive p-values $(d/dt)(A\dot{R}) < p\dot{P}^{ap}$, whereas for negative p-values $(d/dt)(A\dot{R}) > p\dot{P}^{ap}$.

The results for the case $\ddot{E} = 0$ are summarized in Table 18-4, and

Table 18-4   System Receding from Equilibrium

Case: $\ddot{E} = 0$

p-Value	$\ddot{P}^{ap}$	Conditions
Positive	Negative	$0 < \dfrac{d}{dt}(A\dot{R}) < p\dot{P}^{ap}$
Negative	Negative	$\dfrac{d}{dt}(A\dot{R}) > 0, \quad p\dot{P}^{ap} < 0$

Figure 18-7 portrays P^{ap}, $\displaystyle\int_{t_0}^{t} \dot{E}^{p}\, dt$, and $\displaystyle\int_{t_0}^{t} \dot{E}_{c}^{p}\, dt$ as functions of time. Again, this figure assumes that $\dot{P}_{l}{}^{ap}$ is negligible by comparison with $\dot{P}_{t}{}^{ar}$. Considering $\dot{P}_{l}{}^{ap}$ as non-negligible would simply displace the P^{ap} and the $\displaystyle\int_{t_0}^{t} \dot{E}_{c}^{p}\, dt$ curves slightly.

The case corresponding to $\ddot{E} > 0$ remains to be considered. For positive values of p, the first alternative of (18-6) is compatible with (18-12) under the condition

$$\dot{E}^{p} > \frac{\dot{E}^{p}}{p}\left[\dot{p} - \frac{d}{dt}(\Delta_{m}p)\right] > 0$$

(the last inequality is asserted by theorem 18-3). In consequence, phenomena characterized by the conditions {positive p, $\ddot{E} > 0$, $\dot{P}^{ap} > 0$, $\ddot{P}^{ap} > 0$} fall under the provisions of the theory.

The second alternative of (18-6) is also compatible with (18-12), but under this pair of conditions:

$$0 < \ddot{E}^{p} < \frac{\dot{E}^{p}}{p}\left[\dot{p} - \frac{d}{dt}(\Delta_{m}p)\right] \quad \text{and} \quad 0 < \frac{d}{dt}(A\dot{R}) < p\dot{P}^{ap}.$$

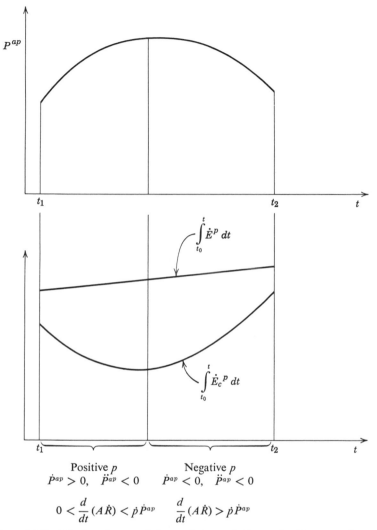

Figure 18-7 Relative shapes of the variations of P^{ap}, and of input and output, as functions of time, for system receding from equilibrium and with $\ddot{E} = 0$. Not to scale.

Therefore the theory also provides for phenomena characterized by {positive p, $\ddot{E} > 0$, $\dot{P}^{ap} > 0$, $\ddot{P}^{ap} < 0$}.

Turning now to negative values of p, from (18-6′) we have that necessarily $\dot{P}^{ap} < 0$, and this is compatible with (18-12) as long as

$$\ddot{E}^p > \frac{\dot{E}_p}{p}\left[\dot{p} - \frac{d}{dt}(\Delta_m p)\right].$$

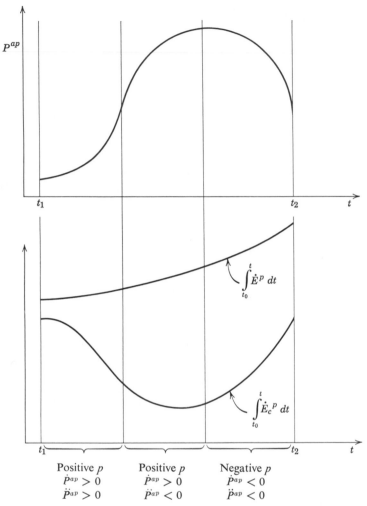

Figure 18-8 Relative shapes of the variations of P^{ap}, and of input and output, as functions of time, for system receding from equilibrium and with $\ddot{E} > 0$. Not to scale.

This inequality will always hold because $\ddot{E}^p > 0$ (in the case being considered at present), while the right side of the inequality is negative for negative values of p. Hence the theory also provides for phenomena characterized by {negative p, $\ddot{E} > 0$, $\dot{P}^{ap} < 0$, $\ddot{P}^{ap} < 0$}.

For the case $\ddot{E} > 0$ we then have functional relations of P^{ap} and $\int_{t_0}^{t} \dot{E}_c^{p} \, dt$ as functions of t that are representable by curves of the types shown in Figure 18-8 and under the restrictions listed in Table 18-5.

Table 18-5   System Receding from Equilibrium

Case: $\ddot{E}^p > 0$

p-Value	$\ddot{p}^{ap}$	Conditions
Positive	Positive	$\ddot{E}^p > \dfrac{\dot{E}^p}{p}\left[\dot{p} - \dfrac{d}{dt}(\Delta_m p)\right] > 0$
	Negative	$0 < \ddot{E}^p < \dfrac{\dot{E}^p}{p}\left[\dot{p} - \dfrac{d}{dt}(\Delta_m p)\right]$
Negative	Negative	None necessary

It is interesting to observe that, as p increases through positive and negative values, the curve $\displaystyle\int_{t_0}^{t} \dot{E}_c{}^p\, dt$ multiplies the number of oscillations of the curve $\displaystyle\int_{t_0}^{t} \dot{E}^p\, dt$. This is shown in Figure 18-9, in which the appropriate portions of Figures 18-6, 18-7, and 18-8 have been combined.

The quantity $\dot{E}^p$ is the rate of change of E^p-transfer that will be input from $\mathcal{E}$ (or from $\mathcal{C}$) to $\mathcal{S}$, while $\dot{E}_c{}^p$ is the rate of change of output from $\mathcal{S}$ to $\mathcal{E}$. In consequence, the quantities $\displaystyle\int_{t_0}^{t} \dot{E}^p\, dt$ and $\displaystyle\int_{t_0}^{t} \dot{E}_c{}^p\, dt$ represent the actual input and output at instant t. From Figures 18-6 to 18-9 it may be seen that the variations in the slope of $\displaystyle\int_{t_0}^{t} \dot{E}_c{}^p\, dt$ are much more pronounced than the variations in the slope of $\displaystyle\int_{t_0}^{t} \dot{E}^p\, dt$. In fact, variations in $\displaystyle\int_{t_0}^{t} \dot{E}^p\, dt$ that, because of their slowness, might not be detectable with the measuring instruments available are in correspondence with variations in $\displaystyle\int_{t_0}^{t} \dot{E}_c{}^p\, dt$ that could be considered to be of an explosive kind. These larger variations in $\displaystyle\int_{t_0}^{t} \dot{E}_c{}^p\, dt$ are due to the variations of P^{ap} with time, which are superimposed on the variations of $\displaystyle\int_{t_0}^{t} \dot{E}^p\, dt$ with time.

Phenomena such as the above may be associated with observations made in the astrophysical, cosmic, and subnuclear realms. In any one case the parameter p may be the temperature, the pressure, or any other parameter in terms of which the gradient is predicted.

It should be rewarding to study now the characteristics associated with the phenomena of return or motion towards equilibrium in a system that is still far from equilibrium. To do this we shall analyze the relations that correspond to $\dot{E}^p = \dot{E} < 0$.

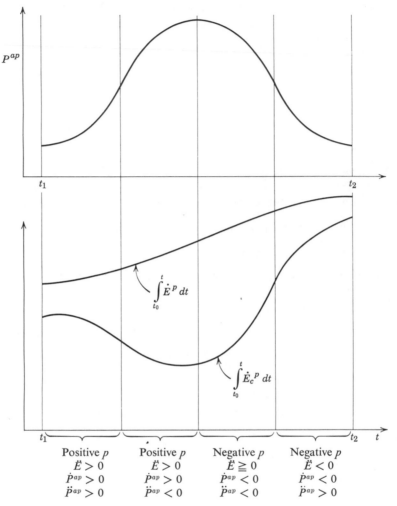

Figure 18-9 Relative shapes of the variations of P^{ap}, and of input and output, as functions of time, for system receding from equilibrium. Not to scale.

From part III of the G.G.L. it follows immediately that $\dot{p} < 0$ whenever $\dot{E}^p < 0$, since earlier in this chapter it was shown that the systems studied in it satisfy the condition of definition 4-4b for quasi-static systems.

Relations (18-4), (18-5), and (18-6) are derived from equation (18-1) and lemma 18-1. Because in the last two the sign of the quantity $\dot{E}^p$ does not enter at all, the first three will not depend on the sign of that quantity either. Therefore they remain valid for systems returning towards equilibrium.

Also theorem 18-2 and its equation (18-12) remain applicable when $\dot{E} < 0$, for in the demonstration of that theorem only the absolute value of $\dot{E}^p$ was employed. However, the thesis of theorem 18-3 must be modified for systems returning towards equilibrium, for in establishing this thesis the positivity of $\dot{E}^p$ is essential.

It has been shown already that both $\dot{E}^p$ and $\dot{p}$ are negative when the system is returning towards equilibrium. It has also been shown (paragraph preceding theorem 18-3) that, if secondary internal gradients are negligible, $|\dot{p}| > |(d/dt) \Delta_m p|$. Therefore

Theorem 18-10. In systems returning towards equilibrium, if secondary internal gradients are negligible, the quantities $\dot{E}^p$, $\dot{p}$, and $[\dot{p} - (d/dt) \Delta_m p]$ are all negative.

In the light of theorem 18-10, the thesis of theorem 18-9 may have to be revised for systems returning towards equilibrium.

For systems returning towards equilibrium at negative values of p the quantity $\dot{p} \dot{P}^{ap} < 0$. In fact, $\dot{P}^{ap} > 0$ because p is negative (theorem 18-7), and $\dot{p} < 0$ because the system is returning towards equilibrium ($\dot{E}^p < 0$; theorem 18-10). Since by lemma 18-1a the quantity $(d/dt) (A\dot{R}) > 0$, it follows that the expression $[(d/dt)(A\dot{R}) - \dot{p} \dot{P}^{ap}] > 0$.

Because from (18-1) we have

$$p\ddot{P}^{ap} = \ddot{E} + \frac{d}{dt}(A\dot{R}) - \dot{p}\dot{P}^{ap},$$

we are now in a position to assert

Theorem 18-11. The following relations hold for systems returning towards equilibrium at negative values of p:

$$\left. \begin{array}{l} \text{For } \ddot{E} < 0: \quad p\ddot{P}^{ap} \gtreqless 0 \quad \text{according as} \\[2mm] \qquad |\ddot{E}| \lesseqgtr \dfrac{d}{dt}(A\dot{R}) - \dot{p}\dot{P}^{ap}; \end{array} \right\} \tag{18-4''}$$

$$\text{For } \ddot{E} = 0; \quad p\ddot{P}^{ap} > 0; \tag{18-5''}$$

$$\text{For } \ddot{E} > 0: \quad p\ddot{P}^{ap} > 0. \tag{18-6''}$$

Now we are in a position to analyze the process of returning towards equilibrium, as the system passes from negative to positive values of p.

The first alternative of (18-4), $p\ddot{P}^{ap} < 0$ for $\ddot{E} < 0$, applied to (18-12), imposes the condition

$$\ddot{E}^p - \frac{\dot{E}^p}{p}\left[\dot{p} - \frac{d}{dt}(\Delta_m p)\right] < 0.$$

The fact that now $\dot{E}^p$ and $[\dot{p} - (d/dt)(\Delta_m p)]$ are negative means that, when p is positive, that inequality is always satisfied. Therefore, the first alternative of (18-4) implies that $\ddot{P}^{ap}$ will be negative for positive values of p.

Because the system is returning towards equilibrium, $\dot{p} < 0$ (G.G.L., part III), and from theorem 18-7 we have that $\dot{P}^{ap} < 0$ for positive p-values. Considering the thesis of lemma 18-1a and the second alternative of (18-4), it follows that $(d/dt)(A\dot{R}) > \dot{p}\dot{P}^{ap}$ is a necessary condition for $p\ddot{P}^{ap} > 0$. This inequality, applied to (18-12), implies

$$\dot{E}^p > \frac{\dot{E}^p}{p}\left[\dot{p} - \frac{d}{dt}(\Delta_m p)\right].$$

Because now $\dot{E}^p < 0$, and $\dot{E}^p$ and $[\dot{p} - (d/dt)(\Delta_m p)]$ are also both negative, it follows that this inequality cannot be satisfied whenever p has a positive value.

When p is negative and $\ddot{E} < 0$, we must use (18-4'') of theorem 18-11. It presents three alternatives for consideration.

Starting with (18-12), we see that, because $\dot{E}^p$ and $[\dot{p} - (d/dt)(\Delta_m p)]$ are now negative, to negative values of p correspond the relations $p\ddot{P}^{ap} \gtrless 0$ according as

$$|\dot{E}^p| \lessgtr \left|\frac{\dot{E}^p}{p}\left[\dot{p} - \frac{d}{dt}(\Delta_m p)\right]\right|.$$

Conjoining this with the first thesis of theorem 18-11, we obtain the results covering the case $\ddot{E} < 0$; they are schematically presented in Table 18-6.

Passing now to the case $\ddot{E} = 0$, we find from (18-12) that

$$p\ddot{P}^{ap} = -\frac{\dot{E}^p}{p}\left[\dot{p} - \frac{d}{dt}(\Delta_m p)\right].$$

Because of theorem 18-10, both $\dot{E}^p$ and $[\dot{p} - (d/dt)(\Delta_m p)]$ are negative. Consequently, to positive p corresponds $p\ddot{P}^{ap} < 0$.

Passing to (18-5), we can infer that positive p corresponds to $p\ddot{P}^{ap} \gtrless 0$ according as $(d/dt)(A\dot{R}) \gtrless \dot{p}\dot{P}^{ap}$. In fact, $(d/dt)(A\dot{R}) > 0$ by lemma 18-1a. Furthermore, $\dot{P}^{ap} < 0$ from theorem 18-7 (return towards equilibrium with positive p), and $\dot{p} < 0$; hence $\dot{p}\dot{P}^{ap} > 0$.

Combining the inferences from (18-5) and (18-12), we find that, for positive p-values, $p\ddot{P}^{ap} < 0$, and hence $\ddot{P}^{ap} < 0$, under the condition $(d/dt)(A\dot{R}) < \dot{p}\dot{P}^{ap}$.

Table 18-6   System Returning towards Equilibrium

Case: $\ddot{E}^p < 0$

p-Value	$\ddot{P}^{ap}$	Conditions
Positive	Negative	None necessary
Negative	Negative	$\|\ddot{E}\| < \left\|\dfrac{\dot{E}^p}{p}\left[\dot{p} - \dfrac{d}{dt}(\Delta_m p)\right]\right\|$ and $\|\ddot{E}\| < \dfrac{d}{dt}(A\dot{R}) - \dot{p}\dot{P}^{ap}$
	Zero	$\|\ddot{E}\| = \left\|\dfrac{\dot{E}^p}{p}\left[\dot{p} - \dfrac{d}{dt}(\Delta_m p)\right]\right\|$ and $\|\ddot{E}\| = \dfrac{d}{dt}(A\dot{R}) - \dot{p}\dot{P}^{ap}$
	Positive	$\|\ddot{E}\| > \left\|\dfrac{\dot{E}^p}{p}\left[\dot{p} - \dfrac{d}{dt}(\Delta_m p)\right]\right\|$ and $\|\ddot{E}\| > \dfrac{d}{dt}(A\dot{R}) - \dot{p}\dot{P}^{ap}$

When p goes through negative values, equation (18-12) predicts $p\ddot{P}^{ap} > 0$, which is compatible with (18-5″) in theorem 18-11.

In consequence of the preceding we have Table 18-7.

The final case to consider is $\ddot{E} > 0$.

When p is negative, equation (18-12) predicts $p\ddot{P}^{ap} > 0$, which is compatible with (18-6″) in theorem 18-11. Then $\ddot{P}^{ap}$ has to be negative.

Table 18-7   System Returning Towards Equilibrium

Case: $\ddot{E} = 0$

p-Value	$\ddot{P}^{ap}$	Conditions
Positive	Negative	$\dfrac{d}{dt}(A\dot{R}) < \dot{p}\dot{P}^{ap}$
Negative	Negative	None

For positive values of p, equation (18-12) predicts that $p\ddot{P}^{ap} \gtrless 0$ according as

$$\dot{E} \gtrless \frac{\dot{E}}{p}\left[\dot{p} - \frac{d}{dt}(\Delta_m p)\right].$$

The positive sign in these inequalities is compatible with the first alternative of (18-6).

The second alternative of (18-6),

$$0 > p\ddot{P}^{ap} > \frac{d}{dt}(A\dot{R}) - \dot{p}\dot{P}^{ap},$$

demands that $\dot{p}\dot{P}^{ap} > 0$ and $\dot{p}\dot{P}^{ap} > (d/dt)(A\dot{R})$. The inequality $\dot{p}\dot{P}^{ap} > 0$ holds because both $\dot{p}$ and $\dot{P}^{ap}$ are negative for systems returning towards equilibrium through positive values of p.

Table 18-8 presents the results that hold for this final case.

Table 18-8   System Returning Toward Equilibrium
Case: $\ddot{E} > 0$

p-Value	$\ddot{P}^{ap}$	Conditions
Negative	Negative	None
Positive	Negative	$\dot{p}\dot{P}^{ap} > \dfrac{d}{dt}(A\dot{R}) > 0$
	Positive	$\ddot{E} > \dfrac{\dot{E}}{p}\left[\dot{p} - \dfrac{d}{dt}(\Delta_m p)\right]$

The results obtained for the three cases in which the system may be found when returning towards equilibrium are graphically portrayed in Figures 18-10 to 18-12.

Figure 18-13 combines several portions of the preceding curves, showing them as a connected whole. The left half of the figure portrays relative variations of P^{ap}, of $\int_{t_0}^{t} \dot{E}^p \, dt$, and of $\int_{t_0}^{t} \dot{E}_c{}^p \, dt$, as the system moves far from equilibrium and receding from it. The right half of the figure shows the relative variations of the same three quantities as the system, still far from equilibrium, is returning towards it.

With regard to the characteristics of the functional relations obtained, several are of significance. They may be observed by an examination of Figure 18-13.

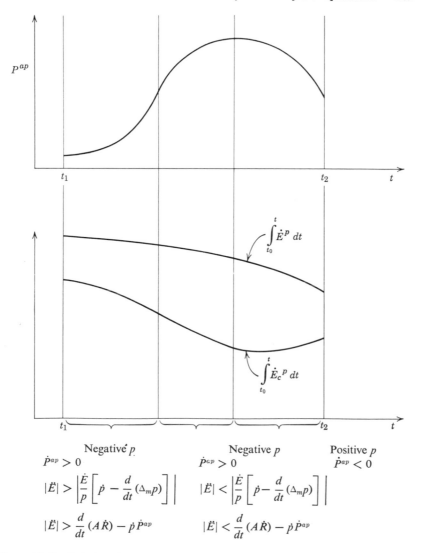

Figure 18-10 Relative shapes of the variations of P^{ap}, and of input and output, as functions of time, for system returning to equilibrium and with $\ddot{E} < 0$. Not to scale.

The first observation is that each of the functions P^{ap} and $\int_{t_0}^{t} \dot{E}_c{}^p \, dt$ has a frequency of change that doubles the frequency of change of $\int_{t_0}^{t} \dot{E}^p \, dt$. The second is that the amplitude variation of $\int_{t_0}^{t} \dot{E}_c{}^p \, dt$ is appreciably larger than that of $\int_{t_0}^{t} \dot{E}^p \, dt$. This is so because $\dot{E}_c{}^p = \dot{E}^p - \dot{P}p_0$, where p_0 is a constant, in conjunction with the relative disposition along the time axis of the points of maxima and minima of the curves for P^{ap} and $\int_{t_0}^{t} \dot{E}^p \, dt$. In fact, the points of minima of P^{ap} coincide in time with the points of maxima and of minima of $\int_{t_0}^{t} \dot{E}^p \, dt$, whereas the points of

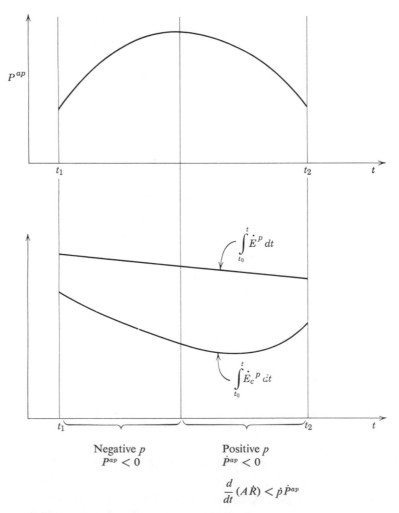

Negative p Positive p
$P^{ap} < 0$ $\dot{P}^{ap} < 0$

$$\frac{d}{dt}(A\dot{R}) < \dot{p}\dot{P}^{ap}$$

Figure 18-11 Relative shapes of the variations of P^{ap}, and of input and output, as functions of time, for systems returning to equilibrium and with $\ddot{E} = 0$. Not to scale.

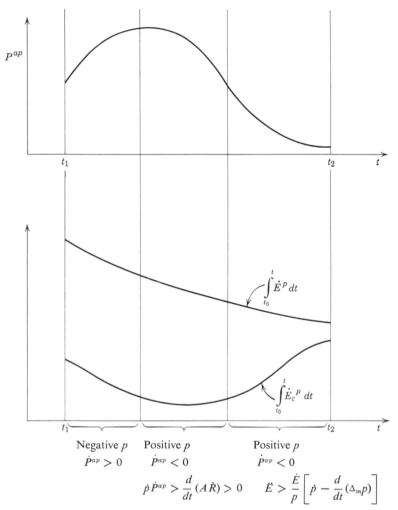

Figure 18-12 Relative shapes of the variations of P^{ap}, and of input and output, as functions of time, for systems returning to equilibrium and with $\dot{E} > 0$. Not to scale.

maxima of P^{ap} coincide in time with intermediate values of $\int_{t_0}^{t} \dot{E}^p \, dt$.

The third observation is a consequence of the preceding two, in connection with the interpretation of $\int_{t_0}^{t} \dot{E}^p \, dt$ and $\int_{t_0}^{t} \dot{E}_c^{\ p} \, dt$ as, respectively, input and outputs of the system during the time interval $[t_0, t]$.

It is an almost immediate consequence of the G.G.L. that, when $p(\mathcal{E})$ remains unaltered, the difference between the input and output rates

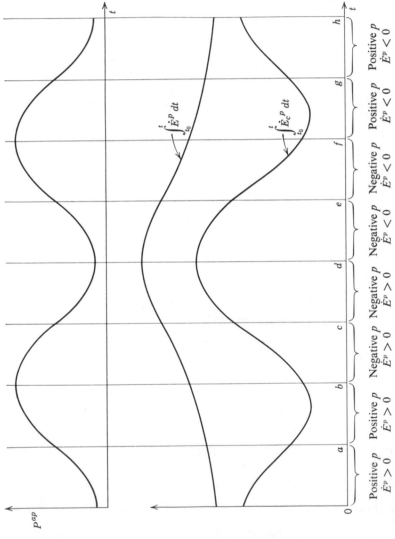

Figure 18-13 Relative shapes of the variations, with time, of P^{ap}, and of input and output, for system receding from equilibrium and then returning to it. Not to scale.

determines the rate of change of the gradient between S and $\mathcal{E}$. In particular,

$$\int_{t_0}^{t_2} \dot{E}^p \, dt - \int_{t_0}^{t_2} \dot{E}_c{}^p \, dt > \int_{t_0}^{t_1} \dot{E}^p \, dt - \int_{t_0}^{t_1} \dot{E}_c{}^p \, dt$$

will have as consequence a p-gradient at t_2 that is larger than the p-gradient present at t_1. Reversely,

$$\int_{t_0}^{t_2} \dot{E}^p \, dt - \int_{t_0}^{t_2} \dot{E}_c{}^p \, dt < \int_{t_0}^{t_1} \dot{E}^p \, dt - \int_{t_0}^{t_1} \dot{E}_c{}^p \, dt$$

results in a diminished p-gradient at t_2, by comparison with the p-gradient that was operative at t_1. This follows readily from definition 4-4b and part III of the G.G.L.

Looking now at Figure 18-13, we see that between instants 0 and b of the time abscisa we have

$$\int_{t_0}^{b} \dot{E}^p \, dt - \int_{t_0}^{b} \dot{E}_c{}^p \, dt \gg \int_{t_0}^{0} \dot{E}^p \, dt - \int_{t_0}^{0} \dot{E}_c{}^p \, dt.$$

By part III of the G.G.L. it then follows that $p(S, b) > p(S, 0)$. Because $p(\mathcal{E}, b) = p(\mathcal{E}, 0)$, the p-gradient from S to $\mathcal{E}$ at b will be significantly larger than the p-gradient that was present at 0.

Applying a translation to the measuring scale, we bring the process at instant b under part I of the G.G.L., and as corollary we may assert that the ratio of output rate to input rate will be positive in the neighborhood of b.

System S now satisfies condition β of definition 4-4b for a quasi-static subsystem of $\mathcal{U} = S \cup \mathcal{E}$, again to within a translation of measuring scale.

Part III of the G.G.L. is now applicable and asserts that the gradient will decrease. The curves of Figure 18-13 confirm the prediction, since

$$\int_{t_0}^{d} \dot{E}^p \, dt - \int_{t_0}^{d} \dot{E}_c{}^p \, dt \ll \int_{t_0}^{b} \dot{E}^p \, dt - \int_{t_0}^{b} \dot{E}_c{}^p \, dt.$$

We see that S will oscillate between condition α and condition β of a quasi-static system as characterized in definition 4-4b. For either of the two conditions, part III of the G.G.L. specifies the rate of change of $p(S)$. Because $p(\mathcal{E})$ remains unaltered, the rate of change of $p(S)$ will determine the rate of change of the p-gradient. This in turn will affect the ratio of output rate to input rate, which will then shift S from condition α to condition β, or vice versa, for a quasi-static system, and so on. Therefore

Theorem 18-12. If $p(\mathcal{E})$ remains a constant quantity, either a change in rate of input to S, and/or a change in rate of internal transfer within S, will produce temporal variations in the output rate from S.

Corollary 18-3.   If $p(\mathcal{S})$ is constant, and $\mathcal{S}$ recedes from equilibrium going through positive to negative p-values, and then returns to positive values of p, the output rate of $\mathcal{S}$ will have a local maximum in the neighborhood of the point of change from recession to return, and local minima near those instants at which $p(\mathcal{S})$ changes sign.

We must now pay closer attention to phenomena associated with the curve $\int_{t_0}^{t} \dot{E}^p \, dt$.

Because as $\mathcal{S}$ approaches the condition of point d in Figure 18-13 it is moving through negative p-values from $-\infty$ in the direction of $A_0{}_-{}^p$, it seems advisable to inquire whether or not the phenomena discovered in Chapter 16 in connection with the approach to $A_{0+}{}^p$ through positive p-values are extensible to the approach to $A_0{}_-{}^p$ through negative p-values. An examination of the theorems of Chapter 16 shows that in the demonstrations only three kinds of physical considerations enter:

1. The finiteness of inputs.
2. $\Delta P_{\mathrm{irr}}^{ap} > 0$.
3. The boundedness or unboundedness of the other quantities entering into the expressions (either as fixed quantities or as limits).

Property 1 is an assumption throughout our whole study.
Property 2 was extended to negative values of p in theorem 18-6.
Properties 3 are independent of the signs of the quantities involved.
In consequence:

Theorem 18-13.   Theorems 16-1 to 16-6 and corollaries 16-1 to 16-3 are extensible to systems operating at negative values of p and approaching $A_0{}_-{}^p$.

When referring to theorems 16-1 to 16-6, as extended to the domain of negative p-values and the neighborhood of $A_0{}_-{}^p$, we shall use the notation "theorems 16-1a to 16-6a." Observe that theorems 16-5a and 16-6a are compatible with the P^{ap} curve in Figure 18-13.

From theorem 16-4a or corollary 16-3 and the finiteness of inputs, *for the converter* $\mathcal{C}$ there follows

Theorem 18-14.   In a process consisting of a conversion and an out-transfer, if q is the conversion parameter and p the out-transfer parameter, then

$$\lim_{p \to A_0{}_-{}^p} \dot{E}^p = 0.$$

PROOF.   From theorem 16-4a it follows that $\lim_{p \to A_0{}_-{}^p} (\partial p / \partial \dot{E}^q) = 0$. The finiteness property of $\dot{E}^q$ then assures us that $\lim_{p \to A_0{}_-{}^p} \dot{p}(\mathcal{S}) = 0$. But it is the

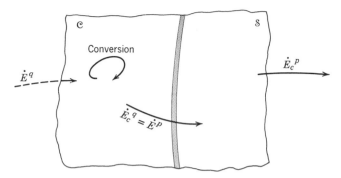

Figure 18-14 Converter output entering $\mathcal{S}$ as input to system that out-transfers energy to environment E.

p-gradient from $\mathcal{C}$ to $\mathcal{E}$ that produces the out-transfer from $\mathcal{C}$ (S.L., and G.G.L., part I). In consequence it follows that $\lim\limits_{p \to A_0-^p} \int_{t_0}^{t} \dot{E}^p \, dt = \text{constant}$ function of t, and thus $\lim\limits_{p \to A_0-^p} \dot{E}^p = 0$.

Theorem 18-14 is compatible with the curve for $\int_{t_0}^{t} \dot{E}^p \, dt$ in Figure 18-13, as the curve behaves near the point $t = d$.

Observe that the quantity $\dot{E}^p$, which all through this chapter has been considered input rate to $\mathcal{S}$, in theorem 18-14 is considered also as rate of output from the converter. The quantity $\dot{E}_c{}^p$ remains the output rate from $\mathcal{S}$.

Figure 18-14 illustrates the situation being considered.

In the figure the input $\dot{E}^q$ to $\mathcal{C}$ is shown dashed, rather than continuous, to suggest that it may well have been an input rate to $\mathcal{C}$ long before the process came under study. If $\mathcal{C}$ represents a star, for example, we may consider ΔE^q as having been totally introduced when the star was created. After that creation no more input enters the star (at least, in this model), but internal conversions and outputs take place as long as the star remains active.

Some of the phenomena studied in this chapter and associated with systems far from equilibrium bear resemblance to phenomena observed in quasars (see [43]), in particular, the variations in the energy output $\int_{t_0}^{t} \dot{E}_c{}^p \, dt$ of the system when contrasted with the variations in the converter output $\int_{t_0}^{t} \dot{E}^p \, dt$. Quantitative estimates of the magnification ratio of those two outputs have not yet been made; therefore we cannot at present relate the observed variations in the output of quasars to phenomena studied in this chapter.

The results established here apply to *any* intensive parameter p, as long as the process satisfies the hypotheses of the theory. Several interesting questions suggest themselves. Could the gradients of two such intensive parameters operate simultaneously and with such a kind of coupling that the maxima and minima of each $\int_{t_0}^{t} \dot{E}_c{}^p \, dt$ curve reinforce the maxima and minima of the other? Could there be resonance or beats? And, if pressure is one of the operating intensive parameters, could a physical picture be constructed for negative pressures? Could matter, under conditions of negative pressure, have a density greater than the densities of its constituent elements under positive pressure?

Appendix C

The Degree of Reaction Progress and the Chemical Affinity

It was shown in Chapter 14 that the fundamental physicochemical equation for systems undergoing reversible processes is of the form

$$E = E(P^{ap_1}, P^{ap_2}); \qquad dE = p_1\, dP^{ap_1} + p_2\, dP^{ap_2},$$

the case where the system and process being studied has more than two degrees of freedom having a fundamental equation with more terms (as many as degrees of freedom) but of exactly the same form.

It was further established in Chapter 14 that, for systems undergoing real (irreversible) processes,

$$dE = p_1\, dP^{ap_1} + p_2\, dP^{ap_2} - dE_{irr},$$

every term being independent of the path, and consequently

$$E = E(P^{ap_1}, P^{ap_2}, E_{irr}).$$

The term dE_{irr} was then decomposed into two factors (and thus expressed in the same form as the other terms of the fundamental physicochemical equation): one factor, R, being considered a measure of the degree of advance, progress, or evolution of the irreversible process under study; the other factor, A, being a measure of the effect that the degree of evolution of the process has upon the function E of the state of the system. Therefore, the fundamental physicochemical equation, in its general form for any number of degrees of freedom, is

$$dE = \sum_i p_i\, dP^{ap_i} - A\, dR.$$

It is evident that the parameter to use as a measure of the degree of evolution of the process (or, more exactly, of the system under the process

177

of interest) may differ from one kind of process to another. Furthermore, this parameter is not unique, for any other one that is a strictly monotonic function of the first one will do as well. In this appendix will be presented an example of a parameter suitable to measure the degree of evolution of processes of a chemical nature.

The degree of progress of a chemical reaction may be characterized, at any instant of the reaction, by specifying the number of moles,* or the mass, of each chemical species present and active in the reaction vessel. This, however, is a multiple-valued function: to each state or degree of evolution of the process, as many numbers correspond as there are chemical species participating (as reactants or as products) in the reaction. The following question now presents itself: is it possible to find a uniform (single-valued) function to characterize the degree of evolution of the process? Evidently, this uniform characterizing function must be intimately related to the multiform (multiple-valued) function that also characterizes the same phenomenon.

In more general terms the problem at hand is the following: given a process the degree of evolution (or advance) of which is characterized by a multiform function, is it possible to establish the same characterization by means of a uniform function? If the possibility exists, how is the realization to be carried out?

It is clear that the answer to the first query is negative if at least two of the branches of the multiform function are independent. If the answer is to be affirmative, there must be a *relation of constraint* binding together the various branches of the multiform function. Does such a relation of constraint exist when the process is a chemical reaction? Indeed yes, for such a binding relation between the amounts of the chemical species active in the reaction is established by the stoichiometric equation of the reaction:

$$\sum_{i=1}^{l} c_i Z_i = \sum_{i=1}^{u} c_i Z_i; \qquad -\sum_{i=1}^{l} c_i Z_i + \sum_{i=1}^{u} c_i Z_i = 0.$$

The set of numbers $\{c_i\}$ is the set of stoichiometric coefficients of the reaction; Z_i denotes the molecule of species i. In the second mode of expression, the stoichiometric coefficients of the reactants are taken to be

---

* A mole or gram-molecular weight of a substance is the molecular or formula weight of the substance expressed in grams; it is thus equal to the sum, in grams, of the atomic weights for all the atoms appearing in the molecular formula. For example, carbon dioxide has the molecular formula CO_2; since the atomic weights of carbon and oxygen are 12 and 16, respectively, the molecular formula weight, or gram mole, of carbon dioxide is 44 grams. Engineers also use the pound mole. It is more exact but less convenient to use the mass of each chemical substance, rather than the number of moles of it.

negative (because the amount of each reactant diminishes as the reaction proceeds), and those of the products as positive.

The possibility of characterizing the degree of progress of a chemical reaction by means of a uniform function having been established, it remains to derive the means of implementation for such a characterization.

From the chemical meaning of the stoichiometric equation of the reaction process, it follows that the stoichiometric coefficient of each chemical species is a number characterizing the *relative* rate of change of the number of moles of that chemical species as the reaction proceeds. Thus, in the reaction

$$O_2 + 2H_2 \to 2H_2O, \qquad -O_2 - 2H_2 + 2H_2O = 0$$

the coefficients mean that, for each mole of O_2 that is consumed in the process, two moles of H_2 must also react, and two moles of H_2O must be produced. If only a fraction λ of a mole of oxygen has been consumed, then 2λ is the quantity (in moles) of hydrogen that has also reacted. Hence, if the initial quantities of the chemical species of interest are known, a knowledge of the stoichiometric coefficients suffices to provide the data on the quantities of each chemical species that will be on hand after the reaction has proceeded to a degree measured by λ.

Denote by n_i^0 the initial quantity, in moles, of chemical species i, and by n_i the quantity of the same chemical species at a later instant of interest. Obviously, n_i is a function of time and hence of the degree of progress of the reaction. Then, from what has already been said,

$$n_i = n_i^0 + c_i\lambda.$$

In fact, at $t = t_0$ (initial instant, measuring the start of the reaction), $\lambda = 0$, and the equation reduces to $n_i = n_i^0$, as should be.

Let the reaction proceed and its degree of progress be measured by λ. Eventually one of the reactants will disappear; label this reactant with the index q. Then, at the precise instant at which reactant q has disappeared, the above equation, applied to reactant q, takes the form

$$n_q = n_q^0 + c_q\lambda = 0,$$

and thus

$$\lambda = -\frac{n_q^0}{c_q}$$

The reaction cannot proceed any further, and this value of λ is the maximal for this reaction under the conditions stipulated. This maximal value λ_m is evidently a function of the initial quantities (i.e., the initial conditions) of the system. Thus, if the reaction reaches completion "to the right" (i.e., one of the reactants, q, disappears), $\lambda_m = -(n_q^0/c_q)$, and if $|n_q^0| = |c_q|$, then $\lambda_m = 1$.

Observe that λ_m is always positive, for $n_q^0 \geq 0$ for any chemical species, and $c_i < 0$ for any reactant. Indeed, λ will always be positive when calculated on the basis of reactants, for then both $(n_i - n_i^0) < 0$ and $c_i < 0$, and $\lambda = (n_i - n_i^0)/c_i$.

If i stands for one of the products of the reaction, the following may be said. At $t = t_0$, $n_i = n_i^0 = 0$ and $\lambda = 0$. At completion of the reaction to the right, $n_i^0 = 0$ and $\lambda = n_i/c_i$. Thus, λ will always be positive when calculated on the basis of products, for $n_i > 0$ and $c_i > 0$ for products. Furthermore, if $|n_i^0| = |c_i|$ for at least one reactant, $\lambda_m = n_i/c_i = c_i/c_i = 1$, no matter which product index i represents.

Finally observe that, at any one instant t of time, the value of λ is independent of the product that is used to calculate it, because if, say, $c_j = kc_m$, then also $n_j = kn_m$, and $\lambda = n_j/c_j = n_m/c_m$. If λ is determined on the basis of reactants, however, it is independent of the reactant used in the calculation only if $n_i^0 = lc_i$, where l is the same constant for every i. In fact, $\lambda = (n_i/c_i) - (n_i^0/c_i)$ and again $c_j = kc_m$ implies $n_j = kn_m$; but λ will not be invariant under a change of reactant for the calculation unless the ratio n_i^0/c_i is invariant under a change of reactant i, and this means that there exists a constant l such that $n_i^0 = lc_i$ for all i.

The expression for n_i is linear in λ, and in it λ is a strictly monotone (linear) function of the mass of the product of the reaction, as well as being also a linear function of the mass that has been consumed of the reactant.

Therefore, the following definition seems to be an adequate mathematical representation of the degree of evolution of a chemical reaction as it is conceived by the physical chemist:

Definition C-1. The *degree of evolution or progress of a reaction* will be determined by the expression $\lambda = (n_i - n_i^0)/c_i$, where i stands for any one of the reactants or for any one of the products.

When the process consists in the dissociation of a single reactant, λ measures the *degree of dissociation*; if the process consists in the ionization of a single reactant, λ measures the *degree of ionization*.

The degree of evolution λ of the chemical reaction is an adequate measure of irreversibility R in processes which consist of chemical reactions.

Nota Bene. The preceding study and characterization of the degree of reaction progress has presupposed that the system, during the process in question, is a closed system (i.e., it has no mass transfer with the environment).

From the defining equation for λ it follows that

$$\frac{dn_i}{dt} = c_i \dot{\lambda} = c_i v$$

and

$$\frac{dm_i}{dt} = c_i M_i v,$$

where m_i, n_i, and M_i are, respectively, the mass, the number of moles, and the gram-molecular weight of the ith constituent of the chemical system. If V is the volume, the *molar concentration of constituent i* is n_i/V (a specific quantity!). Then the rate of change of the molar concentration is given by

$$\frac{d}{dt} C_i = \frac{d}{dt}\left(\frac{n_i}{V}\right) = \frac{c_i v}{V} - \frac{n_i}{V^2}\frac{dV}{dt} \; ;$$

at constant volume:

$$\frac{dC_i}{dt} = c_i \frac{v}{V}.$$

When the process is a chemical reaction and thus $R = \lambda$, the coefficient A of $d\lambda$ in the expression for dE is called the chemical affinity function. Naturally, the chemical affinity has all the properties of the general affinity function studied in Chapters 14 and 17.

Appendix D

Some Physicochemical Potentials

In Chapter 13 the physicochemical potentials were defined in terms of the Legendre transforms of the energy. It was there demonstrated that every Legendre transform of the energy is, like the energy function itself, a function of state. The necessary and sufficient conditions for unconstrained physicochemical equilibrium were given in Chapter 15 in terms of the Legendre transforms of the energy.

In this appendix will be presented, as examples of physicochemical potentials, those that have thus far shown themselves to be of greater usefulness in physical chemistry, and especially in chemical thermodynamics. In most problems of this latter science a complete set of characterizing parameters consists of a mechanical parameter, a thermal parameter, and the mass or mole number of each component or chemical species in the system (or of some of them, depending on whether or not binding relations exist between the components of the system).

Nomenclature. A *closed* system is one having no mass transfer with its environment; an *open* system has mass transfer with $\mathcal{E}$. The mass transfer considered may be that involved in a heat transfer by convection.

Examples of closed systems are batch processes in chemical industries; examples of open systems are continuous processes in chemical industries, a biological cell, or the human body.

In order to find the physicochemical meanings of the Legendre transforms to be derived from the energy, it is most expedient to consider them in the simplest form. Therefore we shall first derive their expressions for closed systems entering into processes that are sufficiently near to reversibility to permit this approximation, then we shall seek the physicochemical interpretation of these expressions, and finally we shall extend them to open systems and to processes that do not permit neglect of their irreversible character.

THE ENTHALPY FUNCTION

The enthalpy function (symbol: H) is the Legendre transform of E (or U, whenever K and L may be neglected) for the independent variables P and S. Thus, if the independent variables $\{V, S\}$ of U are transformed into $\{P = -(\partial U/\partial V), S\}$, applying the Legendre transformation to the internal energy U gives $H = L(U)_V = U - (\partial U/\partial V)V = U + PV$, and H becomes the potential of T and V with respect to S and P, respectively. That is,

$$T = \frac{\partial H}{\partial S} \quad \text{and} \quad V = \frac{\partial H}{\partial P}.$$

From the definition it follows that

$$H_2 - H_1 = (U_2 + P_2 V_2) - (U_1 + P_1 V_1) = (U_2 - U_1) + (P_2 V_2 - P_1 V_1).$$

If the system of concern is under constant pressure, $\Delta H = \Delta U + P\,\Delta V$. Introducing the first law (Appendix A) in this expression,

$$\Delta H = \Delta Q - \Delta W + P\,\Delta V.$$

In the particular case in which the only work transfer is work of expansion, $\Delta W = P\,\Delta V$, and thus $\Delta H = \Delta Q$. As a consequence of the foregoing:

Theorem D-1. The equality $\Delta H = \Delta Q$ holds in a system undergoing a process in which the work transfer is subjected to the condition

$$\Delta W = P_2 V_2 - P_1 V_1.$$

Corollary D-1. The equality $\Delta H = \Delta Q$ holds in a system undergoing an isobaric (constant-pressure) process whenever the only work transfer is work of expansion.

Observe that theorem D-1 is not restricted to closed systems; the corollary, however, is restricted to such systems, since by hypothesis the only work transfer allowed is work of expansion (or compression). Theorem D-1 is a particular case of another theorem having wider applicability:

Theorem D-2. The equality $\Delta_1{}^2 H = \Delta_1{}^2 Q$ holds in a system undergoing a process in which the work transfer is subjected to the condition

$$\int_{t_1}^{t_2} \frac{dW}{dt}\,dt = \int_{t_1}^{t_2} \frac{d}{dt}(PV)\,dt.$$

PROOF.   From

$$\Delta H = \int_{t_1}^{t_2} \frac{dH}{dt}\, dt = \int_{t_1}^{t_2} \frac{dU}{dt}\, dt + \int_{t_1}^{t_2} \frac{d}{dt}(PV)\, dt$$

and the F.L.

$$\int_{t_1}^{t_2} \frac{dU}{dt}\, dt = \int_{t_1}^{t_2} \dot{Q}\, dt - \int_{t_1}^{t_2} \dot{W}\, dt.$$

THE HELMHOLTZ FREE ENERGY

The Helmholtz free energy F is the Legendre transform of E corresponding to the change of variables

$$\{V, S\} \rightarrow \left\{ V, T = \frac{\partial E}{\partial S} \right\}.$$

Such a transformation brings E to correspond to $E - TS = F$. The function F is thus the potential of S and P with respect to T and V, respectively:

$$S = -\frac{\partial F}{\partial T}, \qquad P = -\frac{\partial F}{\partial V}.$$

When K and L are negligible, $F = U - TS$.

Introducing the F.L. into the definition of F,

$$\frac{dF}{dt} = \frac{dU}{dt} - \frac{d}{dt}(TS) = \frac{dQ}{dt} - \frac{dW}{dt} - \frac{d}{dt}(TS)$$

$$= \frac{dQ}{dt} - \frac{dW}{dt} - T\frac{dS}{dt} - S\frac{dT}{dt}.$$

But

$$\frac{dS}{dt} = \frac{dS_{\text{rev}}}{dt} + \frac{dS_{\text{irr}}}{dt} = \frac{1}{T}\dot{Q} + \dot{S}_{\text{irr}}.$$

The quantity $\dot{S}_{\text{irr}}$ is the particular case of the quantity $\dot{P}_{\text{irr}}^{\text{ap}}$ (end of Chapter 5) that is of interest in the present context. Substituting the relation $T\dot{S} = \dot{Q} + T\dot{S}_{\text{irr}}$ into the preceding relation,

$$\frac{dF}{dt} = -\frac{dW}{dt} - S\frac{dT}{dt} - T\frac{dS_{\text{irr}}}{dt}.$$

It is thus seen that

Theorem D-3.   In a process for which $\int_{t_1}^{t_2} S\dot{T}\, dt = 0$,

$$\Delta W = -(F_2 - F_1) - \int_{t_1}^{t_2} T\dot{S}_{\text{irr}}\, dt;$$

the theoretically maximum work thus is attainable with a reversible path, and it is then equal to the decrease in the Helmholtz free energy during the process.

PROOF.   It suffices to note that $\dot{S}_{irr} \nless 0$.

Theorem D-3 justifies the name of *work function* or *maximum work function* that is very often given to the function F.

Why would the function F be called free energy? This name implies a decomposition of the energy of a system into a "free" part and an "unfree" part. "Free" would seem to imply "available to do other things," like being converted into useful work.

From the very definition $F = E - TS$ follows

$$\frac{dE}{dt} = \frac{dF}{dt} + \frac{d}{dt}(TS).$$

From Chapters 6 and 10 it follows that the entropy S may be interpreted as a coefficient of unavailability, and it has been shown above that dF/dt provides a measure of the maximum attainable work (for reversible processes). The preceding equality could thus be considered to decompose the rate of energy transfer into two terms: a "free" and an "unfree" term.

There is, however, a delicate point to reconsider in the reasoning of the preceding paragraph: while it is true that an entropy increase represents an increment in the coefficient of potential unavailability, the fact should be remembered that, except for purely (100%) irreversible processes (with regard to these, see theorem 11-2), the process that brought about the entropy increase has also changed the $\dot{E}_c^T = \dot{Q}_c$ [refer to equation (5-3) and theorem 5-2] of the availability equation

$$\dot{Q} = \dot{Q}_c + \dot{S}T_0 = \dot{Q}_c + \left[\frac{\dot{Q}}{T} + \dot{S}_{irr}\right]T_0.$$

Thus, except for the process in which $\dot{S} = \dot{S}_{irr}$, a positive $\dot{S}$ must be accompanied by $\dot{Q} > 0$, since $T \nless A_0^T$. But $\Delta Q > 0$ (heat in-transfer) is partially converted into useful work; in fact, since ΔS is a function of couples of states, to larger ΔQ between *the same* states corresponds also larger ΔQ_c. It is thus seen that a process which brings about $(d/dt)(TS) > 0$ will also (unless it is a *purely* irreversible process) bring about $dF/dt > 0$, since

$$\frac{dF}{dt} = \frac{dQ}{dt} - \frac{dW}{dt} - \frac{d}{dt}(TS).$$

This shows that the decomposition $\dot{E} = \dot{F} + (d/dt)(TS)$ is a decomposition into terms that *are not independent*.

Another useful interpretation of F is obtained in the study of equilibrium, thus:

Theorem D-4. A system at constant V and T will spontaneously move towards lower values of F; at equilibrium and under the same conditions, the function F is a minimum.

PROOF. This theorem is but a corollary of theorem 15-1, but an independent demonstration and discussion may be enlightening.

In an arbitrary *real* transformation,

$$\Delta S > \frac{\Delta E + P\,\Delta V}{T} = \Delta S_{rev},$$

or

$$\Delta E + P\,\Delta V - T\,\Delta S < 0.$$

Imposing the conditions of the theorem, $V =$ constant and $T =$ constant, we reduce the above relation to

$$\Delta(E - TS) = \Delta F < 0.$$

Therefore, in an actual process at constant V and T, the system will spontaneously transform towards a state of lower Helmholtz free energy. At equilibrium the system has no further tendency for spontaneous change, and therefore F must have reached a minimum.

Observe that the equilibrium state at constant V and T does not necessarily correspond to a state of minimal E. It has been shown that S increases in any spontaneous process within an *isolated* system, and that it reaches a maximum at the equilibrium state (see theorems 12-2 and 12-7). Now, in transforming from one state to another it is possible that both S and E increase in such a way that $T\,\Delta S > \Delta E$. In such situations the equilibrium state may correspond to a non-minimal value of E. This does not contradict the criterion for equilibrium established in theorem 12-5, for there it was proved that the equilibrium state corresponds to minimal E when $S = P^{aT}$ is constant. When both E and S change during a process, neither the criterion for equilibrium given by theorem 12-2 nor that given by theorem 12-5 is applicable for studying the equilibrium conditions for the process; functions other than E and S are thus needed to characterize equilibrium. The Helmholtz function F does precisely such a job for processes in which both V and T are constant, but in which S and E may not be constant. However, the equilibrium criterion in terms of the Helmholtz function is only a very particular case of theorem 15-1; the power of that theorem may thus be estimated.

THE GIBBS FREE ENERGY FUNCTION

The Gibbs free energy function G is the Legendre transform of the energy function E corresponding to the change of variables

$$\{V, S\} \rightarrow \left\{ P = -\frac{\partial E}{\partial V}, T = \frac{\partial E}{\partial S} \right\}.$$

The transformation brings E into $G = E + PV - TS = H - TS = F + PV$. The function G is thus the potential of S and V with respect to T and P, respectively:

$$S = -\frac{\partial G}{\partial T}; \qquad V = \frac{\partial G}{\partial P}.$$

If K and L are negligible, $G = U + PV - TS$.

From the definition,

$$\frac{dG}{dt} = \frac{dE}{dt} - \frac{d}{dt}(PV) - \frac{d}{dt}(TS).$$

Introducing the first law into this equation,

$$\frac{dG}{dt} = \frac{dQ}{dt} - \frac{dW}{dt} + \frac{d}{dt}(PV) - \frac{d}{dt}(TS).$$

But

$$\frac{dS}{dt} = \frac{dS_t}{dt} + \frac{dS_l}{dt} = \frac{1}{T}\frac{dQ}{dt} + \frac{dS_l}{dt},$$

where, as in Chapter 5, $\Delta S_t = \Delta S_{\text{rev}}$ and $\Delta S_l = \Delta S_{\text{irr}}$. Substitution yields

$$\frac{dG}{dt} = -\frac{dW}{dt} + \frac{d}{dt}(PV) - S\frac{dT}{dt} - T\frac{dS_l}{dt}.$$

If we denote by ΔW^P the work transfer due to pressure, and by $\Delta W^{\bar{P}}$ the work transfer not due to pressure, so that

$$\Delta W = \Delta W^P + \Delta W^{\bar{P}} = \Delta(PV) + \Delta W^{\bar{P}},$$

we can state

Theorem D-5.   In a process satisfying the condition

$$\int_{t_1}^{t_2} S\frac{dT}{dt} = 0,$$

the (theoretical) maximal $\Delta W^{\bar{P}}$ is attainable in a reversible path, and is then equal to the decrease of G in the system.

PROOF.   Immediate consequence of the preceding expression for dG/dt.

Because

$$\frac{dW^{\bar{P}}}{dt} = \frac{dW}{dt} - \frac{dW^P}{dt},$$

it is possible for a system to undergo a process in which $|\Delta G| < |\Delta F|$; that is, $G_2 - G_1 < F_2 - F_1$. This is also an immediate consequence of the relation $G = F + PV$.

In *laboratory* physical chemistry (but not, on the contrary, in astrophysics or meteorology) most processes are carried out under conditions of constant pressure and temperature. Then $S\dot{T} = 0$ and $\Delta W^P = P \Delta V$. Therefore, the Gibbs function G is of great usefulness in the physical chemistry of laboratory experimentation, especially in matters of phase and reaction equilibria.

Further insights into the interpretational possibilities of G can be found in the study of open-system processes, equilibria, etc.

Table D-1 of physicochemical potentials, which with minor modifications can be found in several textbooks, is included here for reference purposes. The expressions in the second of the four columns are complete only for closed systems undergoing idealized (reversible) transformations, without change in composition during the process; the system under these conditions therefore has only two degrees of freedom, and two characterizing parameters (independent variables) suffice for its characterization: one thermal and the other mechanical. The last column expresses the fact that dU, dH, dF, and dG are perfect differentials, which means that these four quantities are independent of the path or process between states, that is, U, H, F, and G are functions of state.

It should be observed that knowledge of any one of the physicochemical potentials in terms of its proper independent variables suffices to enable us to express the other physicochemical potentials in terms of the first one and of its own proper independent variables.

Thus, for example, assume that what is known is H in terms of S and P. Then

$$T = \frac{\partial H}{\partial S}, \qquad V = \frac{\partial H}{\partial P};$$

$$G = H - TS = H - S\frac{\partial H}{\partial S};$$

$$F = G - PV = H - TS - PV = H - S\frac{\partial H}{\partial S} - P\frac{\partial H}{\partial P};$$

$$U = H - PV = H - P\frac{\partial H}{\partial P}.$$

Table D-1 Physicochemical Potentials
(reversible processes with no change in composition; closed systems)

Potential	Independent Variables	Conjugate Variables	Relations
Internal energy	V, S	$T = \dfrac{\partial U}{\partial S}$	$\dfrac{\partial T}{\partial V} = -\dfrac{\partial P}{\partial S}$
$dU = T\,dS - P\,dV$		$P = -\dfrac{\partial U}{\partial V}$	$= \dfrac{\partial^2 U}{\partial V \, \partial S}.$
Enthalpy (heat content)	P, S	$T = \dfrac{\partial H}{\partial S}$	$\dfrac{\partial T}{\partial P} = \dfrac{\partial V}{\partial S}$
$H = U + PV$ $\quad dH = T\,dS + V\,dP$		$V = \dfrac{\partial H}{\partial P}$	$= \dfrac{\partial^2 H}{\partial P \, \partial S}$
Helmholtz function Maximum work function Helmholtz potential work function	V, T	$S = -\dfrac{\partial F}{\partial T}$	$\dfrac{\partial S}{\partial V} = \dfrac{\partial P}{\partial T}$
$F = U - TS$ $\quad dF = -P\,dV - S\,dT$		$P = -\dfrac{\partial F}{\partial V}$	$= -\dfrac{\partial^2 F}{\partial V \, dT}$
Gibbs function Gibbs potential Thermodynamic potential	P, T	$S = -\dfrac{\partial G}{\partial T}$	$\dfrac{\partial S}{\partial P} = -\dfrac{\partial V}{\partial T}$
$G = H - TS$ $\quad = F + PV$ $\quad dG = -S\,dT + V\,dP$		$V = \dfrac{\partial G}{\partial P}$	$= \dfrac{\partial^2 G}{\partial P \, \partial T}$

From the expression for the derivative of a quotient with respect to its denominator,

$$\frac{\partial(y/x)}{\partial x} = \frac{x(\partial y/\partial x) - y}{x^2},$$

an analogy is observed with the expression $H = G + TS = G - T(\partial G/\partial T)$ by placing $G = y$ and $T = x$. In fact,

$$\frac{\partial(G/T)}{\partial T} = -\frac{H}{T^2}.$$

Similarly we obtain

$$\frac{\partial (F/T)}{\partial T} = -\frac{E}{T^2}$$

and other analogous expressions.

The purpose at hand now is to expand the table of physicochemical potentials by relaxing the restrictions imposed thus far: system closed, no change in composition, reversibility of processes.

EXTENSION TO REAL PROCESSES

The first extension will be to systems that, remaining closed, are the seat of irreversible (real) processes and transformations. This extension demands the addition of as many degrees of freedom to the fundamental physicochemical equation as parameters are required to characterize the irreversibility of the process being considered. Our interest at present being in chemical processes, it has been seen that, in general, the addition of a single parameter—the degree of evolution of the reaction—suffices to characterize the irreversibility of interest (see Chapters 14 and 17 and Appendix C).

Therefore, starting with the extended fundamental physicochemical equation $E = E(P^{ap_1}, P^{ap_2}, \lambda)$, we may apply the Legendre transformation to various sets of independent variables and obtain the expressions for the corresponding potentials. These are:

$$
\begin{aligned}
U &= U(S, V, \lambda); & dU &= T\,dS - P\,dV - A\,d\lambda; \\
H &= H(S, P, \lambda); & dH &= T\,dS + V\,dP - A\,d\lambda; \\
F &= F(T, V, \lambda); & dF &= -S\,dT - P\,dV - A\,d\lambda; \\
G &= G(T, P, \lambda); & dG &= -S\,dT + V\,dP - A\,d\lambda.
\end{aligned}
$$

Because U, H, F, and G are functions of state,

$$dU = \frac{\partial U}{\partial S}\,dS + \frac{\partial U}{\partial V}\,dV + \frac{\partial U}{\partial \lambda}\,d\lambda;$$

$$dH = \frac{\partial H}{\partial S}\,dS + \frac{\partial H}{\partial P}\,dP + \frac{\partial H}{\partial \lambda}\,d\lambda;$$

$$dF = \frac{\partial F}{\partial T}\,dT + \frac{\partial F}{\partial V}\,dV + \frac{\partial F}{\partial \lambda}\,d\lambda;$$

$$dG = \frac{\partial G}{\partial T}\,dT + \frac{\partial G}{\partial P}\,dP + \frac{\partial G}{\partial \lambda}\,d\lambda.$$

Comparing the coefficients of the last four equations with those of the preceding four, we obtain Table D-2 of relations.

Note in particular the four expressions for the chemical affinity A in terms of the physicochemical potentials. Because the degree of progress of the process, R, is in this case given by the degree of (chemical) reaction progress, λ, the affinity function A may be called the chemical affinity in the cases under consideration.

Table D-2 Partial Derivatives of the Physicochemical Potentials
(irreversible processes; closed system)

$\dfrac{\partial U}{\partial S} = T$	$\dfrac{\partial H}{\partial S} = T$	$\dfrac{\partial F}{\partial T} = -S$	$\dfrac{\partial G}{\partial T} = -S$
$\dfrac{\partial U}{\partial V} = -P$	$\dfrac{\partial H}{\partial P} = V$	$\dfrac{\partial F}{\partial V} = -P$	$\dfrac{\partial G}{\partial P} = V$
$\dfrac{\partial U}{\partial \lambda} = -A$	$\dfrac{\partial H}{\partial \lambda} = -A$	$\dfrac{\partial F}{\partial \lambda} = -A$	$\dfrac{\partial G}{\partial \lambda} = -A$

Notice also that a thermal intensive parameter is obtainable, to within a plus or minus sign, as the partial derivative of either one of two physicochemical potentials with respect to a thermal extensive parameter, and vice versa. An analogous statement applies to the mechanical parameters (intensive and extensive). The reader should remember, however, that the theory of physicochemical potentials and the fundamental physicochemical equation were developed in Chapters 13 and 14 under the convention stated in Chapter 13—that is, the intensive parameters can be considered to have constant values throughout the systems under investigation. This agreement does not do away with the distinction between intensive and extensive parameters (definitions 4-2 and 4-3), but it does place them on an equal basis for purposes of mathematical manipulation, since the convention referred to above implies that *no internal* transfers are to be considered (because of the necessity condition imposed by the S.L.). Observe also that here we are studying chemical conversions, and for the moment disregarding the transfers that may be associated with them.

From Table D-2 of partial derivatives of the physicochemical potentials it is possible to obtain relations between the partial derivatives of the parameters. For example, from the table we read that

$$\frac{\partial F}{\partial V} = -P \quad \text{and} \quad \frac{\partial F}{\partial T} = -S.$$

If the required continuity properties are satisfied or sufficiently approximated (see, for example, [8], pp. 265–267; [16], pp. 165–172; [17], pp. 146–151),

$$\frac{\partial^2 F}{\partial T \partial V} = \frac{\partial^2 F}{\partial V \partial T}.$$

But

$$\frac{\partial^2 F}{\partial T \partial V} = \frac{\partial}{\partial T}\left(\frac{\partial F}{\partial V}\right) = \frac{\partial}{\partial T}(-P),$$

while

$$\frac{\partial^2 F}{\partial V \partial T} = \frac{\partial}{\partial V}\left(\frac{\partial F}{\partial T}\right) = \frac{\partial}{\partial V}(-S) = -\frac{\partial S}{\partial V}.$$

Consequently:

$$\frac{\partial S}{\partial V} = \frac{\partial P}{\partial T}.$$

In deriving relations like the last one, it is advisable to carry along in symbols the parameters that are being kept constant, for occasionally the same relation can follow from different sets of constant parameters.

Table D-3 Partial Derivatives of Characterizing Parameters
(irreversible processes; closed systems)

$$\left(\frac{\partial T}{\partial V}\right)_{S\lambda} = -\left(\frac{\partial P}{\partial S}\right)_{V\lambda} \quad \left(\frac{\partial T}{\partial P}\right)_{S\lambda} = \left(\frac{\partial V}{\partial S}\right)_{P\lambda} \quad \left(\frac{\partial S}{\partial V}\right)_{T\lambda} = \left(\frac{\partial P}{\partial T}\right)_{V\lambda} \quad \left(\frac{\partial S}{\partial P}\right)_{T\lambda} = -\left(\frac{\partial V}{\partial T}\right)_{P\lambda}$$

$$\left(\frac{\partial T}{\partial \lambda}\right)_{SV} = -\left(\frac{\partial A}{\partial S}\right)_{V\lambda} \quad \left(\frac{\partial T}{\partial \lambda}\right)_{SP} = -\left(\frac{\partial A}{\partial S}\right)_{P\lambda} \quad \left(\frac{\partial S}{\partial \lambda}\right)_{TV} = \left(\frac{\partial A}{\partial T}\right)_{V\lambda} \quad \left(\frac{\partial S}{\partial \lambda}\right)_{TP} = \left(\frac{\partial A}{\partial T}\right)_{P\lambda}$$

$$\left(\frac{\partial P}{\partial \lambda}\right)_{SV} = \left(\frac{\partial A}{\partial V}\right)_{S\lambda} \quad \left(\frac{\partial V}{\partial \lambda}\right)_{SP} = -\left(\frac{\partial A}{\partial P}\right)_{S\lambda} \quad \left(\frac{\partial P}{\partial \lambda}\right)_{TV} = \left(\frac{\partial A}{\partial V}\right)_{T\lambda} \quad \left(\frac{\partial V}{\partial \lambda}\right)_{TP} = -\left(\frac{\partial A}{\partial P}\right)_{T\lambda}$$

Table D-3 is available for reference purposes. The variables P and V are often said to be *conjugates* of each other (see Appendix B and Chapter 13); likewise T is called the conjugate of S and vice versa, and A and λ are said to be conjugate chemical parameters. With that terminology, Table D-3 obeys the following law: the partial derivative of a thermal parameter with respect to a mechanical parameter equals, to within a sign factor, the partial derivative of the conjugate mechanical parameter with respect to the conjugate thermal parameter. Likewise, the partial derivative of a thermal parameter with respect to a chemical parameter is equal to the partial derivative of the conjugate chemical parameter with respect to the conjugate thermal parameter, to within a sign.

EXTENSION TO OPEN SYSTEMS

It remains to effect the second extension desired on Table D-1 of physicochemical potentials, by removing the restriction that the system be closed.

This extension, like the preceding one, requires the addition of some degree of freedom to the system, to care for the characterization of the more complex phenomena being considered. However, whereas in the preceding extension only one additional characterizing parameter sufficed (λ, to characterize the degree of evolution of the chemical reaction), in the present extension as many additional degrees of freedom will be needed as there are chemical species or constituents in the system, because there may be mass transfer of any one of the constituents in the input and/or output of the system (besides the change in the amounts of the constituents that may result from chemical reactions within the system).

The changes in the amounts of constituents resulting from the chemical reaction are interrelated by the stoichiometric equation of the reaction. The changes in the amounts of constituents resulting from mass transfers are independent of each other. For the characterization we shall use the mole numbers of the constituents, rather than their masses.

The fundamental physicochemical equation becomes, for open systems of concern in chemical thermodynamics, $U = U(S, V, n_1, n_2, \ldots, n_m)$.

Because U is a function of state, we also have

$$dU = \frac{\partial U}{\partial S}\, dS + \frac{\partial U}{\partial V}\, dV + \sum_{i=1}^{m} \frac{\partial U}{\partial n_i}\, dn_i.$$

It has been seen that $\partial U/\partial S = T$ and $\partial U/\partial V = -P$; therefore

$$dU = T\, dS - P\, dV + \sum_{i=1}^{m} \frac{\partial U}{\partial n_i}\, dn_i;$$

this is the fundamental physicochemical equation for open chemical systems.

Nomenclature. The quantity $\partial U/\partial n_i$ is called the *chemical potential of constituent i in the system* and is denoted by μ_i.

It is easy to see that, in situations in which kinetic and potential energy transfers cannot be neglected, $\mu_i = \partial E/\partial n_i$.

From the fundamental physicochemical equation for open systems we obtain

$$U = TS - PV + \sum_{i=1}^{m} \mu_i n_i,$$

and from the two expressions above and theorem 13-2 the following may be deduced:

$$\frac{\partial E}{\partial n_i} = \frac{\partial U}{\partial n_i} = \frac{\partial H}{\partial n_i} = \frac{\partial F}{\partial n_i} = \frac{\partial G}{\partial n_i} = \mu_i;$$

$$H = U + PV = TS + \sum_{i=1}^{m} \mu_i n_i;$$

$$F = U - TS = -PV + \sum_{i=1}^{m} \mu_i n_i;$$

$$G = U - TS + PV = \sum_{i=1}^{m} \mu_i n_i;$$

$$dU = T\,dS - P\,dV + \sum_{i=1}^{m} \mu_i\,dn_i;$$

$$dH = T\,dS + V\,dP + \sum_{i=1}^{m} \mu_i\,dn_i;$$

$$dF = -S\,dT - P\,dV + \sum_{i=1}^{m} \mu_i\,dn_i;$$

$$dG = -S\,dT + V\,dP + \sum_{i=1}^{m} \mu_i\,dn_i.$$

Finally, using the equation $n_i = n_i^0 + c_i\lambda$, we can express the relations existing between the chemical affinity and the chemical potentials; in fact,

$$A = -\frac{\partial E}{\partial \lambda} = -\sum_i \frac{\partial E}{\partial n_i}\frac{dn_i}{d\lambda} = -\sum_i c_i\mu_i,$$

and

$$\mu_i = \frac{\partial E}{\partial n_i} = \frac{dE}{d\lambda}\frac{\partial \lambda}{\partial n_i} = -\frac{A}{c_i}.$$

Observe that the chemical potentials are defined in such a way that they are applicable to any process in any open system, whereas the concept of chemical affinity is applicable only to processes which are of the nature of a chemical reaction—this is so because the chemical affinity is the coefficient of $d\lambda$ (where λ measures the degree of reaction progress) in the fundamental physicochemical equation. But it must be remembered that λ is only a particular case of R, the degree of progress of the irreversible process; for processes which are not of the nature of a chemical reaction, and for which in consequence the parameter λ is not suited, another and adequate parameter R must be employed. To be suitable, however, any parameter R must satisfy condition (14-6): R must be an extensive quantity such that $dE_{\text{irr}} = A\,dR$.

References

1. E. M. Patterson, *Topology*, Oliver and Boyd, Edinburgh and London, 1956.
2. Federico Grabiel, "Concerning the First Law of Energy Transfers and Conversions," *Mathematicae Notae*, XVIII, Vol. I (de Homenaje a Beppo Levi) pp. 217–231, 1962.
3. Federico Grabiel, "Geometría Diferencial Global en las Mediciones Físicas," *Revista de la Unión Matemática Argentina y de la Asociación Física Argentina*, Vol. XVII (de Homenaje a Beppo Levi) pp. 69–71, 1955.
4. N. Gunter, *Sur les Intégrales de Stieltjes et leurs applications aux problèms de la physique mathématique*, Chelsea Publishing Company, New York, 1949.
5. Federico Grabiel, "Set Functions and Tensors," *Tensor* (New Series), Vol. 10, No. 1, pp. 1–20, January 1960.
6. Federico Grabiel, "Algebra of Set Tensors," *Tensor* (New Series), Vol. 14, pp. 53–59, 1964.
7. Maurice A. Biot, *Mechanics of Incremental Deformations*, John Wiley and Sons, New York, 1965.
8. James Pierpont, *Lectures on the Theory of Functions of Real Variables*, Vol. I, Ginn and Company, Boston, 1905; also in Dover reprint.
9. Ulisse Dini, *Grundlagen für eine Theorie der Functionen einer veränderlichen reellen Grösse*, Druck and Verlag von B. G. Teubner, Leipzig, 1892; also the original (Italian) edition.
10. Paul Dubreil, *Algèbre*. Tome I: *Équivalences, Opérations, Groupes, Anneaux, Corps*, Gauthier-Villars et Cie, Paris, 1946.
11. Nathan Jacobson, *Lectures in Abstract Algebra*. Vol. I: *Basic Concepts*, Van Nostrand Company, Princeton, N.J., 1951.
12. Constantin Caratheódory, "Untersuchungen über die Grundlagen der Thermodynamik," *Mathematische Annalen* Vol. 67, pp. 355–386, 1909 (*Gesammelte Mathematische Schriften*, Band II, pp. 131–167, C. H. Beck, München).
13. Wilhelm Maak, *Differential und Integralrechnung*, Vandenhoeck und Ruprecht, Göttingen; 1960; English edition published in 1963 by Holt, Rinehart and Winston, New York, and entitled "An Introduction to Modern Calculus."
14. Mauro Picone and Gaetano Fichera, *Trattato di Analisi Matematica*, Vol. II, Tumminelli Editore (Città Universitaria), Rome, 1955.
15. R. Creighton Buck, *Advanced Calculus*, McGraw-Hill Book Company, New York, 1956.

16. Ulisse Dini, *Lezioni di Analisi Infinitesimale*. Vol. I: *Calcolo Differenziale*, Stab. Tipografico Succ. FF. Nistri, Pisa, 1907.
17. Otto Stolz, *Grundzüge der Differential- und Integralrechnung*. Erster Theil: *Reele Veränderliche und Functionen*, Druck und Verlag von B. G. Teubner, Leipzig, 1893.
18. R. H. Fowler and E. A. Guggenheim, *Statistical Thermodynamics*, Cambridge University Press, Cambridge, 1949.
19. W. Nernst, *The New Heat Theorem*, E. P. Dutton and Company, New York, 1926.
20. Walter Nernst, *Theoretical Chemistry*, Macmillan and Company, London, 1923.
21. J. G. Kirkwood and I. Oppenheim, *Chemical Thermodynamics*, McGraw-Hill Book Company, New York, 1961.
22. Georg Helm, *Die Energetik, nach ihrer geschichtlichen Entwicklung*, Verlag von Veit, Leipzig, 1898.
23. Max Planck, *Das Prinzip der Erhaltung der Energie*, Vierte Auflage, Verlag von B. G. Teubner, Leipzig und Berlin 1921, first part.
24. Paul Epstein, *Textbook of Thermodynamics*, John Wiley and Sons, New York, pp. 27–34, 1937.
25. C. Caratheódory, *Vorlesungen über reele Funktionen*, Zweite Auflage, B. G. Teubner, Leipzig, 1927, p. 475.
26. A. Duschek and A. Hochrainer, *Tensorrechnung in analytischer Darstellung*. II: *Tensoranalysis*, Zweite Auflage, Springer-Verlag, Vienna, 1961.
27. P. Dienes, *The Taylor Series-An Introduction to the Theory of Functions of a Complex Variable*, Oxford University Press, Oxford, 1931; corrected edition by Dover Publications, New York, 1957.
28. Nathaniel Coburn, *Vector and Tensor Analysis*, The Macmillan Company, New York, 1960.
29. M. J. Klein, "The Laws of Thermodynamics," pp. 1–23, of "Thermodinamica dei processi irreversibili," *Rendiconti della Scuola Internazionale di Fisica "Enrico Fermi,"* Corso X, Nicola Zanichelli-Editore, Bologna, 1960.
30. E. W. Hobson, *The Theory of Functions of a Real Variable and the Theory of Fourier's Series*, Vol. 1, Third Edition, Cambridge University Press, Cambridge 1927; reprinted by Dover Publications, New York, 1957.
31. Sophus Lie, *Geometrie der Berührungs transformationen*, dargestellt von Sophus Lie und Georg Scheffers, Druck und Verlag von B. G. Teubner, Leipzig, 1896.
32. Charles Cailler, *Introduction Géométrique a la Mécanique Rationnelle*, ouvrage publié par H. Fehr et R. Wavre, 1924; Gauthier-Villars et Cie, Paris, and Georg et Cie, Geneva.
33. Max Born, *The Mechanics of the Atom*, G. Bell and Sons, London, 1960; Frederick Ungar Publishing Company, New York.
34. Th. de Donder, *L'Affinité*, redaction nouvelle par Pierre Van Rysselberghe, Gauthier-Villars et Cie, Paris, 1963.
35. Kortüm, Gustav, *Einführung in die chemische Thermodynamik*, Dritte Auflage, Vandenhoeck und Ruprecht, Gottingen, 1960.
36. W. C. Graustein, *Introduction to Higher Geometry*, The Macmillan Company, New York, 1937.
37. Ott-Henrich Keller, *Analytische Geometrie und Lineare Algebra*, VEB Deutscher Verlag der Wissenschaften, Berlin, 1963.
38. Federico Grabiel, "On the Definition of Primitive Concepts in Physics," (to be published).
39. Georg Hamel, *Theoretische Mechanik*, Springer-Verlag, Berlin, 1949.
40. E. M. Purcell and R. V. Pound, "A Nuclear Spin System at Negative Temperature," *Physical Review*, Vol. 81, pp. 279–280, 1951.

41. N. F. Ramsey, "Thermodynamics and Statistical Mechanics at Negative Absolute Temperatures," *Physical Review*. Vol. 103, pp. 20–28, 1956.
42. Hans-Georg Schöpf, "Zur Thermodynamik negativer Temperaturen," *Annalen der Physik*, 7 Folge, Bd. 9, pp. 107–123, 1962.
43. Jesse L. Greenstein and Maarten Schmidt, "The Quasi-stellar Radio Sources 3C48 and 3C273," *Astrophysical Journal*, Vol. 140, pp. 1–34, 1964.
44. E. Perucca, *Fisica Generale e Sperimentale*. Vol. II: *Meccanica-Calore*. Sesta Edizione, Unione Tipografica-Editrice Torinese, Torino, 1949.
45. D. B. Spalding, *Convective Mass Transfer*, McGraw-Hill Book Company, New York 1963.
46. E. R. G. Eckert and R. M. Drake, *Heat and Mass Transfer*, McGraw-Hill Book Company, New York, 1959.
47. A. V. Lykov and Yu. A. Mikhailov, *Theory of Energy and Mass Transfer*, Pergamon Press, Oxford, 1965.
48. M. Fishenden and O. A. Saunders, *An Introduction to Heat Transfer*, Clarendon Press, Oxford, 1950.
49. Federico Grabiel, "Ordered Operations in Linearly Ordered Systems," *Bollettino della Unione Matematica Italiana*. Serie III, Anno XXI, N.1 (March 1967), pp. 1–20.

Some Notations and a Few Abbreviations

iff	If and only if.
$\dot{x}$	$(d/dt)x$.
$\mathcal{S}$	System.
$\mathcal{E}$	Environment.
$x \in X$	Element x belongs to set X.
$S \times S_2$	Cartesian product of sets S_1 and S_2.
$\cup$	Union (set-theoretic).
$\mathcal{U}$	Universe. Usually $\mathcal{U} = \mathcal{S} \cup \mathcal{E}$, but in some cases $\mathcal{U}$ stands for the universe of all systems having a certain property.
$\mathcal{P}$	Process.
$\mathcal{B}$	Boundary of $\mathcal{S}$.
E	Energy.
$\mathcal{C}$	Converter. (In Appendix A only, $\mathcal{C}$ stands for the set of all equivalence classes of coterminal processes.)
F.L.	First law of energy transfers and conversions (law of conservation of energy).
S.L.	Second law of energy transfers.
G.G.L.	General gradient law.
ΔE	Finite increment of energy.
q	Conversion parameter.
p	Intensive parameter of the transfer. (When no distinction needs to be made between conversions and transfers, p is used to symbolize the parameter of either a transfer or a conversion.)

p_0	Lowest available value of p for the process under study.
s	Gradient parameter (see Chapter 5).
$A_0{}^p$	Absolute zero value of p in the whole universe $\mathcal{U}$.
ΔE^{pi}	Input energy transfer, in-transfer.
ΔE^{po}	Output energy transfer, out-transfer.
$\Delta E^{p_k o}$	System output p_k.
$\Delta E^{p_i c}$	Conversion product p_i.
ΔE^{pci}	Input to converter.
ΔE^{pco}	Conversion output (conversion product leaving $\mathcal{C}$).
ΔE^{pcr}	Retained conversion product (not leaving $\mathcal{C}$).
ΔE^{pcor}	A conversion output that is retained in $\mathcal{S}$.
ΔE^{pir}	Part of in-transfer that is retained in $\mathcal{S}$ but not entering $\mathcal{C}$.
$E_K = K$	Kinetic energy.
$E_L = L$	Potential energy.
V	Volume.
T	Temperature.
P	Pressure.
S	Entropy.
ΔW	Work transfer.
ΔQ	Heat transfer.
ΔE^p	Finite increment of energy associated with gradient of parameter p; it usually stands for an input.
$\Delta E_c{}^p$	Convertible (or retransferable) part of ΔE^p.
$\Delta E_t{}^p$	Part of ΔE^p that is inconvertible because of existence of process subject to conditions (a) and (b) of Chapter 5.
$\Delta E_l{}^p$	Part of ΔE^p that is inconvertible because of the peculiar nature of the process in question.
$\Delta E_{ic}{}^p = \Delta E_t{}^p + \Delta E_l{}^p$	Inconvertible part of ΔE^p.
P^e	Exterior pressure.
P^i	Interior pressure.
ΔE^{Tc}	Conversion product in form of heat transfer.
$\Delta E^{(md)c}$	Conversion product in form of mechanical deformation.
ΔE_f	Energy transfer due to frictional dissipation.
ΔS_f	Entropy increment due to frictional conversion.

$\Delta E_{\text{irr}}^{p}$	Irreversible part of ΔE^{p}-transfer; $\Delta E_{\text{irr}}^{p} = \Delta E_{l}{}^{p} = \Delta P_{\text{irr}}^{ap} p_0.$
$\Delta E_{\text{rev}}^{p}$	Reversible part of ΔE^{p}.
$L(E)_x$	Legendre transform of E with respect to x.
E_T	Total energy.
ϕ	Potential; $L = -\phi$.
ΔW_c	Work transfer into S against internal conservative force; $\Delta_1{}^2 W_c + \phi_1 - \phi_2 = L_2 - L_1 = \Delta_1{}^2 L$.
P^{ap}	Associated extensive parameter; coparameter.
$\Delta_1{}^2 P^{ap}$	Coparameter increment between states 1 and 2.
$\Delta P_{\text{rev}}^{ap}$	Reversible part of ΔP^{ap}.
$\Delta P_{\text{irr}}^{ap}$	Irreversible part of ΔP^{ap}.
ΔP^{af}	Part of $\Delta P_{\text{irr}}^{ap}$ due to frictional conversion.
R	Degree of progress or evolution of the irreversible process.
λ	Degree of advance, evolution, or progress of a chemical reaction.
v	Reaction velocity.
A	Affinity function (also, the chemical affinity function).
n_i	Mole number of constituent i of system.
U	Internal energy.
H	Enthalpy.
F	Helmholtz function (maximum work function, Helmholtz potential).
G	Gibbs function (Gibbs potential, thermodynamic potential).
μ_i	Chemical potential of constituent i of system.
Eff.	Efficiency of process.
t	Time.
Z_i	Molecule of species i.
c_i	Stoichiometric coefficient of Z_i.
n_i	Quantity, in moles, of Z_i at the instant of interest.
$n_i{}^0$	Initial quantity of Z_i, in moles.
λ_m	Maximal value reached by λ in a chemical reaction.
$A_{0+}{}^{p}$	Absolute zero value of p in the whole universe $\mathfrak{U}$, for positive p-values.
$A_{0-}{}^{p}$	Absolute zero value of p in the whole universe $\mathfrak{U}$, for negative p-values.

Index